FORCES OF THE ZODIAC

Companions of the Soul

FORCES OF THE ZODIAC

Companions of the Soul

by Robert R. Leichtman, M.D.
& Carl Japikse

Illustrations by D. Kendrick Johnson

ARIEL PRESS
The Publishing House of Light

This book is made possible by a gift
to the Publications Fund of Light
by Louise Swanson

ISBN 0-89804-038-8

Library of Congress Card Catalog Number: 85-70204

Contents

To the force of Aquarius,
which blesses and inspires
the whole of the new age

FORCES OF THE ZODIAC

Companions of the Soul

Foreword

As two people with a deep interest in astrology, we have long thought that the conventional treatment of this science does not adequately honor the remarkable potential of the forces of the zodiac. Instead of using astrology to understand how to activate and apply our creative and spiritual resources, most astrologers today devote themselves to understanding the *personality*, so they can cater more successfully to its wishes and wants. A major reason for this materialistic orientation is undoubtedly the fact that the average user of astrological advice is primarily interested in the fulfillment of his or her most mundane and egotistical desires. But by continually pandering to those who crave more money, power, and romantic gratification, conventional astrology has reduced itself to a study of the lowest planetary influences, ignoring the higher aspects.

This orientation has alienated most of those people who focus their lives at a higher level. Serious spiritual students recognize that there is a great deal more to self-development and the life of spirit than just understanding our personal weaknesses and strengths. They know that there is more to living a successful life than just timing our moves to coincide with the cosmos and finding clever ways to manipulate others and our environment. These people are more interested in discovering the profound meanings of life than in pursuing the eternal quest for more power, recognition, money, and romance. They are looking for help in finding the wisdom, goodwill, and strength they can use *to change themselves*—not just strengthen their defenses and bribe fate. They are looking for a better contact with spirit. Conventional astrology, unfortunately, is too preoccupied with its selfish cravings to provide it.

This need not be the case, however. Through many years of experimentation and intuitive research, the two of us have come to appreciate the immense value of the forces of the zodiac in stimulating and guiding the process of self-development and spiritual enrichment. We have found that if the focus

of astrology is shifted to a *higher* level than that which is cus-
tomary in conventional practice, it is possible to harness astrological forces as a powerful resource in human living. Instead
of being a passive victim of these forces, we can actually tap
their unlimited reservoirs of love, wisdom, and power—to help
us transform our human weaknesses and vulnerabilities,
expand the scope of our creative involvement in life, and fuel
our service to spirit. We can likewise gain a much deeper
understanding of our unique spiritual destiny and *how spirit
seeks to direct us* as a personality. And by recognizing that the
forces of the zodiac are designed to act as companions of the
soul, we can begin to work with them skillfully to facilitate the
integration of the life of spirit into our character and daily self-
expression.

There are many people on the spiritual path who have this
higher interest in interacting with divine forces, yet they do not
know how well suited astrology is to help them. Because conventional astrology has virtually ignored these people and their
interests, many of these people have chosen to ignore—and
perhaps even scorn—the conventional practice of astrology.

This book has been written to address and correct this
problem.

It is not, however, our intention to replace or undermine
the work of conventional astrology. There is still great value in
properly constructed and interpreted natal horoscopes. These
charts can provide considerable insight into personality characteristics, strengths, and weaknesses, the patterns of problems
we face, and the most successful directions for self-expression.
We write not to condemn but to inspire reform, to point out
some of the limitations of modern astrology, and to suggest a
powerful way of using the forces of the zodiac which will complement and enrich the standard practices of astrology—and,
we hope, help astrology aspire to greater heights.

For those who are steeped in conventional astrology, it

may be tempting to think that we have written just one more book on "sun sign" astrology and have ignored the unique and potent influences of the planets and other astrological forces prominent at the time of birth. This would not be accurate, however. We do appreciate the deeper complexities of astrology, but are more interested in enriching the study and use of astrology than in following all of its traditions. The position of the natal sun and ascendant do not limit and define the character of our personality and self-expression as much as they provide "open doors" for spirit to reach into our life to enrich our divine potential and channel our long-range evolution as a spiritual being. This may be of little interest to an astrologer who devotes himself to predicting the love life of his clients, but it is of immense and practical importance to the spiritual aspirant. The influences of the planetary forces are issues the spiritual aspirant must learn to master—not be limited by. As our individual consciousness becomes spiritualized, our spiritual will assumes more and more of a role in guiding the daily habits and thoughts of the personality. Ordinary planetary forces simply become another environmental factor which we must learn to control and use productively! The forces and qualities of the twelve major zodiacal signs, on the other hand, become more and more meaningful to us as powerful sources of enrichment and opportunity, both for our growth as a spiritual person and for our creative self-expression.

In writing *Forces of the Zodiac,* we have sought to provoke thinking—even controversy. To our minds, the current practice of astrology, like so many ancient traditions, has developed a rather rigid mind set—somewhat like the fundamentalists in religion. The practice of astrology is filled with rules which are accepted just because "it has always been done this way," with interpretations and dogma which are rarely challenged. Traditional explanations from standard texts are too readily embraced, instead of seeking a fresh revelation of

15

the meaning of zodiacal forces. In addition, there is a materialistic focus which represents the projection of personal wants, fears, and assumptions—not a true study of heavenly influences. We would like to see astrology grow up and recognize its mature promise—not remain an adolescent pseudoscience forever—and hope this book will be read in this spirit.

To those who have been alienated by conventional astrology, we hope this book will show that astrology can be approached intelligently, as part of the spiritual life. Instead of being a tool for imposing our personal will more successfully on others, astrology should be a powerful resource for genuine self-improvement. When approached intelligently, astrology can be a tool of practical psychology, giving us direction and power to discipline our habits of thought and action, and also a tool of practical spirituality, leading us to insights into how to harness the life of spirit in our character and daily work.

And to those with an interest in esoteric astrology, who already see the applicability of astrological knowledge to spiritual growth, we hope this book will prove to be an invaluable resource. All too often, esoteric students get caught up in their fascination with solving the mysteries of the cosmos and forget to apply these insights to enrich human life and improve conditions on earth. It is always difficult to turn abstract ideas, theories, and hard-to-grasp principles into a practical system for daily living, but this is precisely the challenge which every spiritual aspirant and every esoteric student must confront and learn to conquer. We view *Forces of the Zodiac* as a handbook which can make it easier to translate abstract force into practical self-expression, and hope esoteric students will use it for this purpose.

It is not our intention to present a huge collection of esoteric facts and theories for debate and discussion. Instead, we seek to offer a guide to understanding and harnessing the *living power* of divine forces. For this reason, we spend as much time describing the best ways to discipline ourself, so that we can harness these forces, as we do describing the actual nature of the energies. We have written the book, in other words, to be *used*, not just studied. We hope spiritual aspirants will use it year in and year out, until they have become so familiar and intimate with these forces that they truly do become their "companions."

For those who cannot live without esoteric facts, we would recommend reading *Esoteric Astrology* by Alice A. Bailey. The contribution Mrs. Bailey made to the proper study of astrology is tremendous. We would encourage every serious student of the life of spirit or astrology to make a thoughtful study of her works.

Because we hope that *Forces of the Zodiac* will be used as a practical guide to spiritual living, we do not recommend reading it from cover to cover all in one gulp. Instead, we would suggest reading chapters one through five, the chapter which describes the current sign of the zodiac, and chapters eighteen and nineteen. Then, as each new sign is entered during the year, turn to the appropriate chapter describing its forces and digest it thoroughly. In this way, you can avoid a bad case of astrological "sunburn"—overexposure to too much information all at once. Some people, of course, will want to skim through the chapters describing the forces of the twelve signs as part of their initial reading; for them, we would recommend reading the keynotes, the description of the archetypal nature of the forces, and the symbolism of the sign—the first five or six pages of the commentary on each sign.

Since this book will be read and used by people of differing levels of interest, we have kept the actual commentaries as practical as possible, and have chosen to put some of the material which was included in our original monthly reports in appendices at the end of the book. There is, for example, a listing of the Graces and the Muses which could be used each month to balance our reactions to the forces of that time. The Graces and Muses are personifications of divine archetypes* such as joy, patience, and courage which we can learn to tap to make our work of integration more effective. They are taken from essays we wrote which appear in volumes IV and V of *The Art of Living*.

The planets esoterically associated with each sign are also listed in an appendix. This material is taken from the writings of Alice Bailey, as is the listing of the rays connected with each sign.

It has not been our intention to write a complete statement about esoteric astrology. Our intention has been far more practical—to provide an introduction to a different way of harnessing and using astrological force. Astrology is a subject which is exceedingly vast and complex. Ultimately, it leads us to a study of the mind of God, its structure and influence in our life, and how we can best interact with it. As such, there can be no end to the revelations which can be gleaned from a thoughtful study of the forces of the zodiac.

Our hope is to inspire each reader to take a new and deeper look at the full potential of spiritual astrology.

—Robert R. Leichtman, M.D.
Carl Japikse

---

* Divine archetypes are patterns of perfection which God has created to assist in bringing the life and glory of heaven into manifestation on earth. These patterns are the design and living force from which all life has been created. Divine archetypes exist at the level of the higher self, not the personality, and therefore are not to be confused with Jungian archetypes, which are usually the creations of human thinking.

1

The Time God Chooses

HEAVENLY INFLUENCES

We live in the midst of divine and not-so-divine influences. These forces affect and condition our life and activities in ways that most people only casually recognize. The not-so-divine forces are largely the collective thoughts, wishes, hopes, expectations, and urges of human consciousness. Sometimes these influences are pleasant, sometimes unpleasant; their effects can be both constructive and destructive. But they are of human origin, and they vary with planetary and national mood.

The divine forces are different. They originate in heaven—not in the physical constellations we can see in the sky, but in the higher realms of divine consciousness. These forces flow through the universe in orderly, purposeful patterns and cycles. And because earth is part of God's cosmic scheme, we the inhabitants of earth are influenced by these divine forces. They are our sustenance, our support, and our source of guidance and creative power.

Most people are unaware of these intangible forces; they are directed largely by their whims, the subculture they live in, and their reactions to life's events. They are victims of their wishes and fears—pawns of the intangible forces around them. Intelligent people, however, gradually become aware of their individuality; they learn that it is possible to discipline themselves and not be automatically controlled by strong desires, environmental pressures, and their reactiveness. They also come to appreciate the power of the forces which surround and influence them—and seek to understand it. The determined effort to identify and harness these forces helps them gain a deeper knowledge of their life, the nature of spirit, and the nature of the cosmos. It enables them to build a powerful relationship with transcendent, divine forces—and use these forces to add wisdom, love, and strength to their character, enrich the quality of their daily activities, and enlighten their lives.

These divine forces work through many agencies; this is part of their nature. It is ridiculous to think that there is just God—a supreme, omnipotent, transcendent Intelligence dwelling apart from physical life—and us. The creative power and intelligence of God reaches us through many avenues: the indwelling light of our soul; divine archetypes; inspired works of art, music, literature, and science; the revelation of illumined scripture—and astrology! All of these sources reveal important aspects of the nature and power of God. None should be excluded as a means of contacting and interacting with divine life—lest we seriously limit our potential for success.

Throughout history, astrology has worked to discover, chart, and explain divine forces and their impact on humans. The practice of astrology has often been cheapened by ignorant and silly people, who have used it only to speculate about the future. It has likewise been tarnished by the rage of religious bigots, who have not understood what they criticized. For these reasons, the usefulness of modern astrology has been greatly crippled. But the forces that astrology studies can never be cheapened by our stupidity nor tarnished by our prejudice. They still exist and continue to influence our lives, day after day, cycle after cycle.

Over the past six years, the two of us have carefully researched the forces of the zodiac as a source of guidance, love, creativity, and power for intelligent living and spiritual self-realization. During this time, we issued our findings in a series of monthly reports, producing a new report for each new sign of the zodiac. These reports described the nature of the forces which would prevail during the month and how they would affect human consciousness. We tailored these reports to the needs of the serious spiritual student, stressing the special opportunities which arise in each sign for healing, growth, the enrichment of character, and creative work, as well as examining the kinds of problems which were likely to arise.

This research was prompted by the original observation that the forces of the zodiac affect us all alike as they move from sign to sign through the year, and that we can benefit greatly from a knowledge of the dominant influences of these forces in any particular cycle. As we conducted our investigation, we confirmed this hypothesis, and found many other benefits in becoming aware of and responsive to these forces. Our deeper awareness of the rhythms of the universe, for example, enabled us to adapt ourselves more intelligently to them, seize opportunities we might otherwise have missed, and manage problems more successfully. We learned, through direct experience, that we share more than we suspect with the rest of life.

The value of our findings has been confirmed by those who used the reports during the six years we produced them. Now that our research is complete, we are gathering the data here, with a chapter devoted to each of the twelve signs of the zodiac. These commentaries provide a detailed explanation of how astrological forces influence and guide us, month by month, throughout the zodiacal year.

The significance of the divine forces which work through the zodiac is enormous. They bring to each of us a vast potential for psychological and spiritual enrichment, gently conditioning mass consciousness to create a suitable climate for change and healing while encouraging each of us, and society as a whole, to expand our responsibilities, resolve our problems, and find new and more creative ways to approach life. In other words, they behave very much like other divine forces! Astrology is a vital part of the mainstream of divine, intangible forces which influence human thought and behavior—even if we are unaware of it.

In order to harness this great resource, however, we must become aware of how it influences us and what it means to respond intelligently to it. This is the story of *Forces of the Zodiac*.

A LIVING, DIVINE PRESENCE

In evaluating human nature, many people are notoriously influenced by styles and appearances: the way others talk, dress, and gesture. But such superficial examinations can be very misleading, especially since some people go to great lengths to perfect style while neglecting the substance of self-expression. Unless we are gifted with considerable intuition, most of us come to know the real character of people only through a lifelong study of how they respond to opportunities and responsibilities—and how they manage problems, criticism, authority, and crises of integrity. This type of deeper study probes beyond the veneer of style and reveals the real nature of our friends' values, convictions, abilities, and relationship with spirit—their inner humanitarian core.

A superficial study of the heavenly influences of life would be equally misleading. It would be a mistake, for instance, to believe that the forces of the zodiac are mysterious energies emanating from a select group of constellations many light years away. The *physical* zodiac is just a collection of separate orbs of hot gases; it has no special influence on us. But just as physical people have an inner, spiritual reality, the physical constellations likewise embody a deeper reality—*the spiritual zodiac.* This spiritual zodiac is nothing less than the collective planetary and stellar consciousnesses in which we live and move and have our being. Its influences, which are divine, are constantly bathing the whole of creation, including humanity.

To the superficial observer, the spiritual character of the zodiac is even less obvious than is the inner core of values and spiritual qualities in the human being. Yet it does exist, and it influences our thinking and behavior, both directly and indirectly, just as the soul conditions our thinking and behavior, even when we give no indication of being responsive to it.

There is another factor as well which complicates the study

24

of these influences. The spiritual zodiac is constantly changing, both in its focus and its impact on us. The reason why is simple. We dwell in a living, evolving universe which is structured by a great cosmic intelligence. As we grow individually, develop new abilities, and take on new responsibilities, more opportunities open up for us. In much the same way, as divine creation proceeds toward its destiny, according to its design and plan, the configuration of the spiritual zodiac changes. In terms of the whole, these are minor changes; nonetheless, these shifts in the zodiac can create significant new directions on earth.

The force of Scorpio, for example, is concerned with the phenomena of death, among other things. In recent years, it has been modified by the influence of Uranus, which stimulates innovation. This has brought about a renaissance of interest among humans in the processes of death and dying. As a result, society has been led to develop more compassionate methods of caring for the dying. Likewise, the constellation of Aquarius, which embodies the spirit of humanitarian and community consciousness, is also influenced by cyclic forces. During a period when it is strongly conditioned by Mars, the forces of Aquarius will tend to promote an interest in serving the needs of others. But when the forces of Aquarius are modified by Saturn, the emphasis would shift from the urge to serve to the urge to resolve the accumulation of old problems and conflicts.

Yet it is not just the influences of the planets which condition the "raw" zodiacal force as it enters our solar system. At a very subtle and powerful level, there are also certain Great Intelligences Who adapt, qualify, and give special focus to these divine influences. These Great Intelligences are known to humanity by various titles—the Church Invisible, the Hierarchy, the Lords of Civilization, or the Great White Brotherhood. In a figurative sense, these giant intellects form the supraconscious mind for the whole of humanity. As they work together, they filter, adapt, and condition the zodiacal forces as they enter the earth's system, giving them special emphasis, focus, or rhythm.

Some of this conditioning of the forces of the zodiac is noticeable only over a very long period of time—hundreds and even thousands of years. These describe the larger cycles of the zodiac. But much of the subtle management of these forces is directed at harnessing the shorter cycles of the zodiac which arise as each year unfolds and we repeat the journey through all twelve signs, from Aries to Pisces.

From month to month, as the major signs change, the Hierarchy uses the spiritual aspects of each zodiacal force to energize some specific part of the divine plan for civilization. The net result of this is that when the sun moves into each new sign of the zodiac, the spiritual force of that constellation is shaped to form a "window of opportunity" through which we can attune ourself to the work of the Hierarchy—if we respond intelligently. This may involve learning new ways to repair our character, finding new outlets for our creative self-expression, or learning to work more effectively in groups.

The implications of this idea are tremendous. Life is not static; it is constantly bringing us new opportunity. As the zodiac shifts, it subtly enriches our life—stimulating our awareness, adding inspiration to our understanding, drawing in new support for our creative work, and arranging new responsibilities and opportunities to serve. During Taurus, for example, the planet is flooded by an extra measure of goodwill. The Hierarchy harnesses this force to motivate humanity to cultivate more tolerance and goodwill in its dealings with one another.

All of this occurs within the context of divine law. Indeed, to put the proposition in religious terminology, it could be said that it is the mind of God which conditions these astrological forces, producing a special blend of heavenly qualities and influences which becomes the *atmosphere* for spiritual, psychological, and creative activities on the planet.

This atmosphere stimulates and enriches the collective unconscious of all humanity. As shifts occur at a zodiacal or cosmic level, corresponding tides in the lives and affairs of human beings emerge. But the primary impact on each of us individually is *unconscious*—meaning that we do not have a choice in whether we will be influenced by these forces and factors. Because we are alive and active on the planet, we are conditioned by this atmosphere and the tides which characterize it. Some type of response by us is guaranteed and will be automatic.

The way in which we interact with this atmosphere is similar to the kind of reaction we may register after visiting someone who is sick in a hospital. We may have a very pleasant visit with this person, despite his sickness, but after we leave, we begin to notice that we are more lethargic, gloomy, or afraid than usual. The "sick atmosphere" of the hospital has influenced us unconsciously in a way that is directly contrary to what we have felt consciously. The overall quality and focus of our moods and reactiveness to life have been subtly affected in powerful—and automatic—ways.

The influence of the forces of the zodiac is essentially uniform throughout humanity. This is a point which can be confusing, since conventional astrology has placed so much emphasis on the natal horoscope and transits, thereby generating a number of misconceptions in mass consciousness which are not easily erased. Many people, for instance, believe that a person born in Taurus will be influenced only by Taurian conditions, while a person born in the sign of Libra will be influenced only by Libran forces. This is not the case.

Just as the same sun and moon shines for all of us, whether or not we were born during the day or the night, so also the forces of the zodiac influence all of us. Our personal reactions to these forces are likely to be highly individualistic, but the

27

forces themselves are universal—they do not vary from one person to the next.

There are many reasons why each person reacts differently to these forces, even though their influence on us is the same. Our needs, values, level of awareness, capacity for self-discipline, and interest in growing are all important factors. So is the natal horoscope. There *is* great value in natal astrology, in which a horoscope is constructed charting the position of the planets and the signs of the zodiac at the time of birth. The position of these forces at the moment of birth establishes in our consciousness a specific magnetic harmony or dissonance to a precise combination of astrological influences. Knowing what this magnetic structure is can be enormously helpful in understanding our tendencies in life. But it should be understood that the analysis of the natal horoscope is limited, in most cases, to a study of our *personal reactiveness*—not our capacity to respond spiritually to the forces of the zodiac. There is a need, therefore, for an examination of the transcendent and unifying elements of the divine forces which *influence all of us alike*. And this kind of examination is just as much a legitimate part of astrology as is the use of the natal horoscope.

This is what the commentaries of *Forces of the Zodiac* are designed to do—to indicate the transcendent relationship between the cosmos and the sincere spiritual aspirant. The chapters which follow are designed to give insight into the nature of the zodiacal forces themselves, how they are conditioned by the solar system, and how they are focused and adapted by the great intelligences of our planet. In one sense, they can be thought of as commentaries on the unfoldment of the divine plan on earth.

This will not be of interest to everyone, of course. People who are primarily preoccupied with their personal wishes, habits, and concerns—and who want to learn how to manipulate the world, rather than change themselves—will find little of interest in this book. They would be better served by a good conventional analysis of their natal horoscope and transits. But the person who is attempting to discover the larger perspectives of life and seeks to act in accordance with divine intention will find the commentaries in this book to be an invaluable guide to the work of detachment, the understanding of our purpose, the cultivation of right timing, the development of the mind, and daily living.

It is important to understand, however, that the forces of the zodiac are *not* under our personal control. We have the opportunity to respond to them wisely or foolishly. The more we know about the nature of the forces influencing us, the more wisely we will be able to act. The more we are ignorant of them, the more we will act the part of the fool. Certain signs of the zodiac, for instance, encourage introspection, spiritual insights, and the enlightened reform of our habits. Other periods are best suited for focusing our energies in creative self-expression or using the spiritual will to achieve breakthroughs in ongoing projects. If we foolishly act when it is better to reflect, and hesitate when it is time to strike, we will miss the natural opportunities of life. But if we understand and work with the spiritual forces of the zodiac, we can harness them effectively for our self-understanding, growth, and creativity.

It is part of our obligation as a human being to increase our knowledge of God and life as much as possible. Since our welfare, and that of all humanity, is influenced by the forces of the zodiac, it is important for every thinking person to learn to harness these forces intelligently. This responsibility includes:

• Knowing the nature and quality of the heavenly forces which are the dominant influences during each sign of the zodiac, and how they are likely to affect humanity. This might be the will to grow in Aries, the cultivation of goodwill in Taurus, or the focusing of aspiration in Sagittarius.

• Recognizing our need to discipline ourself so that weak

29

elements of our character are not overly strained by the dominant influences of the month. The heavenly influences of the zodiac *do not cause* personal problems, but existing weaknesses and flaws may well be aggravated by the inflow of certain energies. If we are already possessive, for example, this flaw would probably become more pronounced during a sign when love was a dominant influence. Others, who do not have a vulnerability toward possessiveness, would not be troubled in this way, however. In fact, the force of love would stimulate their unselfish goodwill and compassion.

• Seizing opportunities to pursue worthwhile goals. The dominant influences of any given zodiacal period can open up opportunities for growth, productivity, and creativity which can be seized by those who are alert to them. Pisces, for example, is a good time to explore the inner dimensions of life to assess our attitudes and principles, establish new priorities, and work on mental housecleaning. Gemini is a good time to heal and enrich our attitudes toward our relationships—and to recognize the symbolic significance of certain people in our life, as well as repeated patterns of our behavior.

• Understanding something of the transcendent elements of life which reveal to us the purpose of spirit and guide us along the path we share with all humanity. Knowing that everyone faces challenges and testing in Scorpio, for example, can help us put our own experiences of that time in a healthier context. Knowing that Leo can stimulate everyone to refocus and revise his identity, we can take extra time to review our principles and redefine the roles we play in life. This can help us avoid embarrassing ourself during this period.

• Broadening our perspectives and attitudes toward others, by better understanding why they are prone to behave as they do. If we realize that the forces of Gemini, for example, can stimulate immature people to be more intemperate and partisan in their views and behavior, we can adjust our own speech and behavior to avoid being drawn into this kind of problem.

By pursuing these deeper understandings of life, the zodiac becomes something more than a ribbon of stars in the sky. It becomes a living, divine presence within each one of us and our life—a source of support that we can understand and rely on, as the signs of each year come and go.

This is the true power of the forces of the zodiac: they can come to life within the mind and heart of every human being.

THE INTELLIGENT OBSERVATION OF LIFE

The commentaries on the forces of the zodiac included in this book have not been prepared through conventional astrological calculations. We did not plot the course of the constellations as they moved from sign to sign, nor cast horoscopes. Instead, we researched the movement of these forces into humanity *intuitively*, checking our findings carefully with an evaluation of how people actually responded to the astrological influences. This research has covered six years.

The format of our research was simple and could easily be duplicated by any careful, intuitive thinker. Just prior to the start of each sign of the zodiac, we studied the archetypal nature of the forces for the month to come. After determining the dominant influence of the period, we then identified how these energies were being modified and adapted for that particular year. These subtle changes do not alter the actual nature of the zodiacal energy, but they do give it a specific focus appropriate to that point in time. It is this focusing which produces variety in life and generates the ever-changing opportunities for our growth and creative self-expression.

Being students of human nature, we recognized that not everyone responds equally to opportunity; there are differing levels of awareness and maturity in people. We therefore evaluated the impact of the forces on each of the following three types of people:

• The average person, who is still controlled largely by the wish life of the personality and its reactions.

• The spiritual aspirant, who seeks to be directed by the inner life and to discipline the reactions of the personality.

• The advanced person, who is solidly focused in spiritual principles and qualities, and is able to conduct himself accordingly.

Conventional astrologers, of course, assume that most of these variations in how we are affected by astrological forces can be defined by charting what is called the transits—which show the relationship of the current position of the planets to their position at the time of birth. This relationship is relevant, but not nearly as important as is the level of our maturity and our interest in working with the spiritual elements of the forces of the zodiac.

This is the reason why the information in these commentaries is based not on mathematical calculations but on psychic perceptions. Our whole approach is to deal with the invisible or spiritual zodiac, not the physical one. It is therefore not necessary for the reader to have a thorough background or interest in conventional astrology to benefit from these commentaries. All that is needed is a mature and intelligent interest in personal growth and spiritual unfoldment.

The intent of this book is to help the reader become more aware of the transcendent influences about us, and learn how to use them intelligently in life. As a result, we have deliberately chosen not to make specific predictions, or to emphasize periods of good or bad luck. *Forces of the Zodiac* is designed to be used as an integral part of an intelligent effort to achieve personal growth—not to pander to the wish life of the personality or to help us cheat our fate.

We are also trying to illustrate the value of intelligent observation of life. We are not interested in spoon-feeding the reader with predigested conclusions or rules of conduct. Instead, we have designed the book to stimulate the reader to observe, think, and evaluate the forces of the zodiac on his or her own. This is not a book to be read and then forgotten; it is a book to be used as part of an ongoing exploration of life. If it is used in this way, it can lead to *direct* experience with the spiritual forces of the zodiac—which is much more useful than our usual, indirect reactions to them at subconscious levels.

It is therefore important to understand the growth potential of working with these commentaries. The patterns and forces which shape our destiny and growth lie in the higher, unconscious aspects of our mind. These are stimulated by the forces of the zodiac, as well as our daily behavior and moods. By learning to work intelligently with them, we open the door to many new discoveries.

One of the most significant of these new discoveries is a greater awareness of all aspects of divinity. If we tend to think of God as a remote, inaccessible, omnipotent force, this practical use of astrology can help us contact the aspects of divine will, love, intelligence, and creativity which can enrich our daily life. If we feel alienated from what we assume to be a dead universe, working with the forces of the zodiac can help us appreciate that we dwell in a universe which is alive, changing, evolving, intelligently organized, and filled with active forces which influence the whole planet. If we are stuck in concrete assumptions about life, the regular study of the forces of the zodiac can help us look beyond these superficial levels of thinking to find the abstract power in life itself. The mature study of these forces can help us appreciate the fundamental intelligence of life itself and recognize and respect divine law as a potent force. As a result, we will be able to work much more effectively in integrating divine forces with our individual needs.

33

We will learn what it means to be a co-creator with God—not just in potential, but also in reality.

For this reason, it is important to understand that astrological forces influence multiple levels of consciousness. All too often, the study of astrology is limited to examining only the impact these forces have on our moods and emotional reactiveness. But the real drama of working with the forces of the zodiac often embraces the unconscious aspects of our mind— and it is at this level that the seeds of our growth and contact with divine life germinate and flourish.

Indeed, as we make the effort to discern and understand the spiritual influences of our life, we will find it is possible to tap these heavenly forces before they are distorted or conditioned by mass consciousness—*or our own reactiveness!* And this is of tremendous importance to anyone who wants something more out of personal growth than the cliches and psychobabble so popular today. The modern emphasis on individual self-fulfillment has often reduced personal growth to a level of undisguised selfishness. But this need not trap us. As we discover that there are spiritual forces in life which *transcend* self-concern and self-interest, the significance of our activities and pursuits acquires an entirely new focus and perspective. We can then tap these esoteric forces as the intelligent basis for self-healing, enriching consciousness, and pursuing the art of living.

It is possible, even in this modern age, to rediscover what it means to live and move and have our being within the life of God. This book is written to help us make this discovery.

THE SPIRITUAL ZODIAC

The intent of our research and writing is to lead us to a more intelligent way of cooperating with God in daily life. Some people try to live a spiritual life through a blind belief in

God and the attempt to live by rules and dogma. But as we learn more about the fact that we live in an orderly, intelligent universe, we can come to understand the nature of *divine* laws and principles—not just our manmade rules and assumptions. As we discover the reality of these principles and seek to harmonize ourself with them, we gradually verify the fact that they are real and helpful in our life. We can then appreciate more fully our ability to build a relationship with them and use them to guide our life toward success and fulfillment. This is one aspect of what intelligent cooperation with God means.

We also need to appreciate that divine forces are not nearly as inaccessible as many people believe. God is not dead—or even asleep. Quite the opposite, God is awake, active, and continuously moving through our life and the activities of humanity in subtle and mysterious ways. There are principles, laws, and cycles to the movement of these divine forces. We need to know about them and respond harmoniously to them.

The commentaries in *Forces of the Zodiac* are written to be used by spiritually inclined individuals who want to discover more about the mind of God and the way it works to influence us all. Those who seek to discover the amazing intelligence of God's plan for humanity can find evidence of it in the zodiacal cycles which constantly focus new elements of spiritual will and love on earth. Those who seek to comprehend the nature of divine wisdom can find proof of it by studying how the new directions and activities which are set in motion sign after sign are precisely what humanity needs to become more aware of the life of spirit and begin honoring it in its conduct of life.

These concepts may seem strange to those who have always assumed that the life of spirit can be discovered in full just by relating to God in His omnipotent and indivisible nature. There *is* just one God, but an infinitely diverse number of ways in which God finds expression. The spiritual levels of the forces of the zodiac are some of the most important ways God influences us. The spiritual forces of the zodiac are in fact the forces of love, goodwill, joy, wisdom, dignity, inspiration, harmony, beauty, charity, faith, forgiveness, hope, and peace. All are divine!

Some might object that God's love and wisdom are constant, and they are—in the sense that they can always be relied on. But they are also constantly involved in creative expression, and therefore focused in many different ways. It is with these varied focal points of divine expression and their influence on human aspiration and creativity that *Forces of the Zodiac* deals. As the writer of Ecclesiastes put it:

> *Everything that happens in this world happens at the*
>   *time God chooses.*
> *He sets the time for birth and the time for death,*
> *The time for planting and for pulling up,*
> *The time for killing and the time for healing,*
> *The time for tearing down and the time for building.*
> *He sets the time for sorrow and the time for joy,*
> *The time for mourning and for dancing,*
> *The time for making love and the time for not making*
>   *love,*
> *The time for finding and the time for losing.*
> *He sets the time for saving and the time for throwing*
>   *away,*
> *The time for tearing and for mending,*
> *The time for silence and the time for talk,*
> *The time for war and the time for peace.*

Let us therefore take heed of the times God chooses.

2

The Zodiac and Us

THE SEARCH FOR MEANING

Conventional astrology describes the relationship between the heavens and the individual human being—but not as fully as it should. It does a fairly good job of explaining the way we are, but fails to tell us what we can become. It tells us about our patterns of reaction and our character strengths and weaknesses, but overlooks our deeper potential. It tells us when to act to be successful, but leaves it to us to find out if these moves are truly the right ones for us. It tells us how to avoid problems and conflicts, but does not teach us how to change our values or habits. Conventional astrology, in other words, is a useful tool for learning to be more successful in expressing *what we already are* as a personality, but it largely fails to help us call on our spiritual potential to *change* what we are. It does not help us tap the real significance of astrological influences in our life.

Indeed, the magnitude and scope of the zodiac has so confounded the majority of astrologers that they have mostly stopped searching for meaning. They devote their time instead to refining their methods of constructing horoscopes and recycling traditional concepts about astrology. These pursuits serve to establish the fact that there is order and intelligence in the universe, and patterns in the zodiac. But the fact that God figuratively speaks to us through astrological forces is largely missed. The potential of these forces to heal and enrich our awareness, our values, and our lifestyle is all but ignored. Even those who call themselves "esoteric astrologers" tend to be mundane astrologers in disguise, renaming old traditions with new labels—but without adding any significant new spiritual orientation or direction to astrology.

As a result, the capacity of the individual to interact with astrological forces, intelligently and skillfully, has been discounted and demeaned. To many astrologers, the influences of the zodiac are so powerful and our personal resources as an individual are so limited—at least in comparison—that the individual appears to be nothing more than a *pawn* whose character, opportunities, health, relationships, talents, and problems are determined by the position of the stars and planets at the time of his or her birth. As the stars and planets move through the heavens, they seem to propel the individual through life as well. And there appears to be little or nothing we can do to change or gain control of this course.

This view of astrology, however, is a grave distortion of the real significance of zodiacal forces. There is no question that the capacity of an individual to change the direction of a cosmic force, as it travels through the universe, is nil. But the *capacity of the individual to modify and direct a cosmic force as it influences his own self-expression is enormous.* The ability of the individual to learn to harness and direct the full range of the forces of the zodiac, not just the ones which were prominent at the time of birth, is unlimited. And the opportunity for the individual to learn to plot his own course through life is barred only by ignorance, laziness, and self-centeredness.

Unfortunately, ignorance, laziness, and self-centeredness are often reinforced by conventional astrological practices. The kind of person who habitually lacks initiative, for example, can usually find a justification for this trait in the unfavorable aspects of the position of the planets at the time of his birth. This encourages him just to preserve this limitation and expect others to adjust to it. Such a person will say, "Well, Mars is not in a favorable house, you know," and assume that this excuses his passive approach to life. A more intelligent approach, however, would be to recognize that he is a victim of his own self-deception; he lacks the enthusiasm to make any breakthroughs in his lifestyle, and has not bothered to cultivate the ideals and goals which could fire up a stronger measure of motivation. If he truly wanted to change himself, he could tap into the force of Leo to attract the *power* of the soul and the *power* behind his duty to learn and work. This would provide him with the energy to refuel his initiative and focus his self-expression. And anyone could do this—not just those who have the sun or ascendant in Leo. In fact, it is not even necessary to wait until Leo! Even though such forces of initiative are stronger in July and August, the power of Leo can be tapped intuitively at any time of the year for self-improvement or creative work.

One of the problems of conventional astrology is that it often reduces human nature to cliches. People born in the sign of Scorpio, for example, are supposed to have a strong erotic drive. And when the moon is moving through Scorpio, this passion is supposed to become almost *unbearable*—and, of course, uncontrollable. People who are born in Gemini are supposed to be flaky and indecisive. Leos are supposed to be bossy and sneaky. Worst of all, these people are doomed to stay these ways their whole life—as if they had been stamped out by some Great Cosmic Cookie Cutter and cannot change.

But this type of thinking does a great disservice to human intelligence and our capacity to discipline ourself and transform our character. It just encourages people to ignore the challenges of life and surrender to their problems and conflicts. In point of fact, it is probable that Scorpios simply give in more often to the temptation to be seductive—or be seduced—not that they are more erotic than anyone else. The bossy type of Leo is not really impelled to be obnoxious, either; he has just failed to master self-discipline and add goodwill to his personal relationships. Nor is the poor, indecisive Gemini doomed to eternal flakehood; he can learn to balance and focus his thinking as he strives to act with moderation and self-control.

The way the natal or birth horoscope is usually interpreted by conventional astrologers shows lack of insight into the true potential of astrological forces. Much of our unique, personal mix of magnetic harmonies with the heavens *is* set at the time of birth, but too much significance is given to the positions and the influences of the planets. Forgotten is the fact that the real power comes from the twelve major signs which work through the planets. The planets, of course, condition these forces, but are less important than is commonly believed.

In some ways, the natal horoscope is like the home we live in. It is unique and ours. But the forces of the zodiac are like the weather; they influence everyone alike. When it rains, we all get wet—not just people born on rainy days. Similarly, when it is Sagittarius, we are all "rained on" by the power to focus our goals and ambition. We all need to focus our desire to attain our goals from time to time, so we all can benefit from the force of Sagittarius. It is naive to think that only Sagittarians can use this force—or that we have to wait for the magic period between November 23 and December 21 to put this force to work in our life.

Conventional astrology has educated us to recognize and appreciate the powerful and intelligent cosmic forces which preserve order and regulate change throughout the universe. It is now time for us to recognize that there is a similar system within each individual which likewise establishes and preserves order and regulates activity in our life. We are not a mere object tossed about on the waves of fate. We are a miniature system of divine life and light, a microcosm within the macrocosm, and therefore able to respond intelligently and maturely to astrological forces, even while being influenced by them.

Our adult consciousness is a complete system with a full potential for flexibility, alertness, intuition, affection, goodwill, analysis, assertiveness, authority, discipline, idealism, benevolence, optimism, exuberance, accountability, memory, conscience, change, inventiveness, creativity, mysticism, aspiration, godliness, destruction, and stability. No matter when we were born, the seeds—if not the mature expression—of these qualities and capacities are alive and active in our character.

It is quite valid to view this complex group of capacities as a personal system which is the counterpart to the macrocosmic zodiac. The astrological qualities attributed to all the planets are well represented in our personal consciousness—and as we grow in maturity and spirituality, we become progressively more responsive to the divine forces of the constellations as well. This is a fact which has been proven time after time in careful astrological research. In a powerful way, therefore, this personal system constitutes a *zodiac within us*, which we must learn to master.

As the stellar and planetary forces of the macrocosmic zodiac interact and produce focal points of divine expression, there is a corresponding interaction in our personal system of consciousness, producing new insights, the renewal of old problems and strengths, fresh opportunities for growth and creativity, and a greater self-understanding. If we ignore these changes within our own awareness, the forces of the zodiac will do little to enrich our life, except by accident. In fact, the passive, unintelligent response to these forces may result in an increase in unwanted and unnecessary problems. But if we study them and endeavor to use them wisely, to improve the quality of our self-expression, our capacity to act "at the time God chooses" will increase tremendously.

The period of Taurus, for example, is a good time for attempting to change our habits, for we can draw on the focus of goodwill of this period to seek a more enlightened orientation to our life. Self-indulgent people, however, will merely find their stubbornness and selfishness increased. The period of Leo is an excellent time to work on achieving a better focus and integration in our thinking and behavior, yet people who scorn self-discipline will nevertheless manage to slide through Leo without significant change.

As we learn to work consciously with the interaction between our personal system and the macrocosmic zodiac, we begin to appreciate that the environment which influences us each day is much larger than that of our home, office, or neighborhood. It also includes the intangible forces of the whole solar system and the cosmos. This is not to suggest that we draw the total substance of our character from these forces, or that we are in any way a victim of planetary influences. Our fate is in our own hands *unless we abandon it*—to others, or to the stars. Yet the tides which sweep through universal consciousness and condition the planetary environment also sweep through our personal system of consciousness, conditioning us in much the same way, though on a smaller scale. We must therefore be prepared to respond wisely to them, lest we be swept away by them. This means practicing self-control.

If we are able to control our emotional reactiveness, we will be able to control the tides of sentimentality caused by Venus. If we are able to keep pessimistic feelings in check, we will be able to mute disturbances in our psyche resulting from the influence of Saturn. Likewise, if we are able to meet aggressiveness with self-restraint and goodwill, we will be able to continue striving toward our goals wisely, even though the tides of Mars may be influencing us. By controlling the way in which these forces are focused and expressed in our own personal system of consciousness, we can attune ourself more readily to the spiritual forces of the macrocosmic zodiac, and not be swept away in the tides of mass reactiveness.

Our response to the forces of the zodiac is therefore not something we can afford to leave to chance. Because there are many levels of maturity in our character and self-expression, we are able to interact with astrological forces at just about any level of maturity we choose. If we are habitually focused in what we want for ourself and what we expect life to provide for us—a very immature level—then we will intersect with these forces at a level which will seem to serve these selfish interests. On the other hand, if we are interested in understanding the patterns of our behavior, overcoming our weaknesses, and healing our conflicts with others, then we can interact with these same forces at a higher level—a level which stimulates self-discipline, understanding, and goodwill. And if we are interested in exploring the life of our spiritual self, we can interact with these very same forces at still a higher level—a level which promotes insight, intuition, an awareness of oneness, unconditioned love, and the will to serve.

Just understanding this principle is not enough, however; we must also beware the traps of self-deception. Some people who believe they are interested in personal growth are really only interested in getting more of what they want, and so they interact with astrological forces at the lowest level, even while professing to be spiritually inclined. Others are strongly motivated to take care of their responsibilities in life and work hard at achieving personal success, yet their idea of "duty" and "success" is also largely selfish, not spiritual. Among astrologers, most people who refer to the "spiritual life" are using the phrase only to refer to a capacity to avoid frustration and fulfill their desires. Yet any such distortions of our interest and motivation will keep us in the thrall of the lowest levels of astrology, and undermine our use of the forces of the zodiac.

The commentaries on each sign of the zodiac which form the heart of this book are written to help us focus on and respond to the highest levels of these forces. They are designed to be used by intelligent individuals who are seeking a clearer understanding of the unseen forces conditioning life—by people who are striving to become more responsive to the plan of God. As such, these commentaries are written as much to reveal the forces active in our own consciousness as to reveal the cosmic forces of the zodiac.

It is pointless, after all, to know what forces are in opposition in the heavens if we do not know which forces *in us* are in opposition with one another and with our best interests! It is useless to know which factors are increasing or decreasing in interplanetary relationships unless we know our own attitudes, plans, and goals. It is impossible to harness and focus the forces of the zodiac unless we are able to harness and focus our own will and intelligence.

The commentaries trace the impact of the forces of the zodiac at work in each sign, not only on a cosmic level but more importantly at the individual level, within our personal system. These analyses do not treat us as an object which will "suffer the slings and arrows of outrageous fortune"—good or bad—no matter how we act, but rather as a thinking, conscious being who can activate, organize, and implement these forces for constructive change and creative self-expression.

And yet, even though these commentaries are written to energize our own capacity to respond harmoniously to the forces of the zodiac, it does not follow that reading them will automatically cause this to happen. In order to work effectively with this knowledge, it is necessary for the reader to digest the ideas in this book and then apply them intelligently to his or her life. Since we are each an agent for change and creativity, not an object or victim of fate, we must work to harness these forces productively.

In specific, there are four lines of activity to cultivate:

• We must show an interest in understanding more about ourself and our potential. This means learning about our higher self and its involvement in our growth. Those who try to define who they are merely by collecting a history of their problems and frustrations are not doing enough. We need to frequently examine the relationship between what happens to us and what we have done to cause it—as well as what we can do to improve it.

• We must be willing to grow beyond our current weaknesses and vulnerabilities. There is a real trap in thinking we can cure our problems just by "understanding" them. Understanding without action leads to a state of intellectual detachment that actually preserves our problems intact, giving us the illusion of transformation but not the reality. We need to heal, transform, and enrich the aspects of our character which have caused our problems. Then we can truly put an end to them.

• We need to grasp that much of the drama of life unfolds first at subconscious and unconscious levels. What we do and what happens to us consciously is just the final result of the development, refinement, and precipitation of more subtle patterns. By using our imagination and intelligence to discern this fact, we will learn to pinpoint the real battlefield where we must confront our problems and launch effective resolutions. We will also discover more fully the influence of the forces of the zodiac at these levels.

• We must be willing to cooperate with the patterns and directions of our spiritual self. If we seek only happiness and peace, we will end up stuck in the endless frustration of trying to escape reality through the medium of wishes and fantasies. Instead, we must recognize the fabric and design of our inner life and seek to remold our attitudes, thinking, and habits to embody these patterns. In this way, we honor our spiritual life.

As we nurture these four lines of activity, we will shape the foundation from which we can successfully launch our individual search for meaning—into the structure of our own consciousness, the macrocosmic zodiac, and the relationship between the two.

OUR RESPONSIBILITY

As we study astrology and seek to use it for our benefit, we incur a responsibility to use the forces of the zodiac wisely, maturely. All too many people, unfortunately, are willing to gloss over this responsibility. Their interest in astrology is primarily a selfish one; they are attracted by the possibility of finding short-cuts to success. As a result, they interact only with the *idea* of astrology, not with the actual forces of the zodiac. This problem is similar to the one created by spiritual aspirants who strive to respond to divine love, wisdom, and power, yet interact with them only at the abstract level. They touch the power of spirit, but do not use it to enrich their lives.

To work effectively with these forces—both the forces of our spiritual self and the forces of the zodiac—we must do more than draw on their inspiration. We must *tap the forces which lie behind our concepts,* or we will miss their full potential. We must learn to translate both our ideas and the power they represent into enlightened behavior. It is God's responsibility to set in motion the forces of the zodiac—but it is *our* responsibility to integrate them into our own ability to act.

The conditions and circumstances which arise in any given monthly period of the zodiac, in other words, are determined by two factors: the selective focus of the forces of that sign, and our individual responses to them. The selective focus of the forces of the sign is determined by the progressive unfoldment of the plan of God. It is always the precise blend needed to stimulate the proper advancement of divine intention at the time. Unfortunately, our response to this blend of energies is seldom so precise. Sometimes we do rise to the challenge and use the forces of the zodiac maturely. But all too often, we distort their purpose and focus, creating problems and difficulties, rather than seizing the opportunities they present us.

In striving to understand the nature of our responsibility in using these forces, it is helpful to keep in mind that the value of a gift is determined by how well the recipient of the gift uses it—not by the intention of the giver. A surprise party, for example, should fill us with delight and appreciation for our friends, yet if we respond instead with irritation, because other plans have been disrupted, we change its meaning to us drastically. A promotion at work should fill us with optimism and a sense of new responsibility, but if we react instead with dread and fear of what the future holds, we cancel its beneficial impact. A well-deserved compliment should help us see our value as a human being, yet if we respond by feeling guilty about other inadequacies and failings, we distort its value to us.

The forces of the zodiac, being the focused expression of the plan of God, are always noble and beneficial. They are truly gifts from God. Yet our responses to them often radically change their basic nature and quality as they manifest through the structure of our consciousness. This is true not only for our individual responses, but also for the responses of mass consciousness. The basic force of Taurus, for example, is designed to stimulate within us, both individually and collectively, the power of our motivation. Some people respond to this basic force by renewing their dedication to major responsibilities and opportunities to grow. But others use it only to intensify selfishness and stubbornness. Contrary to popular opinion, it is not the forces of Taurus which produce either of these extremes. The work of Taurus is to stir up motivation. We choose what these motivations will be.

In practical terms, therefore, we have a great measure of control over the way in which the forces of the zodiac influence us. This idea may come as a rude awakening to those who like to believe it is God's sole responsibility to run the universe smoothly, thereby relieving themselves of any worry. It *is* God's responsibility to run the universe smoothly at the cosmic level—and He does. But at the level of our own individuality, it is *our* responsibility to manage problems and opportunities wisely. As a result, we cannot afford to be passive, waiting for the forces of life to shove us this way or that. The forces of the zodiac challenge us to be active and demonstrate initiative in our use of them.

The average student of astrology, unfortunately, does

approach the power of the twelve signs passively. Instead of working to translate the forces of a sign into constructive self-expression, he follows what is known esoterically as "the line of least resistance." He responds to the forces of the zodiac by going with the momentum of whatever mood, habit, or impulse dominates the personality. If he happens to be angry by nature and the forces of Scorpio intensify this anger, he will excuse himself from any responsibility and blame the problem on the excesses of Scorpio. If he happens to be possessive and materialistic by nature and the forces of Cancer heighten these attitudes, he likewise denies his own culpability and blames the stars. In the end, however, he finds that he has not escaped personal accountability at all. He has enslaved himself to the stars by default and condemned himself to a prison of his own habits, misconceptions, and selfishness.

To break out of this self-imposed prison, we must interact skillfully with the forces of the zodiac. To do this, we must understand ourself. We need to understand the elements within ourself, constructive and destructive alike, that may be stimulated by these forces. We need to be aware of those habits and tendencies which undermine our long term success. We need to know where we are limited in patience, tolerance, or stability, so we can guard against undue strain. We must likewise understand the zodiac. We need to understand the archetypal qualities of each zodiacal sign and the role they play in God's plan to perfect humanity. More specifically, we need to know how the force of each sign can help us with our special needs for greater strength, love, wisdom, or joy. Most importantly, we must be able to combine our knowledge of ourself with our knowledge of the zodiac, using the energies of each sign to change our habits, correct our flaws, develop new skills, penetrate old illusions, and free us from the grip of mass consciousness.

The effort to work in this way with the forces of the zodiac requires courage, discernment, aspiration, and dedication. But most of all, it requires a deep respect for the life of spirit. Without recognition of the light of our soul and devotion to its benevolent intent, the effort to work with zodiacal forces becomes a shallow and meaningless exercise.

COMPANIONS OF THE SOUL

We have a fundamental choice in life: to respond to circumstances with the best and noblest elements within us, or to abandon ourself to our selfishness and respond with the worst within us. In a busy life, there are many circumstances which demand a response from us. Whether this response is one of compassion or anger, joy or sadness, patience or impatience, admiration or jealousy, calmness or anxiety, courage or fear, it is still a choice we must make.

The kind of choice we habitually make in confronting the circumstances of life will also reveal to us the type of choice we make in responding to the forces of the zodiac. If we habitually give into impulses of anger, sadness, impatience, jealousy, worry, or fear in our interactions with others, we will probably respond to the forces of the zodiac in much the same way. Yet if we generally respond to our challenges and difficulties with the noble elements of human consciousness, we can conclude that we are well prepared to embrace the forces of the zodiac and use them wisely in daily living.

It is not possible to interact maturely with the forces of the zodiac unless we continually seek to rise above the immature and selfish elements within us. The forces of the zodiac originate in the heavens themselves. In a very real way, they are designed to be the *companions of the soul*, in the sense that they encourage and facilitate, but do not rule, the life of our soul. They are catalysts for our spiritual potential, stirring up the noblest elements of our character and mobilizing our will to act. As such, they are designed to work in harmony with the soul, supporting and helping to implement our divine purpose and plan. Immaturity and selfishness dishonor the forces of the zodiac and corrupt our capacity to respond wisely to them, causing us to fall out of step with the cosmos. To interact wisely with the forces of the zodiac, therefore, we must shun immaturity and selfishness and learn to embrace the energies of each sign with respect and dedication, just as if they were our companions. As we become more attuned to the soul, we can participate in this companionship more and more fully.

We make the difference in how much we benefit from the opportunities around us. If we watch a play while burdened with worries and emotional distractions, we are likely to miss its drama and entertaining value. If we dine while angry or irritated, we are apt to end up with indigestion instead of a pleasant evening. It is neither the play nor the dinner which is at fault—only our own blighted focus of attention. If we gave them *our best attention,* we would tap their enriching and nourishing potential.

The same is true with the forces of the zodiac. During Leo, the sense of selfhood is stimulated, giving opportunity to everyone. It does not really matter whether we are a Leo, a Taurus, a Pisces, or a Virgo, for everyone has a sense of selfhood and is therefore affected by this dominant focus. What *does* matter is how we respond to it. If we spend the time of Leo "looking out for number one," we are focusing our attention on the most immature and irresponsible elements within our character. But if we use the opportunity of Leo to increase our self-respect, learn to manage strength maturely, and subordinate the personal will to the spiritual will, we are giving our attention to the best and noblest elements within us.

The average person is largely controlled by the emotional reactions he experiences from moment to moment. This is because he has not developed a stable core of values and convictions which sets him apart from mass consciousness. He wants the usual gratifications that "everyone else" wants, which means his reactions are strong and predictable. He cannot control the planetary influences any more than he can control himself, and so he has virtually no capacity to harness the forces of the zodiac wisely.

The spiritual aspirant, by contrast, is learning to control his emotional reactions. The advanced person has achieved this, and is learning to focus the quality of his or her character and behavior at a level above mass consciousness. This means that both the aspirant and the advanced person are learning to control the planetary influences in their lives, and are therefore prepared to interact with the forces of the zodiac constructively. The esoteric quality of Mars, for example, is idealism. In the average person, this force stirs up fanatical reactions and a strong congestion in his emotional nature; as a result, the force of Mars is conventionally viewed as disruptive, forceful, aggressive, and explosive. In the advanced person, however, the emotions are controlled and purified, so the strong force of idealism can be focused in an enlightened way and integrated with his values, convictions, and habits. Consequently, the advanced person seldom experiences the disruptive aspects of the force of Mars, and is able to use it constructively and purposefully. He reverses the way in which he is affected by Mars— and takes a significant step on the spiritual path.

The information in the commentaries on each sign is designed to help us focus our attention on the best and noblest elements within us, so we can bring ourself more in harmony with these forces. The intent is to promote a thorough understanding of divine ideals and archetypal forces, and to demonstrate how the power of these forces can be used to improve the quality of our self-expression—by changing habits, refining values, embracing new ideals, activating strengths, and treating others more compassionately.

Properly used, this information can become a guide for reshaping the forces of consciousness within us, so that we become more attuned to the spiritual qualities of the zodiac. As this occurs, our character becomes magnetically responsive to them. Like these forces, we too become a *companion of the soul*, because we are learning to focus and express the forces of spirit on earth in meaningful ways, every day. We become a proper citizen of the universe, a link between heaven and earth.

This is the challenge—and the highest meaning—of working with the forces of the zodiac.

THE POWER TO ACT

In working with the forces of the zodiac, one important factor must be kept in mind: they *are* forces! It is not enough to study them, admire them, adore them, and discuss them at cocktail parties. Being forces, they seek expression. They are designed to be focused, directed, and used.

There are five great ways to use the forces of the zodiac:

• **For healing.** During each sign, we encounter evidence of the imperfection of human nature, which gives us the opportunity to help heal it—whether it is in ourself, our relationships, or society. Yet genuine healing involves much more than just relieving symptoms; it requires us to heal and repair the patterns of consciousness and behavior which are the underlying causes of our illnesses. The forces of the zodiac are ideally suited to help us in this effort. By knowing that self-respect is a keynote of Leo, for example, we will be better prepared to focus the power of self-respect to heal problems of a poor self-image, in ourself or in others, that may arise during Leo. By knowing that a capacity to nurture life is heightened in Pisces, we will be better prepared to use our spiritual treasures of love, joy, and hope to heal pockets of emptiness or depression during Pisces.

• **For transformation.** Transformation is the process of improving the quality of our consciousness by adding transcendent elements—not just feelings of enthusiasm or confidence—to our character and lifestyle. It enriches our character and integrates new issues of spirit into our personality, leading to a permanent growth in consciousness. Each sign of the zodiac presents us with a multitude of opportunities to learn, grow, and transform our values, convictions, habits, relationships, self-image, and orientation toward life. During Cancer, it may be our capacity for generosity which is stimulated. In Libra, the opportunity for growth may be in the area of integrity. In Aquarius, we may find that the urge to reform is quickened. As we identify the primary lessons to be focused on in each sign and work to master them, we tap a significant measure of the power of the sign. In fact, the opportunities for transformation are so important that they will be a special focus in the commentaries on each sign.

• **For creativity.** Human creativity is not limited to the work of writers, artists, musicians, scientists, or inventors. Anyone who enriches life on earth with a greater measure of the wisdom, love, grace, and beauty of spirit is creative. Because the forces of the zodiac are a great resource for the enrichment of consciousness, relationships, and work, they can be a powerful stimulus to creative activity. In Leo, the focus of our creativity may be our ability to use authority benevolently. In Gemini, it might be the development of new ways to integrate our plans with our self-expression. As we learn to work more closely with the forces of the zodiac, we will find they are a rich source of practical creative inspiration and power.

• **For self-expression.** To many people, self-expression is just the habitual recycling of old ideas and automatic reactions to the events about us, but it is meant to be much more. Our self-expression is meant to be the conscious expression of our human love, intelligence, strength, and talents! Genuine self-expression is an act of will; it derives from who we are and what we are determined to say and do. The impact of the zodiac on our self-expression will vary from sign to sign. Scorpio may present us with circumstances in which we must respond with self-control and courage, but if we do not know how to mobilize these strengths, we may well react instead with fear and anxiety. In Gemini, we may confront conditions which call upon us to act with dignity, gracefulness, and joy, but if we have not learned to translate these qualities into our own self-expression, we may react instead with a notable lack of both tact and humor. As we come to appreciate the need to integrate the forces of the zodiac into the fiber of our character, our self-expression is strengthened. Ultimately, we will realize that it is our soul which seeks expression through all that we do. The forces of the zodiac, as companions of the soul, can be a powerful source of help in refining our self-expression.

 • **For building.** No force of the zodiac works by itself, in isolation from the rest. The work of Gemini builds upon the foundation laid in Taurus, and leads to further development in Leo. Whether we are building new habits, relationships, a business, a plan, a family, a personal project, or anything else, skills in harnessing the forces of the zodiac are invaluable. Often, when people receive a flash of insight, they cannot wait to apply it. When conditions do not jell immediately, allowing them to proceed, they become frustrated. They are not good builders. What they do not understand is that ideas and new developments must ripen; if they are significant, they must be exposed to the building power of each of the twelve signs.

They need:

1. The forging of purpose in Aries.
2. The harnessing of motivation in Taurus.
3. The nurturing qualities of Gemini.
4. The breaking up of old patterns and obstacles in Cancer.

5. The focusing of selfhood or definition in Leo.
6. The healing force of Virgo.
7. The balancing of opposites in Libra.
8. The tests of maturity and responsibility in Scorpio.
9. The sharpened focus of idealism and determination in Sagittarius.
10. The will to complete unfinished work in Capricorn.
11. The spiritual sensitivity of Aquarius.
12. The will to serve of Pisces.

Not all of this building is accomplished at a conscious level, of course; much of it occurs subconsciously or even unconsciously. During such periods, the conscious personality may become quite impatient. But the more we understand the direct relationship between the forces of the zodiac and the development of new directions in our life, the more we begin to perceive the value of working intelligently with them.

INSPIRING GROWTH

As we learn to harness the forces of the zodiac and use them productively, these "companions of the soul" will respond in kind, inspiring our growth, both in maturity and understanding. The stronger our relationship with these divine energies becomes, the more they will summon us to live up to the promise of the best and noblest within us.

It is important to look for this growth in the right places, of course. Many people assume that we grow by collecting ideas. This can be a valuable part of growth, of course, but only if we learn to tap the power of these ideas and use it to improve the quality of our self-expression. Others equate growth with the accumulation of power, money, fame, or greater effectiveness in getting what we want. In most cases, however, the accumulation of such things actually stunts our growth!

Genuine growth occurs as we learn to expand our awareness, refine our values, revise our patterns of behavior, add compassion to our character, and strengthen our relationship with our spiritual self. This growth occurs first *within our consciousness* and then finds expression in our life. Working with the forces of the zodiac can inspire this kind of growth in many different ways:

Mentally, we will become more aware of the cyclic ebb and flow of universal forces, leading us to an understanding of the structure of the mind of God. We will gain skill in working with abstract thought—and in recognizing the archetypal themes and ideas which manifest in each sign of the zodiac. In this way, we will learn to work with the *force* of ideas, not just their forms. Perhaps most importantly, however, we will sharpen our skills of careful observation, as we compare the information contained in the commentaries with the actual ways people are behaving.

Emotionally, we will learn to recognize the degree to which our emotional reactions interfere with our ability to understand other people and the events of life, thereby sabotaging the effectiveness of our self-expression. We will become more aware of when we have made major decisions based on our feelings instead of an intelligent evaluation of the facts—and the value of controlling the emotions more objectively. This, in turn, will let us learn to use the emotions to express compassion, affection, and nurturing love—which is their intended role.

In our relationships with others, we will become much more aware of how we influence others and how we, in turn, are influenced by them. We will also be inspired to define the proper role we should be playing in each of our relationships—not just with friends, relatives, and colleagues, but also with authority figures, enemies, subordinates, competitors, and strangers—and to see how we may have distorted our interaction with these people through unrealistic expectations and prejudices. We will also be able to see more clearly how our relationships with others tell us something about our concept of ourself and our general attitude toward people.

In our use of energy, we will learn to seize the opportunity in the conditions of our life and work. As we learn more about what motivates us, for example, we will be able to harness a stronger intention to act in difficult situations. As we learn more about the right use of authority, we will become more effective as a leader—and more at ease with being a loyal subordinate. We will likewise grow in our capacity to set enlightened goals—and reach them.

In our participation in groups, we will become more aware of how these groups either enrich or diminish the quality of our life. And we will grow in practical group skills—for example, the ability to cooperate more effectively with co-workers.

In our relationship with our soul, we will learn more clearly that the soul is constantly involved in our life, using every sign of the zodiac to advance its goals and plans.

Naturally, we will also grow in our ability to respond to the forces of the zodiac! Like anything else worthwhile, this does require skill and sensitivity. Some people, in fact, may register more irritation than enlightenment when they try to tune into these forces. This is not because the forces of the zodiac are irritating, however; it is just an indication that we tend to dwell too much in fear, guilt, anger, or embarrassment. The more we work with the spiritual qualities of the forces of the zodiac, the more we will overcome these problems—and learn to use them to heal, transform, and build in our life.

The ultimate lesson we can learn from the forces of the zodiac is that they are *living, divine forces*, not just abstract ideas. They are alive with power and a purpose of their own. If we can understand this, then we can indeed learn to relate to them as companions of the soul—as companions we can call on for help and inspiration every day of our life.

THE BODY OF GOD

Our soul is our guaranteed passport to universal spiritual experiences. We all enjoy a rich heritage in spirit—and part of this heritage is the forces of the zodiac. And yet, even though this is true, many spiritual aspirants find it difficult to overcome the materialism and provincialism of their culture and religion, so they may enjoy this heritage in the fullest. Instead of identifying with the soul as it actually exists, they identify only with what they have been told to believe about it.

Working with the forces of the zodiac is a powerful way to overcome these limitations. Month by month, we discover how divine force is involved in life—*our life*—weaving richness and diversity into the fabric of our affairs. The forces of the zodiac, in this regard, are like supply lines within the living organism which is the body of God. They bring to us the elements and qualities of life which feed and nourish us, physically, emotionally, mentally, and spiritually.

Our personal system of consciousness is meant to be a support system, too—the supply lines for our conscious self-expression. In some people, unfortunately, it is just a chaotic collection of hurt feelings, personal urges, and undirected thoughts. But it need not be like this. In the enlightened person, the structure of character and self-expression becomes a focal point of stability and wisdom, magnetically attuned to the zodiac of the heavens, which so perfectly regulates and controls the distribution of the life force throughout the body of God.

As the body of God moves and expresses itself, we are affected. But because we are an integral part of the body of God, the effect is always a favorable one—if we are making the effort to interpret it and cooperate with it. It is only unfavorable when we try to move in a different direction than God.

Let us therefore endeavor to move in the same direction as God, and at the time God chooses.

3

Registering the Forces
of the Zodiac

DEFINING THE KEYNOTE

At first, it may seem impossible to make direct intuitive contact with the forces of the zodiac, as complex as each one is. Yet it is not as difficult as it seems. Each sign of the zodiac is characterized by certain dominant qualities which are inherent in the spiritual energies emanating from its constellation. As a result, primary and secondary keynotes can be defined from each of the twelve signs. These keynotes or major themes remain constant from year to year, even though they tend to affect humanity in slightly different ways in each cycle. If we can define and understand the dominant qualities of each sign, then our work of exploring the subtler aspects of these forces becomes much easier.

In defining the keynote or dominant theme, however, it is important to remember that the forces of the zodiac, while pure and benevolent in origin, are quickly distorted as they come into contact with human nature. The collective immaturity and selfishness in mass consciousness act as a filter which changes the quality of these forces before they reach our conscious thoughts and attitudes. We must therefore take into account the possibility of such distortion, and strive to determine the keynote of each sign in its purest form. Unfortunately, this is exactly what many conventional astrologers fail to do, and so they end up studying the imperfect reaction of human nature to these forces, rather than the spiritual essence within them. As a result, many of the traditional interpretations of these forces are quite flawed.

A good example of this would be the way the forces of Gemini are usually interpreted. Traditionally, this sign is supposed to make us intellectually curious, volatile, fickle, devious, and unstable. Yet this is not the true spiritual nature of Gemini—just the way the average person tends to *react* to the forces of Gemini. The true nature of Gemini is the power to promote goodwill and to harmonize the duality in our life—qualities most astrologers completely miss.

Once we have defined the keynote or dominant theme of a sign, we need to anticipate the variety of ways it may influence our life. This means examining each department of our consciousness and self-expression and determining how it will be affected by this force. In doing this, however, we are not just trying to gauge how this force will make us *feel* about the different aspects of our life. We are trying to determine how this keynote will stir up our thinking, our priorities, our approach to work, our values, our integrity, our motivation, our attitudes toward others, and our daily behavior—and what this means to us. Perhaps the most important impact to evaluate is how this force will challenge us to grow.

We can also examine how this force will affect others, and how we can expect to be treated by them. But the major effort should be given to examining the impact of these forces on us.

In order to conduct this examination properly, however, we must rise above our usual focus of emotional reactiveness and desire. If we do not, we will do little more than recycle the wish life of the personality and reshuffle our assumptions and prejudices. The key is to work impersonally, thereby simulating the way in which our soul would examine these same questions and define the dominant keynote of these forces.

DIVINING THE DIVINE

The most important tool we can use to help us study the forces of the zodiac is our own *intelligence*. Our use of intelligence can begin with the careful, thoughtful study of the commentaries in this book, which contain many provocative ideas and hints about the nature of the forces and how to attune ourself to them. Each commentary also provides numerous questions designed to stimulate our intelligent inquiry into the nature of these forces, how they affect us, and what we can do with them.

The intelligent study of other books is also highly recommended—especially *Esoteric Astrology* and *The Labours of Hercules* by Alice Bailey. The intelligent observation of human nature—especially what we can infer from changing patterns of reactiveness and growth—will likewise provide the raw material for many important insights. By paying attention to what actually happens to us and to others in each sign, we can check the accuracy of our interpretations of these forces—and become more aware of the full range of their influence.

Our research into the nature of the forces of the zodiac can extend beyond these intellectual efforts, of course. We can learn to make a direct, intuitive contact with the essence of these forces, thereby discerning their qualities before they are filtered through mass consciousness—and our own subconscious. The skillful use of active meditation can be a valuable tool for transcending the innate life of the personality and attuning ourself to the spiritual forces of the zodiac.

When we do this, it is important to understand that skillful meditation need *not* be a deep trance state beginning with mantra mumbling and proceeding to the suppression of all thought. A far more productive format for meditating would begin with a brief attunement to our spiritual self, followed by careful, reflective thinking on the nature and influence of the forces of the current sign. If we prepare ourself with adequate intellectual research, and then dwell on such questions as "How will this force influence me and others?" in meditation, we will learn to draw valuable inspiration from our higher levels of consciousness. Alternatively, we can meditate on seed thoughts which capture the essence of the dominant spiritual quality of a sign. A seed thought for Libra, for example, would be "the power which balances spirit and form."

Various tools of divination can also be used to elucidate the subtle meanings of the forces of the zodiac. Mantic devices such as the I Ching and the Tarot can be consulted like an oracle to answer questions about the most intelligent way to work with the forces of a particular sign.

Tools of divination are built around systems of archetypal forces which relate divine intelligence to events on earth. These forces are portrayed by physical symbols which, when carefully interpreted, reveal to us the pattern of divine forces relevant to our inquiry. In using such a device, we would ask our question, lay out the symbols in a standard ritual manner, and then proceed to interpret their meaning to us. In this way, we can get some insight into the origins of the situation, the mood of mass consciousness concerning it, the movement of divine forces influencing it, and the most favorable way to proceed.

Astrology itself is commonly used as a tool of divination, so the use of these other tools of divination to discern the forces of the zodiac is consistent with our purpose. After all, at their highest levels, all of these mantic devices plug us into the intelligence of the mind of God.

One of the oldest and simplest mantic devices to use is the I Ching. This is an ancient Chinese system of divination which has sustained its usefulness over several millenia. The consultation is performed by formulating a question and then tossing three coins six times, forming the six lines of a hexagram. The hexagram which is produced—there are only sixty-four possible permutations—can then be interpreted with the help of a text on the I Ching. We recommend the text and technique described in the *I Ching Workbook* by R.L. Wing as being the most consistent with the purposes of *Forces of the Zodiac*.

The usefulness of the I Ching depends on the questions we ask of it, for the question we pose will define the manner in which the oracle of the I Ching will speak to us. For our purposes, the question to ask should be something such as, "How will the forces of Capricorn influence me this year?" Or it could be even more specific: "How can I use the forces of Capricorn to help me be more successful in my career?" Once we have formulated the question, we would toss the coins and determine the hexagram we will be dealing with.

The standard text interpretation of this hexagram will provide general insights into the ways the forces in question will be influencing us, psychologically, sociologically, and spiritually—and how this will affect our relations with others and with groups. It will also give us hints about the most successful way to act during this time, our ability to communicate, what to avoid, when to begin new projects, and how to make headway on blocked projects. If we reflect carefully on these generalizations and thoughtfully apply them to our specific needs, we will gain valuable insights into what the forces of the current or coming sign will mean to us.

The Tarot is another mantic device we can use to help us interpret the nature of the forces of the zodiac. This is a system of archetypal forces represented by seventy-eight symbols, each on a separate card. Each symbol is a colorful and complete image, as opposed to the abstract pictograms of the I Ching. As a result, they are easier to interpret—as well as misinterpret. The value of the Tarot is that it can thoroughly define the relationship between a question we have and a complex array of major and minor divine forces. As such, it can be a very useful aid for understanding the way in which the forces of a particular sign will influence us.

As with the I Ching, great care must be taken in formulating the questions we will ask the Tarot. A good question might be: "How will the forces of Capricorn challenge me to grow spiritually in this cycle?" Or, it might be: "How can I use the forces of Capricorn to nourish my creativity?"

There are many different Tarot decks, layouts, and texts we can use to help us answer these questions. As useful as the

Tarot is, it should be kept in mind that the interpretation of the Tarot has been contaminated by the same kind of distortions that astrology has been subjected to—only they are worse, because the Tarot has, for centuries, been mostly used for personal divination. For this reason, we recommend using the Aquarian Tarot deck; it has been less contaminated by human wishes and fears than most. It also seems to incorporate more of a mental focus.

We strongly encourage each person to discern the meaning of the Tarot symbols on his or her own, rather than rely on the standard interpretations found in most texts. Most of these interpretations are tied too closely to personal divination for our purposes—and too involved in adverse meanings. Since each card in the Tarot represents an archetypal force, none of them inherently has an adverse meaning, either in upright or reversed position. If it is understood that the Tarot is just one more way that divine intelligence—*not unenlightened mass consciousness*—can communicate with us, then we should be able to use it to make accurate interpretations. And if we can, then we will find that it can be a powerful aid for discerning and understanding the special focus of the forces of the zodiac sign after sign, year after year.

We would not recommend that anyone become too involved in any of these methods of discerning the forces of the zodiac, however. The heart of our effort should be devoted instead to *applying* the insights we gain about these forces to the challenges and opportunities of our life. Ideas mean little if we do not use them—for in using them, we test their accuracy and their merit. If Gemini really floods us with large amounts of divine love, and Sagittarius really helps us forge divine purpose into enlightened goals, then we can look for the evidence of this as we try to activate these divine forces in our daily living. In this way, we can find out what works and what does not—as well as add to our practical knowledge about ourself and life.

By using more than one tool for divining the forces of the zodiac, we are able to confirm the basic nature of each force. Even though the insights we gain from one source will often overlap and even duplicate that of another, our understanding will almost always be enriched by the unique perspective and focus of these differing methods. In addition, the use of diverse tools to study these forces will help us substantiate the fact that these forces have a reality of their own, independent of our prejudices and assumptions. It also provides us with a means of studying these forces objectively.

In our own research, which was first done independently and then compared and compiled into monthly reports, we went to great lengths to confirm the basic themes and trends for each sign—and to explore the ways in which they influence humanity as a whole. Meditation was used to anchor the basic quality of the force. Once this was established, we used our intuitive faculties to explore the keynotes of the sign and their general influences on human nature. Then, the tools of the I Ching and the Tarot were used to fill in the details. Sometimes the I Ching would help us understand the general movement of the forces into the earth, and what they would stir up. At other times, the Tarot provided this focus more clearly, especially in terms of the problems which might arise *in our own nature* as we sought to integrate this force into our own awareness. Used together, these types of intuitive research provided us with an objective and complete view of the forces of the zodiac and how they will affect us.

REGISTERING THE FORCES

Having insight into the nature of the forces of the zodiac, however, is *not* the same as registering the quality of these forces in our conscious awareness. Once we have gained some idea of what the forces of a sign are, we must then determine what *our response* to them will be—how we intend to respond to the opportunities, problems, and challenges of the time, how we will treat others, and what issues of growth we will focus on. Making this decision is of great importance, because it selectively attunes us to the particular aspect of the forces we will then deal with.

If our focus of thought and attitude is primarily material-istic and self-centered, for example, this will color our ability to register these forces. Many people, after all, are only interested in astrology to the degree that they think it can help them cheat their fate and take advantage of others. If this is our intention in working with the forces of the zodiac, however, we will be able to attune ourself only to the lowest levels of these energies. As a result, we will end up trapped in the wish life of the per-sonality, unable to respond in meaningful ways to our inner life and the divine patterns of growth inherent in our spiritual potential. In all likelihood, we will only be tapping into *the reaction of mass consciousness* to the forces of the zodiac—not the spiritual qualities of the forces themselves.

The solution is to seek to respond to these forces with the best of our human nature—to identify our noble goals and aspi-rations, focus ourself in the best of our intentions, dwell in a steady and deep respect for our higher intelligence, and stead-fastly pursue what truly is the best for us, not just what we would like to have happen. It is a good idea to set this kind of tone *before* we try to make contact with the forces of any sign— and then sustain it while deciding how we will respond to them.

Another, more obscure problem can also arise in our effort to properly register the forces of the zodiac. For generation after generation, students of astrology have recycled traditional notions about the nature and impact of these forces. Most of these theories and concepts, unfortunately, have now been sub-tly colored by the hopes, expectations, and fears of mass consciousness, thereby distorting their usefulness. Over the years, the psychic potency of many of these thought-forms has become quite strong. As a result, when we try to tune into and register the forces of the zodiac intuitively, we may just plug into these accumulated thought-forms instead—and never know the difference!

Fortunately, there are ways to protect ourself from this kind of psychic contamination. The simplest form of protection is the practice of detachment—simple in concept, if not always in execution. Detachment is the process of learning to identify with our inner capacity for clear thinking and spiritual wisdom, rather than with our wishes, fears, desires, memories, and associations. As we cultivate it, we learn to observe and evaluate the conditions of life without reacting in a personal way to them. As such, it is a key to true objectivity. For a more complete description of this process, see our essay, "The Practice of Detachment," in volume I of *The Art of Living.*

Another effective way of protecting ourself from this psychic contamination is to develop and sustain a sincere love of truth. To do this, we will need to understand that there is a reality to the forces of the zodiac independent of our human perception and analysis. Just as the sun shines whether or not we personally believe that it does, so also the forces of the zodiac move through our life, influencing us with their unique qualities and purposes whether or not we respond wisely to them. We cannot change them, but we can learn to harness them—if we will respect them for what they are and learn to love their purposes. But this means being ready to give up old ideas and assumptions about life and respond to these forces *as they actually are*—not as we would like them to be, or as conventional astrology would have us believe they are.

Being companions of the soul, the forces of the zodiac will always honor our spiritual design—not our personal needs for gratification or success. If we have deceived ourself about what we need or ought to be doing in life, the forces of the zodiac will relentlessly expose this self-deception. If we do not love the truth, we will try to hide from this, and retreat into the comfortable distortions of conventional astrology and mass consciousness. But if we do sincerely love the truth, we can break through all of these distortions—our own included—and tap not only an accurate perception of the forces of the zodiac but also a new level of contact with the soul.

Once we understand what we must guard against, the actual work of registering the forces of the zodiac in our awareness is largely an issue of asking the right questions about what these forces mean to us. All too often, the questions we pose about life are not as helpful as they could be; they betray an escapist and materialistic focus which limits our capacity to act. Having discovered, for example, that the forces of Gemini can aggravate problems of indecisiveness, and realizing that we have this tendency ourself, we may be tempted to ask: "How can I avoid having to make decisions during Gemini?" But this would be a retreat into defensiveness and escapism; it would not help us in any meaningful way. Instead, we should ask: "How can I learn to use the inclusive, harmonizing forces of Gemini to make intelligent decisions and stick by them?" In this way, we register the growth potential of the sign.

The best questions to ask are always those which will lead us to a genuine solution to our problems and new growth through our opportunities—not ones which would just help us gratify our wishes and desires. Our inquiry should be directed at what we need to do in order to become more responsive to these forces—what blind spots and areas of self-deception need to be cleared away, what old habits need to be updated and revised, what new action needs to be taken, and what it means to use these forces to honor our spiritual design. By asking right questions, we identify our needs and set the stage for using the forces of the zodiac to help us meet them.

It is not enough, of course, just to ask questions; we must also answer them. This is done by invoking the appropriate quality of the forces of the zodiac to help us face the challenges of the sign. Having decided, for example, that the inclusive power of the love and harmony of Gemini can help us make intelligent decisions, we would invoke it to help us. This could be done as part of a meditation—or as we confront our problem of indecisiveness during Gemini. And if we continue to have problems with indecisiveness during other signs of the zodiac, we can still invoke the force of Gemini to help us!

The key to invoking the help of these forces is to remember that they are dynamic energies, not just abstract ideas. Each of the forces of the zodiac is a living energy which has the power to influence our habits, understanding, and self-expression. By thinking of this power flowing through us and impelling us to make enlightened changes, we make it possible for it to do precisely that!

To help with the process of learning to invoke these forces as dynamic energies which can become a part of our own life and awareness, we have included a prayer at the beginning of each commentary. The prayer is carefully written to invoke a greater responsiveness to the dominant forces of each sign— and helps us see more clearly what it means to register and express them in our own life. Frequent use of the prayer during the period of the sign will greatly increase our responsiveness to these forces.

We must be prepared to do more than just pray, however. To register the dynamic thrust of these forces fully, we need to look constantly for the opportunities they will create—as well as for the problems which may arise from our own reaction to them. Being alert for opportunities which can arise is a true creative challenge, as it teaches us to think in terms of the unseen potential which is developing in our life. As we try to determine how to harness this unseen potential, we begin to appreciate more completely how these forces actually influence our thinking and behavior. None of these opportunities is handed to us automatically, of course; whether or not these "predictions" come true for any one individual depends entirely on his or her own initiative and right timing in taking advantage of them.

We should also understand that some of our personal problems may be magnified by the dynamic force of each sign—and that this likewise gives us an opportunity for registering the quality of these forces. If we are habitually hostile and argumentative, for instance, the force of Leo will magnify these tendencies—not because Leo brings more anger into our consciousness, but because it highlights our values, needs, principles, wants, and fears, which happen to be saturated with hostility and contentiousness. Yet we need not become further immersed in these conditions. We can rise above our anger and register the essential benignity of Leo, learning to identify with our spiritual capacity for compassion. If we work throughout Leo to express compassion instead of anger, it will be a time of great healing, rather than regression.

It should also be understood, incidentally, that the same forces of Leo which aggravate anger in some people help promote assertiveness and self-confidence in those who are habitually shy and introverted. The forces of Virgo, by contrast, would probably quiet down the anger of the aggressive, hostile person—but magnify the shyness of the introverted person. In this example, we can see more clearly that it is not the forces of the zodiac which cause our problems, but rather what we do with them. We can also appreciate more fully the value of registering these forces intelligently.

If we seek to register the highest qualities of these forces— the wisdom, courage, and goodwill—in our character and self-expression, we will find that they have a powerful impact, month by month, year by year, on our growth and awareness.

To fully appreciate this impact, it may be helpful to keep a journal of the impressions, observations, and insights we have while registering and working with the forces of the zodiac. In this way, we create a permanent record of what otherwise might be fleeting thoughts and realizations—a record that we can go back and consult during later stages of the zodiacal year—and in succeeding years as well.

The more accurately we are able to register the forces of the zodiac in our conscious awareness, the more we will come to appreciate their role as companions of the soul. And, we will set the stage for sharing in their company as well.

THE CYCLES OF EACH SIGN

As we make the effort to register these forces, we will become progressively more sensitive to their presence in our life, and the shift in quality and power which always occurs as we leave one monthly sign and enter into the next. The fact that such changes occur, and are readily observable, demonstrates that these forces are something more than just abstract ideas— they are living energies which exist independently of us.

The shift from one zodiacal energy to another will sometimes generate a brief period of mild instability. It tends to begin a few days before the end of the old sign and last a few days after the beginning of the new one, and is characterized by slight difficulty in concentrating or a mild uncertainty about our beliefs or convictions. In some people, this period of instability might temporarily heighten emotional reactiveness.

The challenge during this period of the "cusp" is to sustain our self-discipline and preserve our principles. If we control our reactiveness and learn to govern our behavior with wisdom, these times of instability will pose no real threat to us.

As we observe these changes in our responsiveness, our

behavior, our daily activities, and the people and events around us, our life becomes a figurative laboratory—a focal point of revelation. In this laboratory, we can study the interaction between the forces of our own consciousness and the forces of the zodiac, and how they shape our character, values, and interest in growing. In this way, we become consciously aware of vital processes of growth and development which are entirely unconscious in the average person, thereby enabling us to cooperate with them and accelerate our progress.

As our sensitivity to these forces increases, we become aware of something else as well: that the forces influencing each sign rise and fall during its monthly period. While this is not a new idea, it is amazing how little awareness most people have of these rhythms—even esoteric students. There are three periods of special importance we should be familiar with. These are called "decanates," and are roughly ten days in length.

The first decanate focuses the basic impulse of the force. This will be the period of our greatest reactiveness, especially in the emotions. It is therefore a time when it is profitable to carefully explore and observe the nature and quality of the forces at work—and the nature and quality of our response to them. In other words, it is a time for attuning to the new forces and for disciplining ourself to use them wisely. It favors the gathering of inspiration about the direction and purpose of these forces, as well as assessing our needs and direction in life. The risk of irritability, self-deception, and the reappearance of unresolved problems is high during this first decanate.

The second decanate or ten-day period in a sign highlights the *quality* of the force. It is therefore a time which is best spent digesting the insights gained during the attunement of the first ten days—a time for new realizations and for integrating the actual quality of the force into our habits, self-image, and attitudes. It favors creativity and the use of the mind. The risk of inaction and disinterest is high.

The third decanate or ten-day period highlights the *appearance* and application of these new forces. It is therefore a time for implementing new decisions and plans. In esoteric terms, this is the time for taking action and grounding new ideas and plans. It favors leadership, self-expression, and the use of the will to act. The risk of exposure, embarrassment, and defeat is increased.

At the end of the zodiacal month, there is a phase we call the time of completion. The major themes of the month come to a head at this time; the final opportunities present themselves and the lessons which have been learned are summarized.

In each monthly cycle, there are two other times of special emphasis—the new and full moons. Just as the physical moon affects the physical tides of earth, so also the subtle body of the moon affects the tides of the subtle forces of the zodiac. These times of special emphasis give us extra opportunities to add to our self-understanding and self-expression.

The period of the new moon is a time for change—and an excellent opportunity for focusing our individuality through planning, initiating action, and improving the self-image. Esoterically, the new moon is the time when the impact of heavenly influences is at its weakest point. The personality is, to some extent, "left on its own" and must rely on its own strengths—although this is true only in degree and not in actual fact. The challenge of the new moon, therefore, is to focus on what we can do with the talents and capacities we have, both in thought and deed. It is a good time for introspection and self-assessment—as well as for inaugurating new projects or reforms.

The difficulty of the new moon is that it is a time when we must often stand alone, unsupported by others. For this reason, we need to guard against self-pity, unreasonable fears and doubts, and inertia. If we view the new moon as a challenge to our resourcefulness, we will harness its special opportunity.

The period of the full moon is the time of greatest response to stimulation. The forces of spirit and the zodiac are at "high tide." For the advanced individual, it is a marvelous time for inspiration, new ideas, and guidance, especially in the context of group work. We should therefore involve ourself in assessing the nature of our spiritual self and what it means to express its plan for us. It is also a good time to review the nature of our spiritual service and group work—and the revisions we must make in order to serve more effectively.

For the person who lacks this high perspective and maturity, however, the full moon is often a time of overreaction, conflict, and stress. Since all subconscious and unconscious forces—mature as well as immature—are greatly stimulated, the undisciplined person finds it hard to maintain control. For this type of person, the full moon presents a forceful challenge to learn and practice self-discipline and detachment.

In the commentaries on each sign, a brief "focus" is listed for both the new and full moons. The focus for the new moon is a single word or phrase which sums up the optimum way to use this time within the context of the sign. It will help us focus our self-expression. The focus for the full moon is meant to be used in the same way, but it deals with our active cooperation with spiritual forces and groups.

This kind of active, intelligent effort to register and use the forces of the zodiac enables us to express them more wisely— and build the kind of close, intimate relationship with them that they deserve, as companions of our soul. This ought to be our constant goal in our study of the forces of the zodiac.

4

Putting the Zodiac
To Work

INVOLVING OURSELF

The real power of each sign of the zodiac lies, of course, not in the stars but in what we can do with it in our life—to accelerate our growth, heighten our creativity, strengthen our leadership skills, and enhance our group participation. Harnessing this power and putting it to work in our life is no easy task, however. It is not a question of just waiting for our favorite sign to roll around and then letting it work for us! As with any opportunity, we must be prepared to work hard and intelligently to harness these forces.

Each sign of the zodiac has its own special emphasis on growth, creative work, leadership, and group service. We need to discover what this focus is, then apply ourself to cooperating in practical ways with it. This will not only help us seize opportunities we might otherwise miss, but also link us with the immense reservoirs of practical power that each of these signs represents. This power is available to us for our use in our activities—but only if we act as a responsible agent of it.

To harness the power of these forces, in other words, we must do a great deal more than just intellectually contemplate the unlimited ways we might use them. We must define our individual *needs* for expressing their wisdom, goodwill, strength, harmony, joy, and peace, and then we must vigorously involve ourself in the ongoing effort to use these forces, day by day, to be productive in life.

ACCELERATING GROWTH

Just as the average person usually thinks of health as freedom from sickness, and happiness as having what he wants, he also tends to think of growth *as the process of getting what he desires.* This is the type of person who generally regards himself as either a pawn or a victim of the circumstances of life; as such, he has no motive except to pursue blatantly self-serving goals. But real growth involves much more than just developing a strong ego and learning to dominate our environment! It must take us into the inner dimensions of life, which are the true source of our power to reform and improve the conditions around us—and within us.

Genuine growth focuses on *us*—the refinement of our values, the enrichment of our character strengths, the expansion of our awareness, and the development of our creative abilities—not the changing conditions of outer life. As we cultivate our inner life and use it to transform our character, we become a better, more mature person—not just someone with more power, money, or the ability to control others. The increase in maturity and awareness is the heart of real growth.

Within our spiritual self are patterns of genius and talent, as well as wellsprings of love, joy, and courage. As we recognize and nurture these seeds within us, we grow mentally, emotionally, physically, and spiritually. We grow mentally by developing new talents, refining our perspective on life, and cultivating our inner wisdom. We grow emotionally by learning to discipline our reactiveness and by teaching the emotions to express joy, affection, compassion, and goodwill. We grow physically by learning to act effectively and constructively in daily life. And we grow spiritually as we strive to develop a personality which is a suitable vehicle for use by our spirit in fulfilling its purpose on earth.

It takes intelligent effort to grow in these ways. We must work hard to understand ourself—to define our real needs for growth, not just the distress or frustrations we would like to avoid. We must examine who we are and what we have been, so that we can identify the patterns of problems which must be healed before new growth can be launched. But we do not have to work in a vacuum. The soul is always ready to respond and help us in any sincere effort to grow—and so are the unlimited resources of the forces of the zodiac.

One of the primary ways the forces of the zodiac help us grow is by challenging our limitations, blind spots, outdated habits, and selfishness, so we can reform them more easily.

Aries challenges our initiative by calling us to start new tasks and complete old ones, reform our behavior, and give greater expression to our values and convictions.

Taurus challenges our motivation by calling us to examine our selfish habits and prejudices, mobilize our goodwill, learn cooperation, and strengthen our intention to be helpful.

Gemini challenges our capacity for goodwill by calling us to become more tolerant, practice forgiveness and brotherhood, act more kindly, and pursue constructive service.

Cancer challenges our tendencies to be materialistic by calling us to translate our inner vision of greatness into practical objectives, revise our priorities, and enrich our self-expression with spiritual qualities.

Leo challenges our selfhood and self-expression by calling us to organize our thinking and behavior, revise our sense of purpose, and act with a more enlightened degree of self-control.

Virgo challenges our spiritual development by calling us to review what we are doing to activate it, expand the scope of our service, and nurture the seeds of greatness within ourself, our family, and our work.

Libra challenges our integrity by calling us to review our record of mistakes and accomplishments, examine our accountability, and increase our sense of responsibility.

Scorpio challenges our self-determination by giving focus to the struggle between our commitment to spirit and our emotional immaturity. It calls us to practice detachment, exert self-control, and cultivate a higher orientation toward life.

Sagittarius challenges our idealism by calling us to clarify our aspirations and learn to work wisely with spiritual forces.

Capricorn challenges our involvement in life by calling us to examine where we have failed to honor the fullness of our potential or failed to complete our tasks or act with courage.

Aquarius challenges our relationships by calling us to recognize selfishness and its consequences, strengthen our humanitarian values, and become more aware of our need for one another in solving our collective problems.

Pisces challenges our self-deceptions and illusions by calling us to understand our power to rule our own awareness, act with insight and goodwill, and learn to serve.

As we strive to meet these challenges, we will gain much understanding about ourself—our strengths, weaknesses, priorities, self-deceptions, and values. We will also learn what changes we need to make to transform the patterns of our character that have led to cycle after cycle of repeated difficulty. This is important, because just understanding our problems is not enough; we must *resolve* them so they no longer trouble us.

Some people, of course, try to resolve their problems by finding someone else to blame for them. Others strive mainly to silence the guilt and fear their conscience generates when things go wrong. Still others resort to justifying their hostility, paranoia, selfishness, and aggressiveness through deft twists of clever rationalizations. But these are only childish responses to childish problems. They dishonor our potential for expressing maturity, wisdom, and goodwill. The mature person grows by seeking to *add* new measures of patience, goodwill, trust, cooperation, talent, and courage to his character.

These he can find in the forces of the zodiac. If we suffer from ambivalence and indecisiveness, for instance, the force of Leo can be harnessed to add a greater measure of strength and self-determination to our character. If we have trouble disciplining worn-out habits, the force of Taurus can be harnessed to add a stronger motivation for change to our effort. The important point to comprehend is that we must harness more than just the knowledge of what we need. Knowledge can provide a *basis* for resolving problems, but rarely is the resolution itself. In addition to knowing that we need to be patient, forgiving, or innovative, in other words, we must also express the *power* and *quality* of patience, goodwill, and creativity.

The challenge of harnessing the forces of the zodiac to help us grow in our ability to solve problems is to discover their positive strength and learn to apply them to our daily needs. If we meet this challenge correctly, we will learn to express the dominant spiritual force of each sign *through* the problems and difficulties we face.

We should not think that the only way to grow is by facing and resolving our problems, however! This can be a powerful impetus, but we can also grow by finding opportunities for greater self-expression and fulfillment—and acting on them. Unfortunately, many people define "opportunity" as a chance to get something for nothing—or to get away with something without being caught. Serendipity is a part of life, but there is an obvious distinction to be made between opportunism and opportunities for growth. The former exercises our potential for cheating; the latter, our potential for greatness!

An opportunity is a combination of conditions or forces which give us a chance to expand our self-expression or the contribution we make to life. Whether or not we seize an opportunity depends largely on us. We may have an opportunity to build a lasting friendship by treating someone new we meet with kindness and generosity, but if we act rudely and selfishly instead, the opportunity will evaporate. In most cases, genuine opportunities require us to *make a demonstration* of our talent or goodwill. As a result, they almost always stimulate growth.

The forces of the zodiac present us with many opportunities. Some are fleeting; others will last for the whole period of a given sign. But unlike problems, we have to be alert to our opportunities and seize them when the time is ripe. Problems cling to us and follow us from sign to sign, but opportunities do not. Unless we are oriented to enriching the quality of life, we will miss most of them.

Learning to recognize and seize the opportunities of life is one of the most profound ways we can grow. It teaches us the value of true *insight*—of looking beyond the surface and discovering the forces at work behind the scenes, building new possibilities and prospects. To find opportunities, we must:

Look inside ourself, to determine how we can expand our responsibilities, develop new skills, become receptive to new ideas, enrich our understanding, tap new inspiration for innovative work, tap new leadership potential, or expand our storehouse of goodwill, patience, and courage.

Look inside others, to see how we can improve communication, share common work and problems, cooperate in new endeavors, and stimulate their potential to grow.

Look inside our work, to appreciate its organization and better understand how we can add to its stability and growth.

Look inside society, to recognize the underlying ideals and evolving purpose which should govern its operation—and how we can strengthen and support them.

The more we work with the forces of the zodiac, the more these rich and varied opportunities will stand out to us—even though they remain unseen to others. Moreover, we will have a good idea of what it will take to seize them, for it is nothing less than the dominant spiritual force of each sign which generates the majority of the opportunities of the time. As we work with the primary keynote of the sign, as a close and intimate companion, we will tap the power we need to capitalize on our opportunities.

And, as we strive to meet our opportunities with the best and noblest elements of our character, we also provide our soul with an opportunity—the opportunity to express its wisdom and love on earth through us.

HEIGHTENING CREATIVITY

Creativity is a complex process involving many factors and forces. Some people equate creativity with being different, as though simple, stylistic changes were the substance of innovation. Others think that creativity is cultivated just by becoming more confident and forceful in our self-expression. But glitter and aggressiveness are not really hallmarks of creativity, any more than showmanship is its best measure. Genuine creativity mobilizes our inner potential for genius and nobility and inspires us to honor it through the work we do. It transforms and enlightens the quality of our self-expression, not just our style. It contributes something worthwhile to the world, not just a clever show. It enriches our capacity to be productive, not just our sense of self-confidence.

The process of creativity involves inspiration, planning, talent, experimentation, the germination of new ideas, and the constant improvement of technique. Each sign of the zodiac emphasizes one or more important aspects of this process. The more we understand how the forces of a sign support and nurture our creative self-expression, the more effectively we can cooperate with them.

We all have a vast potential for creative self-expression, even though it lies dormant in many of us. In this regard, it is important to appreciate that creative self-expression is not limited just to the traditional creative arts; it embraces the art of living, our career, enlightened family management, and hobbies as well. Whenever we bring something new from the level of spirit into expression on earth, we are being creative.

To interact creatively with the forces of the zodiac, however, we must approach creative work *intelligently*. Too many people still limit their understanding of the creative process by emphasizing the feeling nature of inspiration. This is probably because we tend to have emotional reactions to good works of art, music, and literature, whether we are creating it or just enjoying it. Too much emotion, however, generates more frustration than beauty and innovation. The creative effort actually has its foundation in the part of the *mind* which deals with abstractions, symbols, and shades of meaning.

Intelligent interaction with the forces of the zodiac trains the mind to work with abstract forces and symbols and relate them effectively to our needs, resources, and opportunities. Learning to manage several dimensions of thought and association simultaneously, thereby blending abstract force with concrete plans for action, teaches us some of the most basic skills of creativity.

As we work with the forces of the zodiac in these ways, we also develop an intimate contact with the energies of joy, beauty, goodwill, justice, harmony, wisdom, serenity, and grace. These are some of the most useful building blocks of creativity. The more skill we develop in expressing these qualities, the more adept we become in investing them creatively in our work and relationships. We also set the stage for using them, eventually, in the larger context of serving spirit.

The forces of Aquarius, for example, stimulate the qualities of unity, wholeness, serenity, and health. As we interact with these forces, we can learn to use them creatively to heal and enrich our relationships with family and friends—as well as the quality of our work. The forces of Aries can help us break through old patterns of thought and behavior to find new ways to deal with ongoing situations. The forces of Libra can help us see the actual side by side with the ideal—as well as ways to bring them into greater balance. The forces of Virgo stimulate our interest in nurturing the development of projects and long range goals. If we seek to use these forces innovatively, we will quickly discover the immense creative power which can be harnessed, sign after sign.

The creative power of each sign is such an important facet

of the forces of the zodiac that we have included a divine song or psalm in each commentary. This song is written as though it were the recitation of the higher self—the means by which the higher self calls upon its companions, the forces of the zodiac, to help develop its creative plans. By reflecting on this song and relating it to our own creative work, we can learn about the symbolic nature of the forces of the zodiac as they seek to interact with the forces of our human awareness. We will be able to sense the inner, dynamic workings of the forces of the zodiac, and how they can be harnessed for creative expression.

STRENGTHENING LEADERSHIP

The forces of the zodiac, being divine powers, can also help us exert dominion over our affairs and become a more effective leader in the affairs of groups. Like creativity, leadership is a complex talent, involving many skills and capacities beyond the simple ability to rule with authority. It requires the ability to be inspired and to inspire others, to search for direction, to communicate, to initiate new projects, to generate practical plans, and to work harmoniously with others.

Unfortunately, the art of leadership is widely misunderstood; it is usually equated with dictatorial control of people and situations. Some people think a good leader is one who can get his own way by being tough and intimidating with others. Others define leadership as the ability to communicate and persuade, write clever memos, and hold well-organized meetings. But this is just the fancy footwork, not the substance, of leadership. Leadership does involve the use of power, but it is the enlightened use of power: the power to motivate others, discern the heart of an issue, choose wisely, gain the respect of others, act at the right time, resolve conflict, and turn dissension into consensus.

The hallmark of leadership is the ability to *take charge.* The most obvious place to begin is by taking charge of ourself— our habits, attitudes, lack of initiative, or need for reform. But there are other areas of life as well in which we can take charge and assert enlightened leadership. We can take charge of the work we do, by increasing our cooperation with others, im- proving the quality of our work, and acting with greater enthu- siasm. In each of these ways, we lead. We can take charge of our relationships, both with family and friends, by putting a stop to manipulation or exploitation, suggesting new lines of activity, and acting with greater responsibility. In each of these ways, we lead. And we can take charge in groups we belong to, by inspiring others with a new sense of group purpose, motivat- ing others to cooperate more fully, and organizing group activi- ties. In each of these ways, we lead. It is not necessary to hold a position of leadership; by acting with the skills and qualities of leadership, we lead.

This is where an ability to harness the forces of the zodiac can be invaluable. By defining the collective needs of those we seek to lead, we can identify specific forces and talents which we can then draw on, as the time is ripe, throughout the zodiacal year. This lets us work to attune the group as a whole to its inner potential and opportunities. By defining the ideals we need to serve and inspire in others, we can identify specific divine qualities which we can then invoke from the zodiac. Our national government, for instance, could be greatly enriched by the goodwill of Gemini, which inspires enlightened leadership. By invoking it on behalf of our nation, we as an individual can "take charge" of problems and responsibilities we usually only complain about.

It is not just inspiration that we can draw from the forces of the zodiac, however, but also the power of divine purpose. This is of great importance to the enlightened leader. If we try to use our personal will to take charge of people and circumstances, we can quickly exhaust ourself—no matter how noble our intentions may be. But if we draw on the impersonal power of the forces of the zodiac, we will find our capacity to stay "at the helm," in charge of our responsibilities, is inexhaustible.

A careful study of the signs will indicate which ones can best help us with our specific needs. In Gemini, for example, our ability to communicate our ideas effectively will be increased. The force of Leo helps us focus our thinking, boost our self-confidence, and act with courage. Aquarius fosters a sense of cooperation and unity, as well as deeper humanitarian concerns. The power of all of these attributes can be used to enrich and expand our leadership abilities.

In addition, the forces of the zodiac can also teach us what it means to be an enlightened *follower*. The ability to follow is actually the complement of good leadership, even though it is usually overlooked by those who want only to control events. Every real leader must be able to follow as well as lead, since someone or some ideal usually leads the leader. To become a good follower, we need to learn what it takes to cooperate with intelligent leaders—and spiritual ideals. We must also learn how to support the creative work of others—to support the best and noblest aspects within a group.

Too often, the twin capacities to lead and follow are missing in human groups—especially in business and government. As a result, leadership positions fall by default to blatant egotists who can neither follow nor lead, but just grab power and exercise it like a petty tyrant lording over his personal fiefdom. And those in subordinate positions, having no incentive to be enlightened followers, follow the line of least resistance and become defensive and highly competitive with their colleagues.

Working with the forces of the zodiac is an excellent way to break out of these traps. The motivating power of Taurus, for example, can help us discover that there are larger purposes and forces at work in a group than the personal will of the leaders; by tapping into these purposes, we can learn to follow them, even though the rest of the group is motivated by baser and more selfish drives. And the forces of Capricorn can help us become more aware of the rich legacy of tradition in a group and how to use it to inspire group members to rededicate themselves to the work at hand.

As we learn to be an enlightened follower in this way, we will discover what it means to be led by spiritual purpose—to practice intelligent obedience to our spiritual will. This, too, is a lesson the forces of the zodiac can help us learn. During Aries, for example, the spiritual will works quietly but powerfully to encourage us to turn away from our selfish priorities and invest ourself more fully in working to make life more sacred. We can respond openly to this encouragement and cooperate with it—or rebel against it.

There are always more subtle lessons to learn about the spiritual will, how to forge it into noble purposes and enlightened motives, and how to serve it in our daily work. The great people of history in government, science, and the humanities have all been led by the noble vision of their destiny. As we learn to be led by the same kind of noble vision, we too will learn what it means to lead.

ENHANCING GROUP WORK

The ability to work in groups is a necessity in this modern world, making collective achievement possible. Yet groups can also be a trap to the unsuspecting. Religious groups and governments, for instance, will often tyrannize their followers with either veiled or unveiled threats. And the sophisticated misuse of appeals for unity and harmony can do nearly as much damage, although they are less obvious. Some spiritual groups make such a big point of achieving harmony that they suppress all dissension and conflict that arises—and all individuality as well. The result is a mediocre group of passive followers who accomplish very little.

Other examples also illustrate the problems of groups. A strong-willed person will bully other members of a family in the name of maintaining "unity." In business, the call for teamwork often leads to the suppression of creativity or differing points of view, cutting off the potential for new ideas and approaches—or even practical solutions to problems.

The forces of the zodiac can be extremely helpful in improving the quality of group work. But it does little good to know that the forces of Taurus support hierarchical reorganization in groups, unless we know what a proper structure would be. The place to begin, in other words, is with a definition of the principles of effective group activity. These are:

1. We must identify and understand the genuine purpose of the group. Secret agendas must be exposed and unrealistic goals discarded in favor of clearly defining the reason why all these people are working together. From this dominant purpose, the power to impel and sustain the group is drawn.

2. Each member must define the proper role he or she must play in fulfilling this collective purpose. If everyone in a group views his or her work in relationship to the central purpose, then they can all cooperate effectively together. They can also accept the need for differing levels of power and responsibility without falling into the trap of equality, which can reduce everyone in a group to the same level of mediocrity.

3. There must be an effective leader. Typically, the ideal leader is thought to be a hard driving, charismatic genius—someone with a flair for showmanship yet the ability to think and work like a computer. These are the kinds of people who get organizations into trouble, however; they notoriously do not make good leaders. A good leader must be able to grasp the dominant purpose of the group and know how it is meant to

evolve. He must be able to generate plans which will implement this purpose, and communicate them effectively to others. Esoterically, the leader holds the vision for the work of the group and wields the energy of the purpose behind it, dispersing it as appropriate to the members of the group.

4. There must be an effective organization. This is not the bricks and mortar of the building which houses the group, nor the hierarchy of committees or executives which manage the group. It is the structure of fundamental policies and plans which convey the dominant purpose of the group. In actual practice, this organization is invested in key people who have the responsibility to formulate and implement policy, plans, and review. Without this structure, there is no framework which can serve to integrate and coordinate group activity.

5. Individual maturity is also of great importance. If we bring our neurotic fears, prejudices, and selfishness into any group endeavor, we risk contaminating others with these poisons. We will also be unable to cooperate effectively. After all, how can we work with others if we are unable to work with our own personal problems?

6. There must also be an ability to share. In any group, we share far more than a common labor. We also share our talents, our goodwill, the problems of the group's work, and the rewards of group success. Esoterically, the ability to share keeps the life energy of the group circulating.

7. We must know when to work as part of the group and when to work independently. This is far more important than is usually understood. Even though it is commonly assumed that cooperation is always good, there are times when it is clearly not in the best interests of the whole. A good example of this principle can be found in the collective farms of communist societies. Too much organization and central planning isolates management from production and the realities of human nature—and mother nature as well. The result has usually been

disastrous. In the West, modern businesses often give their scientists and engineers a great deal of independence, in order to encourage creativity. Clearly, there are times when certain tasks are best left to individual effort.

Once we have a good grasp of the essentials of group work, we can more clearly see how the forces of each sign of the zodiac can help make the groups we are part of more effective. Libra is an excellent time to seek consensus within groups. The forces of Sagittarius can be used to refocus the role we play in groups. And Cancer can be a good time to understand the problems of our family as well as to strengthen family ties.

In some cases, the energy of a sign will stimulate rebellion against the purpose of the group, the authority of its leaders, or specific policies—if the seeds of such rebellion already exist. When this occurs, it should be seen as a group problem, not just a problem of individuals. It may be necessary to redefine the purpose of the collective work more precisely, realign assignments and responsibilities, or even change the composition of the group. More goodwill among group members may not be enough to resolve the underlying problems.

Working with the forces of the zodiac to enhance group work also helps us recognize the need for individual maturity. The force of Aquarius, for example, will tend to evoke a stronger humanitarian interest in the members of a group; the forces of Pisces will help us evaluate the contribution we make and eliminate self-serving motives and objectives. Other signs will help morale by increasing respect for the group endeavor.

The keynote listed for each sign in the commentaries in this book can be used quite productively to focus on the qualities with which we can nurture group life in each sign. As we gain experience in working in this way, we will find that we can tune into these energies consciously and learn to radiate them to other members of the group, thereby enriching the quality of group life—and its work.

THE CYCLES OF THE YEAR

The forces of the zodiac do not just stimulate us for one month and then go away. Just as the sun is always with us even though it shines most warmly during the summer, so also the harmony of Gemini is always with us, even though it is strongest in June, and the nurturing love of Virgo is always with us, even though it is strongest in September. Part of the work of harnessing these forces is to learn to recognize the relationships between the forces of the various signs—and the patterns or cycles they create throughout the zodiacal year.

Conventional astrologers are well aware of these patterns and cycles, but they tend to focus their attention on our subconscious reactions to them, rather than what it means to harness the power of these forces to change ourself. As a result, they miss the real drama of these cycles.

The zodiacal year begins in Aries and runs through Pisces. Although new force from the zodiac emerges in every sign of the year, there is always an unusually strong and directed blast of it at the onset, in Aries. Most of us are unaware of this blast, as it is registered only by the unconscious mind, but it sets in motion new seeds and directions which will govern our growth and creative opportunities for the rest of the zodiacal year. This new life is meant to enrich our consciousness and self-expression, but how much it is able to do depends on how we respond.

As the year progresses, we will become aware of "echoes" of this new blast of energy in Aries, each echo helping us understand it more fully. In Taurus, for example, we may become aware of the emergence of new motivations and a stronger sense of aspiration. In Leo, we may be impelled to update and refocus our sense of identity. In Sagittarius, we may finally focus this energy as the ambition to pursue some new goal. By Aquarius and Pisces, we will be able to appreciate the full maturity of these new directions, and initiate a new line of service.

96

In addition to this basic progression of energy through the zodiacal year, there are many other harmonies and resonances we will discover. Some of these are well known to any student of astrology—the relationship among all fire signs, air signs, water signs, and earth signs, or the harmonies among all cardinal, fixed, and mutable signs. There is also an interesting interplay between signs which are polar opposites.

Other resonances are not so obvious. They will be revealed to us as we work with specific problems or opportunities sign after sign, even year after year. A certain problem, for example, may trouble us for two months and then disappear for a month, only to reappear once more. Often, this is related to the complex relationships which exist among the different signs of the zodiac. If our problem involves a poor self-image, for instance, it will tend to be aggravated by the forces of Leo and become almost unbearable in Virgo. But the forces of Libra would have little effect on it, and we might think we have put it behind us once and for all. This self-deception would be dashed in Scorpio, however, as the problem returns full force. If, however, we use the power of Scorpio to dedicate ourself to resolving this poor self-image once and for all, we may find that we are able to make remarkable progress toward a solution in Sagittarius. In this way, we are able to harness the cycles of the zodiac to our own benefit.

To fully understand these subtle patterns of resonance, we must examine the higher dimensions of these zodiacal relationships. The interaction of polar opposites, for example—signs which are six months or 180° apart—needs to be seen as complementary and constructive, rather than antagonistic. In other words, the line of force which connects Scorpio and Taurus must eventually be harmonized and blended, even though it often seems to split and divide at present. Scorpio provides a "frame" for Taurus, in that the desire of Taurus becomes aspiration in Scorpio. And Taurus provides a "frame" for Scorpio, in that the darkness of the tribulations of Scorpio create the potential for illumination in Taurus. In much the same way, the interplay between Leo and Aquarius eventually results in a synthesis which establishes us as an *enlightened individual* while allowing us to experience and work with an awareness of *universal order*. As we see how one sign can fulfill its opposite, we come to recognize that the twelve forces of the zodiac are actually six well-balanced esoteric strengths we must master.

Harnessing the forces of the zodiac can be a fascinating and rewarding challenge—but only if we do our homework. We need to study thoroughly the inner side of these forces, as well as the opportunities and challenges they present us. We must also study the qualities, organization, and problems of our own character. This helps us identify our real needs—not just the symptoms of our problems—and relate them successfully to the appropriate forces of the zodiac.

In addition, as we understand the divine patterns of our soul and our spiritual potential, we can intelligently compare what we are with what we can become. We can then use the forces of the zodiac as our companions to heal our problems and lift us toward the next step of our evolution.

5

Using
The Commentaries

WHAT TO LOOK FOR

The commentaries which follow in the next twelve chapters are written to emphasize the quality of each force of the zodiac *as it exists prior to its impact on human nature*—and how each one can serve as a companion of the soul. Consequently, our interpretations often differ sharply from the standard definitions given by conventional astrologers, who tend to describe the response of mass consciousness to these forces, rather than the forces themselves.

In working with these forces, we should remember that each one will affect different individuals in differing ways. This is because the needs and maturity of people vary greatly. The interests, emotional tone, and wisdom of an immature person, for example, differ radically from those of an enlightened person. For this reason, we have structured these commentaries to lead from the general to the specific. They do not contain exact predictions of what will happen to any one person, but rather thorough explanations of the ways in which these forces tend to influence human psychology. We have written with the purpose of reinforcing our individual responsibility to work with these forces skillfully—not to undermine it, as so many astrologers do.

We should also keep in mind that human consciousness is complex in both structure and operation. The many operations of our thinking and self-expression are like departments of a large organization, all working together harmoniously in ever changing patterns. In psychology, these departments of our character are known as subpersonalities. Just as the impact of the forces of the zodiac will vary from person to person, they are also likely to influence the various departments of our consciousness in differing ways. We should therefore take care not to focus so intently on one aspect of these forces that we exclude other aspects which are equally important to us.

It is for this reason that it is useful to think of our structure of consciousness as a miniature "zodiac within us." Because we are a complex being, we can always find a potential application for each of the forces of the zodiac. We simply have to take the time to define what our needs are and how we can use the dominant forces of a sign productively. As we work with the suggestions in these commentaries, we will be surprised how we are able to enrich and strengthen the key aspects of our character—and build up a reservoir of force which we can then use in our daily self-expression.

The commentaries have been written to help us relate to the forces of the zodiac in practical ways—to find the special qualities of divine life which can best serve the needs of the "zodiac within us" in any given sign. We simply need to look for those suggestions and recommendations that make the most sense to us—and then act on them.

We should also appreciate, however, that the forces of the zodiac *are* divine in origin. In each sign, therefore, they reveal something about God we may have missed before. To tap the full potential of these forces—and the commentaries which follow—we are meant to look for and respond to these divine qualities, in addition to our own personal needs. Ultimately, the structure of our consciousness is meant to reflect the structure of the divine mind which is the zodiac! The more we are able to focus the zodiac within us so that it reflects the zodiac of the heavens, the more enlightened and effective we become, both in life in general and in our spiritual aspiration in specific.

THE STRUCTURE OF THE COMMENTARIES

The commentary on each sign begins with a definition of its **basic archetypal force.** The description of this archetypal force, however, is not the force itself! The force of each sign is a living, divine energy which has its origin in the heavens. It is an abstract, universal power which transcends mere words and symbols. Archetypes have the power to influence our awareness and behavior at *all* levels of our consciousness—even the unconscious mind.

The definition of these forces should be studied carefully, as it is the linchpin for all of the subsequent sections on the sign. As we read these opening paragraphs, we should try to go beyond the words and tap the power behind them—the abstract power of the archetype itself. If we read only for ideas, we will greatly limit our capacity to interact with the forces of the zodiac. Fortunately, as we begin to digest this information and speculate on how we can use it in our daily life, we do invoke the power of these forces to some degree. If we can also learn to use our imagination to reflect on the inner meaning and power of these ideas, we may well tap the levels of abstract thought where these archetypal forces can be contacted directly.

The **symbolism** of the sign is described next. The arrow of Sagittarius, the scales of Libra, and the other symbols of these signs give us visible clues into the nature of each force. They also reveal something about the dynamic thrust of these energies as they interact with human consciousness. Each symbol can be used as a focus in our meditations as we explore the subtleties of these forces.

The next section of the commentary examines **how the force affects us.** This often begins with a general statement of the impact of these forces on human consciousness, and then goes on to a specific description of the effect on the average person, the spiritual aspirant, and the advanced person. These effects vary tremendously; the average person tends to be drawn into intensified reactiveness of one kind or another; the aspirant must often struggle with the duality between his spiritual and human natures; while the advanced person must deal with the energies as they affect the soul.

This section then goes on to describe the impact of these forces on our motivation, our awareness, the mind, the emotions, and our self-expression. At times this will be a positive, uplifting impact; at other times, it is more likely to stir up our rebelliousness and resistance. Our motivation, for example, might be stimulated by a stronger urge to pursue mental house-cleaning; in the same sign, our awareness may be directed by a stronger interest in searching out the musty corners of our subconscious, so they can be transformed. The mind might be stimulated to rise up to a new perception of our spiritual design for living—whereas the emotions might well plunge into guilt, fear, and self-loathing. At the same time, our self-expression would be dominated primarily by genuine progress in self-improvement and the reform of attitudes and habits.

This description is followed by an examination of **the challenges** of the sign. These challenges reveal what it means to tap and use the spiritual quality of the force in:
- Our effort to cultivate a better tie with spirit.
- Our duties as a parent.
- Our relationships with other people.
- Business and commercial activities.
- Society as a whole.
- Our personal growth.

The creative challenge of growth in Scorpio, for instance, is to triumph over the temptations and weaknesses of our human nature by expressing the life of the soul. A thorough knowledge of these creative challenges will be a great help to the sincere spiritual aspirant in understanding what it means to reach beyond our limitations and mobilize our undeveloped potential.

The commentary then takes an in-depth look at the kinds of **problems** which are likely to arise during this particular sign of the zodiac. We must keep in mind that these problems arise out of the weaknesses of our character, however—not from the forces of the zodiac themselves. It may take a while for some people to become comfortable with this idea—especially those steeped in traditional astrological concepts. The average problem-oriented, negative-thinking person tends to assume that a positive force can never create a problem. But too much success can be just as harmful as too much failure. The stress of success and public recognition, for example, can be a severe strain on the patience, humility, tolerance, and poise of a person who is not prepared to handle it.

The section on problems is designed, therefore, to help us discover whatever potential may lurk in us for an immature response to these forces. It contains a checklist of possible weaknesses, areas of self-deception, excesses, and selfish tendencies which may be exposed or agitated. This checklist is *not* provided for the purpose of helping us avoid or protect ourself against these problems, however; this would be contrary to the spirit of growth. Its purpose is to inspire us to eliminate or control these personal flaws and weaknesses, so we can work more effectively with the spiritual essence of the forces of the zodiac.

In most cases, these problems are clearly negative and harmful to our better efforts, but every now and then they include an attitude or habit that some people may view as positive or helpful. We list rudeness and hostility as problems, for example, even though many people excuse them as "strengths" they need in order to assert themselves. We likewise list passiveness and laziness as problems, even though they are often rationalized as ways to express "gentleness" and "cooperation."

We also include in this section blind spots that we are likely not to view as difficulties, for one reason or another. A blind spot could be a tendency to be overly confident, to rationalize mistakes instead of correcting them, or to long for some condition which is not really beneficial. Many people, for example, have become so skilled at learning how to dispose of all guilt that they have dulled their capacity to respond intelligently to life; their defensiveness "protects" them from the tensions necessary for growth.

Regardless of the type of problem, the commentary endeavors to show how this difficulty distorts the intent of the forces of this sign, and what action can be taken to resolve it.

The section on problems is followed by a commentary on the **opportunities** of the sign for more enlightened self-expression and greater growth in character. This section is *not* to be read as a series of predictions of what we can expect to happen to us. An opportunity is an invitation to us to act in new and more effective ways—not a gift which is delivered to us without any effort on our part. To realize any of the opportunities listed in this section, we will have to act with initiative and intelligent skill.

Some of these opportunities will, of course, be related to the problems we may experience. During a period of increased turmoil, after all, there will also be a great opportunity to use the mind to refocus on our principles and values, thereby stabilizing our behavior. During a time when intolerance is heightened, there is also a strong opportunity to practice forgiveness.

Many of the opportunities involve our creative self-expression and the chance to develop new skills and character traits. Certain signs are ideal for building right human relationships, whereas others are more suited for introspection and the development of our intuitive awareness. There might also be the opportunity to cooperate with forces of charitableness and goodwill sweeping through the universe, opening the door for receiving as well as giving a greater abundance of ideas, friendship, patience, goodwill, and wealth.

Next, there is an exploration of **the best way to tune into the force**. This section often lists a series of questions which, when contemplated in a reflective state, helps attune ourself more directly to the dominant qualities of a sign. The emphasis is placed on defining *our need* for these energies, and then acting *as if* this need was being met by the forces of the zodiac—which it will be.

The best ways to heal, teach, and lead are also briefly listed. This reminds us that these commentaries are designed to help us use these forces actively in daily life—and guides us in determining where we can best invest our energies, sign by sign.

Finally, there is also a mention of **how these forces will echo** during the rest of the zodiac. This section indicates two or three signs in which the work begun in the present sign will be picked up and renewed. This information is provided for those who want to begin studying the complex relationships between the various signs.

The text of the commentary concludes with two special features, a song and a parable.

The **song** helps us understand the special dynamics of each force, helping us realize that it is not just an abstract idea but a living, dynamic force which has a quality, direction, and meaning of its own—as well as a capacity to influence us. The song describes these qualities in action at divine creative levels—and how human life is affected as a result. As such, it can help us touch the mystical essence of these forces.

The **parable** personifies specific aspects of the forces and their interaction with human nature. It dramatizes how the forces work in our life, revealing new hints about their nature and potential influence on us. Reflecting on the parable is an excellent way to activate the symbolic meaning of the sign in our own imagination.

Each of the commentaries also provides a useful listing, found right at the beginning of the chapter, of different characteristics of the sign. This listing describes:

The **keynote,** which summarizes the potential of the force to heal and enrich our consciousness. The keynote makes an excellent meditative focus as we seek to understand the nature of the force and how it can draw us closer to the life of spirit.

The **mantra,** a short phrase which can be used in conjunction with the keynote to explore some of the more esoteric dimensions of the dominant force. It can be thought of as the call of the soul as it evokes the intelligent response of the personality. As such, it is a clue to developing enlightened cooperation with the soul.

A focus of contemplation for the new and full moons. It is suggested that readers acquire a good almanac to find the exact time of the new and full moons in their area, rather than rely on newspapers or ordinary calendars for this information. The full moon focus relates the quality of the dominant force to our potential for self-expression. By reflecting on it, we can gain insight into ways to take advantage of this "high tide" in spiritual force. The new moon focus is a phrase which sums up the optimum way to harness the dominant quality of the sign for our personal growth.

The dominant **rays** associated with the sign. The rays are seven types of divine power. A brief description of the rays is listed in the appendix of this book; for a definitive examination of the rays, read *Esoteric Psychology I & II* by Alice Bailey. These two books contain a detailed description of the qualities, dynamics, and influence of these seven major energies of life.

A knowledge of the rays associated with the forces of the zodiac can be very helpful in determining how they will affect us. The forces of Aquarius, for instance, promote a love of humanity and a desire to assist in its progress; the net result of its influence is to transform selfishness into selfless service to humanity. The rays associated with Aquarius are two, four, five, and seven; these rays are, respectively, the divine powers which bring love and wisdom, the harmonization of conflict, the use of practical knowledge, and the orderly regulation of force and form. As a result, the second ray emphasizes the humanitarian concern and goodwill of Aquarius. The fourth ray stimulates the urge to transform dissension into cooperation. The fifth ray promotes the clarity of thinking and pragmatism of Aquarius. And the seventh ray emphasizes the need to create a new order out of chaos—a new order which demonstrates our spiritual intentions. As we come to appreciate the contribution of the rays to the zodiac, we can deepen our insights into the dynamic impact of these forces. In addition, we can also recognize more fully the relation of the forces of the zodiac to the various aspects of God.

The primary **archetypal forces** which influence us during the sign. Divine archetypes are specific aspects of force and quality which have their origin in the mind of God, not collective human thought and behavior. These forces work by inspiring our mind and conditioning our emotions and behavior along the lines of a specific quality. The archetypes listed in the commentary are the pure qualities of the forces of the zodiac—*not* the characteristics of human nature ordinarily emphasized by these signs. They indicate the qualities we ought to be cultivating during this time.

A **prayer** for the sign. These prayers are designed to help us achieve a direct experience of the actual zodiacal forces, and reorient our awareness so that we are better able to be receptive to the full power and meaning of the forces. Using the prayer to help us transcend the effects of mass consciousness and our own limiting beliefs *before* we begin contemplating the forces of a particular sign can have a powerful effect on the clarity of the contact we make.

THE VALUE OF CAREFUL STUDY

It is not the commentaries which make the forces of the zodiac come alive for us—it is our involvement in using them. As we use the commentaries to guide us through the challenges and opportunities of sign after sign, we strengthen our capacity for self-observation and self-evaluation and understand more about the relevance of these forces in our life.

At the start of each sign, the appropriate commentary should be studied carefully, taking sufficient time to reflect fully on its meaning. As we digest what we have read, we should speculate on how these forces will affect us, and which aspects of these energies will be most influential in our life.

There is always a temptation to scan the chapter quickly and decide whether this will be a "good" or a "bad" sign, but this is a temptation to resist, as it would be nothing more than an exercise in emotional reactiveness. Paralyzing our mind with premature judgments is not a healthy way to study anything. All of the signs of the zodiac are divine forces, and should be approached as healthy, constructive influences. If they do not seem that way to us, then this is an indication that *we* need to change.

We should pay special attention to understanding the quality of the dominant force of the sign, as this sets the tone for the way it will affect us. It should be kept in mind, however, that while the archetypal forces of each sign are largely the same each year, their *impact* can vary considerably from year to year. The primary archetypal force of Gemini, for example, works to bring spirit and form closer together. This is true year in and year out. But the special focus of this force may center on finding higher correspondences to mundane events one year, becoming responsive to the inner, spiritual parent the next year, and working to remove obstacles to the life of spirit yet another year.

There are a variety of reasons why these variations occur year to year. Conventional astrologers would remind us that as the positions of the planets change from year to year, they modify the forces of the zodiac as well as our responsiveness to them. In addition, the Hierarchy changes its focus slightly each year, adding its own special emphasis to the zodiac, especially at the time of the full moon. Perhaps the greatest reason is that *we change*—we become stronger or weaker, wiser or more discouraged, more tolerant or more distressed. Our outer circumstances may also change, producing a change in our needs and our state of mind. All of these factors influence the way in which these forces affect us.

Once the quality of the dominant forces of a sign has been studied, we need to consider how these forces will influence our awareness—the miniature "zodiac within us." We should consider how these forces will condition and stimulate our skills, attitudes, values, relationships, creative projects, thinking, emotional reactiveness, and so on.

Reflecting on what we have read should set in motion a series of questions:

• What do we expect to accomplish during this sign?

• What personal flaws and deficiencies should we be alert to, and how best can we correct and heal them?

• How can we use this period of time to enrich our work?

• How can we translate the major forces of this time into a more enlightened self-expression?

• How can we best honor the keynote of this sign in our thoughts, emotions, and physical activities?

Our use of the commentaries should not stop with the initial reading, however. There is so much to absorb and implement that most people will find it best to reread the commentary several times during the course of the sign—at least at the beginning of each decanate. In the first third of the sign, we should focus on the process of self-inquiry and speculation about how the zodiac can help us. At the beginning of the second decanate, ten days into the sign, a careful rereading of the commentary can help us focus on how we can apply these forces in our life. Yet another rereading at the beginning of the last decanate can inspire us to integrate these forces more completely into our character. Then, at the end of the sign, a final reading can help us synthesize our understanding of these forces and our experiences with them.

While the emphasis of these reports is on building our own self-awareness and self-realization, we should not overlook the fact that each period also brings us many useful object lessons. Our friends and colleagues will face challenging situations which parallel lessons we need to be learning as well—and can learn, indirectly through them, if we are attentive to the possibility of it. The more we are attuned to observing life through our conscious study of the forces of the zodiac, the more easily we will recognize that this person's excess or that person's success is teaching us something important about the influences of these forces—something we may be able to profit from later on.

Because of the variations which occur in the impact of these forces, and the growth we will experience in our own life as we work with them, keeping a journal of our insights and changes is highly recommended. This helps us focus our attention on our intelligent interaction with life—and keeps us watchful for the subtle changes occurring in our own awareness and the forces of the zodiac.

Ideally, if we use these commentaries in this way, by the end of each sign we will be a better person than when it began. There is a tremendous power for transformation in the forces of the zodiac—but it can only be tapped if we are willing to harness them and use them constructively.

6

Aries

ARIES

(March 21 through April 19)

Keynote: The impulse to achieve.

Mantra: "The light of divine life impels me to create."

New moon focus: Cooperation with the plan.

Full moon focus: Implementation of the plan.

Rays 1, 4, 6, and 7 dominate.

Primary archetypal forces:

Strength, harmony, joy, brilliance, the spiritual will

A Prayer For Aries:

Within our heart and mind, we know there is One power which has created and now sustains us. At the beginning of every cycle, this One power speaks to us, summoning us to respond to Its direction, purpose, and guidance. Lord, help us love this divine power from the heart; teach the mind to become absorbed in its greatness; and strengthen us to honor its purpose perfectly in thought, emotion, intention, and activity.

As we dedicate our mind to this creative power, let us be filled with new insights and a better understanding of Your plan.

As we dedicate our heart to this benevolent power, let us be filled with a steady trust in the inner life.

As we dedicate our lives to this sustaining power, let us be directed into the paths of correct living.

May the light of the soul dominate and the personality respond, so that the summons is heeded.

And the plan of God emerges more clearly into day.

Aries marks the beginning of a new revolution of the zodiac, a fresh cycle of opportunity and service. The work of Aries is to set in motion the divine energies which will influence the trends of the coming twelve months. This work, however, begins subtly and quietly, in the deepest regions of our unconscious life. The soul responds to the new energies which have been unleashed, redefining and redirecting its purpose and creative plans in accordance with them. But often the personality is completely unaware of what is transpiring at deeper levels.

The specific forces which burst forth each year in Aries at these deep unconscious levels are the divine will to create and will to manifest. It is often not until Gemini or Cancer that we become conscious of the impact of these forces on us as a personality, but at archetypal levels, the impact occurs in Aries and is like an explosion of new divine life. In fact, the sign of Aries is testimony each year to the fact that divine creation is not finished: God is still very much involved in the creative process.

The work of Aries is to stimulate an *evolutionary* change in our thinking and approach to life. The forces of this time endeavor to change our priorities, perspectives, and what we strive toward, bringing these elements of our character more into alignment with divine will and divine plans.

Of course, this type of change usually means that the residue of the past needs to be swept away in order to make room for the new. If we are unprepared for this kind of change, we may find the forces of Aries to be disturbing, both individually and collectively. We may even get in the way of change, and get run down by it. There are several ways in which the changes of Aries can be traumatic if we do not cooperate wisely with them:

• If we do not focus the new burst of divine will into innovative, constructive activities, it may just become divisive, producing splits, schisms, and arguments where cooperation normally reigns. Indeed, the basic duality of life is heightened during Aries and, unless skillfully managed, is apt to emphasize conflicts. These problems can be avoided, however, if we are able to focus on *purpose* and work with the skills of integration, being exceptionally careful not to get trapped in differences and conflicts.

• Our identification with the status quo may be vigorously challenged.

• There may be disquieting shake-ups in our life, especially in terms of authority. New policies, priorities, and lines of authority tend to be established during Aries. These changes can be very uncomfortable for those who are rigid and inflexible, but they need not be. There is a real opportunity in learning to respond well to new lines of authority, both individually and collectively.

The intent of the forces of Aries is to promote a greater involvement of the soul in our daily life—and consequently a more mature involvement by the personality in our activities and responsibilities. This means that most of the changes of Aries will come to us not through external events, but through subtle and provocative influences from within. If we appreciate that these forces are coming from within, then we can take them more in stride, harnessing and using them with equanimity.

One of the most powerful ways that we, as an individual, can work with these archetypal forces of Aries is to strive for a genuine sense of *wholeness* during this month. Aries is an excellent time to step back a bit and consider the larger picture of anything we may be involved in—to look at the forest as a whole, not just the individual trees. It is also a time to strive for completeness and thoroughness in all that we do. In approaching problems, we should proceed holistically—considering *all* elements influencing any difficulty and striving to correct *all* deficiencies. In approaching opportunities, we should proceed in a spirit of innovation—seeking to expand our contacts with life and our responsibilities. And we should pay special attention to the role we play as an individual within the larger

116

"wholes" of our life—family, work, community, and the human race.

The pursuit of wholeness requires the development of a number of humanistic qualities: cooperation, obedience, commitment, and harmony, to list a few. Harmony in particular is of great importance, and is a major archetypal force of Aries.

The forces of Aries awaken within us our potential to achieve, and begin to shape it in dynamic, new ways. We may not always be aware of what this will mean to us as these forces unfold in our life—but if we are alert to them, we can begin cooperating with them.

THE SYMBOLISM OF ARIES

The symbol of Aries is the ram. Conventionally, the ram is associated with sacrifice. The golden fleece in Greek mythology is a story of sacrifice. In ancient Israel, the ram was a sacrificial animal. In Christianity, Jesus came to represent the "sacrificial lamb." Indeed, Easter—which occurs in Aries—puts great emphasis on the passion and sacrifice of the Christ.

Sacrifice is not meant to be quite so melodramatic, however. It should be thought of as the act of making life sacred— of giving up our intense preoccupation with our personal focus so that we can begin working with wholeness. We sacrifice materialistic priorities so we can begin working with the treasures of spirit. We sacrifice selfishness so we can begin working with divine love. We sacrifice ignorance so we can begin working with wisdom. We sacrifice the personal focus of our habits so we can begin working with spiritual purpose.

These sacrifices are often quite real, and usually require us to give up something we cherish deeply. But the sacrifice is always made with the intent of attaining something much greater. It is made not to appease a whimsical God, but rather to prepare ourself to work more effectively as an agent of divine force. Sacrifice is meant to be a daily part of our creative self-expression. All that we do should be seen as the act of making life a bit more sacred and consecrated.

The true sacrifice is the act of overcoming personal desire and personal motives to act in harmony with the direction and intent of the soul. The best way to learn to sacrifice in this manner is to try to think as the soul would think, speak as the soul would speak, and act as the soul would act. Nothing of importance is lost or surrendered in this kind of sacrifice—we forgo only our weaknesses, selfishness, and confusion. In return, we gain the enlightenment and love of the soul.

The ram of Aries, therefore, symbolizes the *will to make life sacred:* the will to transform selfishness into service, the will to participate cooperatively in life, and the will to unite the soul and personality. By interpreting the symbolism in this way, we can see the true power of Aries and how it differs from the usual descriptions of this force, which emphasize the egotism, arrogance, rashness, and impulsiveness of the average person.

HOW THE FORCES OF ARIES AFFECT US

The average person, who is blind to the inner realities of life, will largely miss the significance of Aries. Instead, he will be almost entirely caught up in the struggle and turmoil of this time. Unable to perceive the purpose of events or harness the force of harmony, he will interpret the conflict he experiences as a personal threat to be avoided, if possible, or beaten back, if it is unavoidable. In addition, the average person will focus his self-interests more intensely than usual.

The aspirant, who knows of the inner life of spirit but does not yet fully understand it, will become aware that new ideas and conditions are forming just beyond his conscious awareness, but will not be able to define just what they are. There will be a greater interplay than usual between the conscious mind and unconscious realms of thought, habit, and meaning, but this may affect the aspirant either positively or negatively. If the individual tries to interpret the clues which arise out of the unconscious and put them in the context of helping him serve spirit, it will be positive. But if he retreats into a very personal focus, and lets his fear of the unknown build, it will be negative. At the very least, there will be a tremendous potential for the aspirant to become distracted by and absorbed in the petty and trivial issues of life. At the worst, there is a possibility of becoming overwhelmed by a sense of conflict. This potential threat can be avoided if the aspirant will use the time of Aries for self-renewal and making a fresh commitment to spirit.

The advanced person, who has risen out of his personal focus and acts and thinks from a spiritual perspective, will be able to work directly with the causal forces of Aries. Aries is a time of great power and regeneration for the advanced person— a time for taking advantage of the creative tides which sweep through the planet and the consciousness of humanity. The key for working with this regenerative power is to act from an understanding of group purpose.

Regardless of the level of our refinement, if we work intelligently with the forces of Aries, they will impel us toward greater active expression of our talents, abilities, and treasures of spirit. These forces need to be used and expressed creatively, lest they stagnate in the deeper recesses of the unconscious. Aries is not a time to sit back and do nothing, letting the swirl of life sweep us onward. It is a time to go forth and participate in the work to be done. We respond best to the summons of this time by saying, "I must be about my Father's business."

The ideal **motivation** of Aries, therefore, would be a strong intent to make a constructive contribution to life—through our work, family, and circle of friends. If we then align our values, convictions, principles, and priorities to this motivation, we will be able to harness the richness of the forces of this time. Yet most people are not motivated by this kind of intent. They are motivated instead by personal desire and selfishness. Aries will not eradicate these limiting motivations, but it certainly will not reward them. The selfish person will tend to find himself caught up in a swirl of conflict and opposition, leading to great frustration. In fact, those who have been motivated by personal desire and selfish expediency will find that Aries gives them a rich opportunity to deepen their relationship with the inner being and become more helpful in the world—if they choose to mend their ways. If they refuse, however, they will deny themselves a new round of experience and satisfaction.

In terms of **awareness,** we are most likely to perceive the impact of the forces of Aries through a greater sense of balance and equilibrium. If we have learned any of the fundamental lessons of harmony and balance, we will find ourself more poised mentally, more in control emotionally, and more in step with the opportunities and demands of daily living. But on the other hand, if we are very self-centered and absorbed in our own needs and wants, the forces of Aries will tend to demonstrate our lack of balance.

The mind will be a major factor in harnessing the forces of Aries properly. In those with a sharp and well-focused mind, Aries will be a time of innovation, reform, rejuvenation, and revision—a time for new bursts of creative thinking. In fact, the forces of Aries affect the well-trained mind by producing even greater clarity of thought and understanding than usual. If we look at life from the perspective of purpose—taking the long view, as it were—we will be able suddenly to put many factors into proper focus. We will see the value of long-range priorities over short-term benefits; we will understand the true issues in difficult situations more clearly. And we will be better able to forgive and begin anew.

The emotions often must be consciously restrained during Aries, as there is a great temptation to engage in petty emotional hassles—arguing over insignificant details, becoming angry or irritated due to differences in opinion, taking umbrage at unintentional slights, and so on. Reactiveness is heightened. Once again, an awareness of the longer view is helpful. If we can realize that the purposes and goals we serve are simply *too important* to be tarnished by such immature behavior, we ought to be able to keep our emotional reactiveness in check. In fact, the best use of the emotions is to focus them in loving the purpose and larger implications of our constructive activities.

In the realm of **self-expression**, we will find that Aries has a way of testing our inner strength and integrity. The struggles we may become immersed in will in fact be symbols of inner fights or struggles. As such, the key to evaluating the outcome of these struggles is not whether we "win" or "lose" the outer conflict. The far greater consideration is: what triumphs within us? Is it our basest and most selfish elements? Or our capacity for goodwill and forgiveness, our willingness to accept new responsibility, and our inner sense of nobility and dignity? If we "win" the outer struggles of Aries at the price of compromising or destroying inner qualities of character, then we have not won at all. We have become weaker, not stronger.

THE CHALLENGES OF ARIES

The great challenge to each of us in Aries is to develop genuine spiritual strength. Where weaknesses exist, we are meant to cultivate strength. Unfortunately, we have rather bizarre cultural notions of just what strength is. We define it almost always in terms of the personality—usually in colorfully rationalized forms of rudeness, aggressiveness, anger, defiance, and stubbornness.

121

To the soul, however, these are weaknesses, not strengths. The true strengths are those inner qualities which endure long after the "strengths" of rudeness, anger, and combativeness have dissipated and proven unreliable. These are examples of the strengths to be cultivated in Aries:

- The capacity to be forgiving in the face of injury.
- The ability to remain patient in the face of delays, setbacks, and interference.
- The ability to remain true to our ideals in the face of temptation.
- The courage to initiate worthwhile new endeavors in the face of opposition—or indifference.
- The capacity to learn from our mistakes.
- Dignity in the face of insult.

These strengths cannot be nurtured by the personality alone; they must draw on the unlimited strength of the inner dimensions of being. To cultivate them fully, we must invoke the support of spirit.

In our effort to build a stronger relationship with spirit, therefore, we should strive to expand its *presence* in our daily self-expression. Many people have found that charisma gives them a presence which is very beneficial in dealing with others. But charisma is largely of the emotions, and as such, is only a pale reflection of the presence of spirit. Aries presents us with a real challenge to expand a genuine sense of this presence, by being continually mindful of the soul's influence on our life, overshadowing us, guiding us, loving us, caring about us, and helping us go about our daily work.

Once we have learned to sense the presence of spirit within us in all that we do, we can then take on the greater challenge of finding ways to convey this presence to others. And the challenge to the advanced person is to act with an appreciation of the *omnipresence* of divine life.

The challenge of Aries to parents is to encourage their children, especially older ones, to begin thinking in terms of the long-term view toward life—to begin thinking about the kind of contribution they would like to make to life, the values they cherish the most, the underlying meanings of the problems they face, the purpose of certain events and activities, and so on.

The challenge of Aries in improving human relationships lies in learning to increase our cooperation and find practical ways to become an agent of harmony in all of our dealings with others. The key to success in personal relationships is to work from a level of purpose—to comprehend the opportunity we have for making constructive contributions to life in conjunction with others.

Aries is also a time when new partnerships and alliances tend to take shape—in personal friendships, business associations, the relationship of a creative person with a Muse, or the relationship of the personality with the soul.

The challenge in business and commercial enterprises is to seize this time for effective planning. Aries is an excellent time for reviewing the purposes and goals of business endeavors, redefining them so they are clearer, and then seeing how well existing policies and plans actually express these purposes. Where our policies and plans are not in harmony with the highest goals of our endeavor, they should be modified or replaced.

The challenge of Aries in society is to find ways to rise above the limitations of convention, tradition, and the status quo, and *think* in intelligent and compassionate ways about the ongoing conflicts which divide humanity. There is great danger at this time in recycling old bigotry, animosity, and defensiveness, even though it is tempting. The true leader is the one who will rise above his factionalism, his nationalism, and the mind set of the group he leads and make bold new overtures to resolve differences and disagreements.

In this regard, it should be understood that the forces of Aries subtly encourage us to think globally, rather than individually. And so, the international scene is an important stage for the forces of Aries. There are many ways the impact of these forces can be seen nationally and internationally:

- New leadership may emerge.
- The urge to reform may clash with the urge to preserve the status quo.
- Trends will suddenly be redefined.
- The internal structure of groups will be rearranged.

To the spiritual aspirant, the challenge of Aries at an international level is to think and act and serve as a person of goodwill, and to identify with the larger group of men and women who share this same perspective.

The challenge of Aries in confronting our personal lessons of growth is to review the dominant themes of our life from a new perspective, seeking to:

- Define the purpose of what we do more clearly.
- Embrace a larger perspective or more inclusive understanding of what has happened to us in the past.
- See the creative potential of every aspect of life.

One way of accomplishing this is to ask ourself the following questions, which are in a very real sense the quintessential questions that Aries asks us all:

What rules my self-expression on earth? Is it my sense of purpose and dedication? Or is it my desires and emotional reactiveness? Where is my self-expression focused? In my highest values? Or in my daily whims and moods? What am I doing to *enrich* life, physically, emotionally, mentally, and spiritually?

There are three basic tools of growth which can be of great benefit to us in answering the challenge of Aries:

1. The tool of integration. It is not enough just to be aware of the forces of Aries; success comes from consciously directing the will to manifest and the will to create into our values, habits, and priorities. This requires integrating the new directions, insights, and responsibilities which emerge at this time into our

124

personal capacity to grow. If we do, then the forces of Aries will be constructive, not irritating, and we will tap a renewed sense of direction in our creative tasks.

2. The tool of self-renewal. In specific, we should work to renew our contacts with our higher intelligence. There will be times in Aries when we *must* be guided by our inner vision and principles, not by outer appearance. Our success at these times will depend on our inner composure, self-assurance, responsibility, and capacity to retain a steady awareness of our convictions and values in the face of outside pressures.

3. The tool of thankfulness. We need to appreciate the value of our own skills and talents—and the value of the qualities and achievements of others. We likewise need to appreciate the blessings and opportunities which have come our way, and the help we have received from others. And we need to appreciate divine order and purpose, as it expresses itself in our life and helps us, day by day, in practical ways. Then, we need to translate this appreciation into an active expression of thankfulness. In this way, we can align ourself with wholeness.

And it is always toward a greater sense of wholeness—the Oneness of life—that the forces of Aries lead us.

THE PROBLEMS OF ARIES

The major source of problems in Aries lies in our own resistance to change. In fact, in many cases our greatest personal strengths will be the cause of our greatest personal struggles and conflicts, as they react against the will to manifest of spirit. As our weaknesses are exposed—or we are forced to try something new and different—we will tend to fall back on our traditional strengths and use them to protect ourself against these threats. Yet in many cases we will be doing nothing more than mobilizing our own resistance to block out the force of enlightenment

125

and new maturity. It is therefore important to approach the problems of Aries with great care and search for new and more effective ways of solving them—not just fall back on what has worked in the past.

Aries is also a time when subconscious urges and drives can unexpectedly overpower us and cause us to act more forcefully and rashly than we had expected. Properly channeled, these forces help us build our impulse to achieve and harness our personal ambition so that they serve the spiritual will. Unfortunately, many more people are controlled by their desires and their ambition than vice-versa. For these people, Aries will usually be a time of heightened ambitiousness and competitiveness, leading to greater conflict and turmoil. It will be a time of restlessness and irritability—and quite possibly a time of increased stubbornness, confusion, and ambivalence. But for those who are focused in meaningful values and have an organized personality, the extra power of Aries will be an advantage, not a curse.

Specific problems which arise from our responses to the forces of Aries include:

1. Discouragement. The exposure of our failures or weaknesses may dishearten us and trigger attacks of self-recrimination. The type of person who is quick to blame himself or others, instead of searching for solutions, may unduly energize his problems and stymie his ability to work out innovative solutions. In some instances, however, discouragement may be a sign of growing discontent with the way things are. If we can then rise above our discouragement and define a constructive new path for future activity, we will be working well with these forces. Most people, however, will just sink into boredom, emptiness, apathy, or a brooding bitterness.

2. Impatience. When the average person is confronted with the force of change, he frequently becomes quite impatient with life—impatient that change is not occurring more rapidly,

that God is not taking better care of him, and that his valuable work and service are not more fully appreciated. The spiritual aspirant in particular is often impatient in this way with the soul. But this suggests that the real problem is not our impatience, but our lack of harmony with the wholeness of life and the plan of the soul. If unchecked, this problem can cripple our relationship with the higher forces of life.

3. Vacillation. One of the major problems attending any period of review is the tendency to hesitate too long before acting, unsure of what a new course in life will produce. Aries opens up many new possibilities, but we cannot afford to waste time waiting to see which one will emerge to carry us into the future. We must apply our values and principles and make intelligent decisions regarding which opportunities to seize—and then act on them innovatively and productively.

4. Snideness. Efforts to embarrass others by asking snide and disparaging questions—or damning with faint praise—are likely to be more commonplace. It is important to practice right speech and use the words we speak wisely and constructively. We can hurt ourself and our best interests more with our mouths than in any other way in Aries.

5. Inefficiency. We may find we are being tied up and exhausted by routine, mundane tasks, leaving no time for creative work. Rather than just lament this problem, we should meet it by developing a more efficient use of our time and energy, so that we are able to use our creative energies in an optimum way.

6. Increased materialism. The seductiveness of physical comforts and rewards is always strong in Aries and can have an insidious impact on our efforts to redefine and refocus our values. We must take care not to debase our values or priorities in response to the pressures of daily living.

7. The petty tyranny of demanding people. We can easily become encumbered by people who make excessive demands and expect us to serve their every need. But if this occurs, we

must understand that we have willingly allowed them to make these demands. In the process of trying to be pleasant, we have made promises or concessions not in our best interest. To reverse this situation, we will have to decide how best to restore a proper equilibrium to the relationship.

8. Excessive enthusiasm. Aries can produce a surge of exhilaration and excitement which can be very pleasant at first but leads us all too quickly on a roller coaster ride of the emotions, blinding us to the practical realities of life. In particular, there is a danger of becoming so drunk on the many possibilities which tend to arise in Aries that we may fail to follow through on any of them.

9. Loneliness. As the differences among people are heightened, we may accidentally overemphasize the psychological distance between ourself and some of our friends. We may feel they are moving away from us or shunning us, but our perception is likely to be as much the result of our own aloofness and changing values as theirs.

10. Rejection of authority. As new impulses stir up change at unconscious levels, we may automatically project our resentment of these changes onto visible agents of authority—at work, in government, and in the family. This may lead us to oppose authority in petty ways. This particular problem will be more prevalent in people who are habitually stubborn and tenacious about their independence. It can be alleviated by cultivating the art of cooperation with spiritual themes—plus a dose of inspired humility.

11. Righteousness. The forces of Aries increase the strength of our convictions, leading to greater stability and poise, but also leading to absolutist positions in those who are prone to be dogmatic anyway. It is one thing to know with conviction; it is quite another to clobber others with it. This tendency will lead us into conflicts which are self-defeating.

12. Vanity and egotism. Our opinion of ourself can easily

be overinflated in Aries, if we are not attuned to the real drama occurring at unconscious levels. But this vanity can be a double danger to us, for it can leave us exposed to personal attack and challenge. Once again, the value of inspired humility is great.

13. Superficiality. Aries stimulates the core issues of life, inspiring us to ask what we are doing to enrich life—evoking us to make the changes which will enable us to do a better job of it. Many people on the spiritual path, however, are not as interested in making fundamental changes as they are in *appearing* pious. They do everything they can to avoid facing the real issues of spiritual growth and competence. This usually involves throwing themselves into the cultivation of superficial signs of spirituality—polite manners, graciousness, and agreeability—and pursuing these expressions so avidly that they never have to think about anything more profound. As a result, they stay trapped in dilettantism and never make any progress.

14. Passiveness. Faced with conflict and disharmony, many people retreat into passiveness. Yet this is not a real option, for it is just an evasion of personal responsibility. Nevertheless, it is a very common problem among spiritual aspirants, who want to love God but are afraid to confront the real problems existing within society—and themselves. So they become very quiet and meek and pretend that this is a helpful approach to life. But meekness is not the way by which we make a constructive contribution to life, enriching it for others. To be a spiritual person, we must be able to take the initiative and be a force of goodwill in life—never by being aggressive or rude, but by being firm, determined, set on purpose, and involved in living.

15. Criticism of others. Faultfinding is always a strong temptation to some people, but it is particularly tempting in Aries. It must be understood, however, that blaming and criticizing others for their errors does nothing to help remove those errors—and that it is even more absurd to blame others for *our*

mistakes! Criticism is a destructive activity. We should therefore make the effort to rechannel the energy of unhelpful criticism into practical and constructive activities, seeking to help
others instead of blaming them.

16. Heightened illusions of the inner life. Because unconscious forces are stirred up in Aries, any illusions or fantasies we
might have about the inner life will be stimulated as well. This
may range from something as simple as overemphasizing the
importance of "Freudian slips" to something as complex as generating elaborate illusions about the nature of Hierarchical
groups, "soul mates," and so on.

17. Free floating fears and worries. The fears and traumas
of mass consciousness can intrude upon our personal awareness, magnifying our individual fears and worries. This can be
a serious problem in clouding our thinking and endangering our
self-control, unless we practice poise.

18. Procrastination. The lure of "goofing off" is stronger
than usual during Aries, but this is just our desires kicking up
their heels in a rather infantile way. We need to remember that
the key to forward progress in Aries is cooperating with the
impulse to achieve of the higher self. It is no time for missing
opportunities or backsliding!

THE OPPORTUNITIES OF ARIES

The work we have done and the contributions we have
made to life in the past become the basis for new opportunities
in Aries. These are, after all, the primary foundation for our
creative talent and power to implement change. But we cannot
just transpose what we have done in the past onto the present.
We must translate the meaning of these contributions into new
ideas, new possibilities, and new opportunities.

In general, the opportunities of Aries help us become more

acquainted with the deeper elements of life. The average person, of course, will have no understanding of what transpires at these deeper levels, except possibly to notice that the unknown and the unexplained seem to increase—that there appears to be more luck and chance and freak accidents than normal. But to a person who has experience in tapping the deeper levels of life, Aries will make more sense. It will be seen that the inner structure of our character is stimulated, revitalized, and redirected at this time—and that this is the basis for overcoming weaknesses and increasing strengths.

In fact, if we observe closely, we will discover that harmful tendencies and weaknesses are actually being removed or deemphasized. In some people, of course, this may produce a sense of loss, but it is really the hand of the soul at work, striving to make the adjustments which will help us continue on our way.

Specific opportunities of Aries include:

1. Renewal. There is a tremendous power in the forces of Aries to renew our interest in worthwhile projects and ideas, and to rejuvenate our dedication to spiritual growth and living. This power may also lead to a rebirth of our belief in the value of our humanity and talent, our enthusiasm for living, and our commitment to personal responsibilities. There may well be a parallel of this renaissance in the life of our community or society as a whole.

2. Spiritual discernment. The greater clarity Aries inspires will make it possible to see the path ahead of us more vividly than ever before. As long as we seek to respond to the plan and will of the soul, we will be able to make correct choices in applying our good ideas. But we should proceed from the top down—from the perspective of our higher intelligence, not just the expediencies of the moment.

3. Breakthrough. The impelling force of Aries gives us an enormous potential to push forward and break through the obstacles before us. Naturally, these obstacles will tend to loom

more clearly than before, and if we have a tendency to hesitate, we could easily be overwhelmed by them. But if we focus the momentum of Aries and the strength of the soul and push onward, we can make impressive gains along our chosen path.

4. Self-analysis. Any effort to make sense of our life will be rewarded with new insights and understanding. When we begin to look at the factors *within us* that have brought about frustration or difficulty, instead of putting blame on external conditions, then we will find the real cause of many of our problems. If we use the opportunity for self-analysis with honesty and integrity, we can break down many areas of self-deception.

5. Creativity. Creative thinking and problem solving get a tremendous boost in Aries. It is almost as though the mind were equipped with an "extra gear" at this time. But this extra opportunity can easily be wasted, unless we make an effort to use the mind in innovative and creative ways, not just in our work but even more importantly in our approach to problems.

6. Directness. Forthrightness is a virtue of Aries—not bluntness, but a capacity to get to the heart of an issue and work consistently from this perspective. In communicating with others, we should avoid long-winded explanations or excuses and strive to be to the point. Instead of trying to present others with full-blown ideas, it is often preferable to give them hints which will get them to start thinking on their own.

7. Purification. It is easier to contact the fires of purification of the soul and focus them into our habits, thoughts, and feelings to burn away the dross, temper our talents and urges, and achieve a greater alignment with the patterns and plans of spirit. Purification does not just involve cleaning away the debris of old attitudes, but also identifying with emerging new forces. Ideally, the work of purification should lead to new insights, a fresh sense of who we are, and a new grasp of purpose.

8. Providence. The providing, supportive nature of divine life and the higher self tends to be more in evidence during Aries

than at other times. The egotist will be so preoccupied with himself that he will miss the signs, but the person who is properly aligned with the soul and accustomed to invoking it will experience a much deeper bond with this aspect of the higher life. To the degree that we strive to enrich life through our contributions and service, we will find our efforts enriched in turn.

9. Dedication. Aries is a marvelous time for the renewal of old pledges and for adding strength to our commitments—especially our dedication to the spiritual life. In this way, we can add strength and courage to our self-expression.

10. Poise. The principle of individual self-expression underlies all aspects of Aries. Our self-assurance, poise, and posture toward life will be greatly strengthened, provided that we strive to cooperate with the plans and emerging new directions of spirit. As we realize that we are truly a *partner* with the soul, our poise and dignity are greatly magnified.

11. Joy. There is always a strong measure of joy inherent in the forces of Aries—the joy which attends the initiation of new plans, energies, and activities. This is a quality of joy which can be tapped by the mature person regardless of what may be happening in his or her outer life, as it is really the joy of divine creation. The key to tapping it lies in being able to entertain the new ideas and projects the soul is setting before us.

TUNING INTO THE FORCES OF ARIES

One of the best ways to tune in directly to the forces of Aries on our own is to discern and understand the direction of the emerging new forces. This can be aided by asking ourself the following catechism:

What needs to be done that I can do?

How can I apply my talents for the good of mankind?

Where can I make a contribution?

How can I increase the quality of my contribution?

What can I share more fully with others?

In striving to answer these questions, we should probe as deeply into the realm of intuition as we can. An excellent way to do this, especially for people who already know how, is to use mantic devices such as the I Ching or the Tarot. The interplay between the conscious mind and the unconscious which characterizes Aries makes it an especially powerful time to explore the nature of archetypal forces with these tools of divination. By pursuing the answers to questions such as these, it will be possible to construct a framework of understanding which reveals a great deal about the forces of Aries.

Aries is also an excellent time to work with myths, allegories, and similar presentations of truth which hint at inner powers. We must always be careful, however, to relate such myths and parables to our own needs and challenges.

Of course, the best way to attune to the forces of Aries is always in our practical use of its energies. In this regard:

• The best way to teach at this time is to inspire others to embark or progress on the path of discovery—to reveal to them the rich, inner dimensions of consciousness and the means by which they can interact with them. The use of mythology and symbolism can be very helpful in this endeavor.

• The best way to heal is by planting the seeds of perfection and nurturing their growth—both by removing weeds which might inhibit it and by tending the seeds with love. We heal most powerfully in Aries by trying to bring the outer form into harmony with the inner ideal or purpose.

• The best way to lead is by inspiring groups to new action based on a clear understanding of the group's purpose.

Finally, it can be helpful to understand where the new directions of Aries will lead us. To some degree, the new energies released in Aries will be echoed in each succeeding sign of the zodiac. But the two signs in which we can expect these new directions to manifest most fully in our life will be Virgo and Scorpio—Virgo being the time when we will complete the work of integration begun now, and Scorpio being the time when we will test how well we have absorbed these new directions.

A SONG FOR ARIES

A fiery power blazes forth, high in the heavens, sending seeds of light to earth, to germinate in coolness.

The seeds grow, but are threatened by weeds. Flames from the fiery power flash through the air, burning away the weeds and purging the stalks of their weakness. Their strength renewed, the seedlings continue growing.

Time after time, the flames sweep down, destroying impurity and cleansing the struggling life within the plants. Every visitation brings a renewed cycle of growth. At last, the light within bursts forth in flower.

One final time, the fiery flames descend, not to scorch or parch, but to enter into the light of the flowers. The flowers glow with the perfect radiance of the fire. Having purged impurity and recreated fire on earth, the fiery power blazes forth from within, becoming a light for other seeds.

A PARABLE FOR ARIES

The instinct of sheep is strong and powerful; it binds them together in the common flock. But other impulses even stronger than instinct do arise. So it was with one young sheep, who gradually became convinced that he must leave the flock to pursue his own destiny.

The thought of striking out on his own terrified him, for he knew not what awaited him, but something stronger than terror led him on. The prospect of leaving the flock saddened him, but something greater than sadness reassured him that he must. And so, one night as the rest of the flock slept, he slipped away.

He knew not where to go, but followed the impulse within him as best he could. It led him through forests and across plains, close to villages and out into the most desolate regions. He frequently encountered danger, and hardly a day went by that he did not doubt the wisdom of his decision to leave.

When he slept, he dreamed of the flock. At first, they gently called him to return. In later dreams, they became more threatening, accusing him of abandoning them and angrily attacking him. But the ram remained resolute, awakening from his dreams bleating, "I *must* do this." He felt terrible to be apart from the flock, but pressed on.

At last, he came to a valley which was different from the others he had traveled through; the fragrance of the flowers was most exotic, as though tended by angels, and the birds sang with unrestrained joy. The whole valley seemed to radiate light. He hesitated to enter, but as he did, his impulse to wander and explore departed. He felt a great sense of release and sank into a deep and peaceful slumber.

When he awoke, the sheep was startled to find, there in the valley of his discovery, the rest of the flock. "Did you follow me here to force me to come back?" he asked.

"No," they responded, "we followed you because you led the way to a much better home, a new beginning. We accept you now as leader of the flock."

"But you attacked me in my dreams."

"We did not share your vision, and were afraid. Now we know you are right. Let us join you here."

The sheep smiled and cried with delight, happy to be one with the flock again. He knew, at that moment, that he had been guided, and his friends had been drawn, by the deepest instinct of all: the instinct to follow a genuine purpose.

7

Taurus

TAURUS

(April 20 through May 20)

Keynote: Harnessing spiritual motivation.

Mantra: "The light of wisdom draws me into the life
of my spirit and shows me the way ahead."

New moon focus: Discovering new measures of light within us.

Full moon focus: Radiating the light of wisdom and goodwill.

Rays 1, 4, and 5 dominate.

Primary archetypal forces:
Truth, unity, freedom, goodwill, wisdom

A Prayer For Taurus:

O Heavenly Mother-Father God, lift up our minds and hearts, so that we may discover the inner light of wisdom and learn to use it to enlighten our life.

Lift up our minds, so that we may respond to the inner realities of spirit, and come to comprehend them. Open our eyes to the spiritual patterns in our daily activities, so we can see that they are part of the path which leads us onto the lighted way.

Lift up our hearts, so that we may respond to the purpose of Your plan. Strengthen our dedication to spirit, so that we may overcome our selfishness, resolve our inner conflicts, and renew our commitments to the life of spirit.

Heal our blindness, for we are ready to see.

Bless the best within us, for we are ready to honor it.

Harmonize the discord of our lives, for we are ready to become peacemakers. And direct us with your spiritual will, for we are ready to play our part in fulfilling it.

Taurus is a time of conflict between desire and duty, between the pursuit of personal pleasure and obedience to spiritual direction. For some, this struggle will be obvious, as it has always been with them. For others, however, it will be less noticeable, focused at subconscious and unconscious levels. Often, the struggle will appear to involve our relationships, but the real conflict is a personal one, within ourself. It is resolved by reconciling our human and our spiritual natures, thereby mastering duality. Desire and duty must be harmonized, not by redefining duty in terms of our desires, but rather by harnessing our personal ambition so it serves our higher purposes.

In many ways, the opening paragraph of Charles Dickens' novel, *A Tale of Two Cities*, captures the spirit of this struggle in Taurus:

"It was the best of times, it was the worst of times, it was the age of wisdom, it was the age of foolishness, it was the epoch of belief, it was the epoch of incredulity, it was the season of Light, it was the season of Darkness, it was the spring of hope, it was the winter of despair, we had everything before us, we had nothing before us, we were all going direct to Heaven, we were all going direct the other way—in short, the period was so far like the present period, that some of its noisiest authorities insisted on its being received, for good or for evil, in the superlative degree of comparison only."

How does a spiritual person handle a period which is the best of times, the worst of times? By seizing it as an opportunity to magnify and focus the best and noblest within us, and to use this to cleanse and purify the worst within us—anything which demeans us, compromises our integrity, or hinders our relationship with spirit. This is what the struggles of Taurus are meant to inspire us to do.

In a very real sense, the forces of Taurus unfold as though they were generated by a wise man striding purposefully on the path before him, drawing opportunities and followers to him with the swirl of his cloak. The "wise man," of course, is the soul or the divine essence within any activity. As it sees the path before it more clearly and fully than before, it moves forward to embrace it, thereby setting new directions and motivations in motion. In this way, the light of divine activity illumines our understanding of divine purpose and awakens us to greater involvement in fulfilling it.

Whether or not we respond to the light of Taurus, it will affect us all. It calls us to commit ourself more completely to investing our energies and skills in fulfilling the responsibilities of our personal growth and career—and our obligations to our higher self, community, and colleagues.

It is easy to miss the meaning of the forces of Taurus, however; like the forces of Aries, their true impact tends to be subtle. They do not just stimulate a stronger urge to work hard, for example; they encourage us to look at *the quality of our goals* and *the quality of our methods* in reaching these goals. Indeed, the secret of Taurus is embodied in the search for meaning and significance, which time and time again takes us into the realm of the quality of life and our response to it—instead of just dealing with results, appearances, and methodologies. Taurus prods us to refine our understanding of who we are, what we are doing, and why we are doing it, so that we can rededicate ourself to these activities with a greater sense of purpose—and stronger motivation to push on toward successful completion.

This, in fact, is one of the central characteristics of Taurus—that it generates a new and more forceful motivation to reach one's goals, pursue one's path, and embrace one's destiny. Our motivations are the inner resource which generates our power to act and achieve. Our motivations move us, physically, emotionally, mentally, and spiritually. The quality of our motivations is therefore of great importance, as it determines the quality of our self-expression and the significance of our accomplishments.

140

Due to the importance of harnessing the right kind of motivating force in Taurus, this period of the zodiac is therefore a time to ponder on where we are heading—and how we will focus the new energies which we have just received during Aries. If we take the time to reflect in this way, new insight and inspiration will emerge to guide us in understanding both where we have come from and where we are going.

This type of reflection is entirely consistent with one other aspect of the archetypal nature of Taurus as well. Taurus is meant to be, above all, a time of *discovery*—a time in which we can go beyond the confusion and ambivalences of the events of our outer life and penetrate to a new understanding of the inner forces and purposes guiding them. Taurus is a time when we can discover more fully the light within us and the light within life. If we are dedicated to spirit and examine our life carefully and objectively, the light of Taurus will lead us to a discovery of the nature of will and its proper expression. Taurus will be a time of many new insights. But if we are basically selfish and driven by our desires, the light of Taurus will magnify our self-deceptions and illusions.

Ultimately, if we pursue this understanding fully, we will find that Taurus is a time for discovering what impels us and the course we are meant to follow in response. If we use this period of time wisely, we will develop new skills in harnessing the basic duality of our nature, putting it to work in our life.

THE SYMBOLISM OF TAURUS

The symbol of Taurus is the bull. Normally, it is interpreted in terms of a heightening of the desire nature, sex, and wildness. In the average person, these elements would certainly be magnified during Taurus. But the esoteric meanings of this symbol are a good deal more profound.

The bull represents independence. For the human, this begins as concentrated selfishness, stubbornness, and defiance, which he mistakes for independence. The individual discovers that he has "free will," which he then believes gives him the license to act wildly, without discipline or higher guidance. But the wildness of the bull only traps him in a restrictive box of his own creation; he discovers that in the pursuit of freedom, free will, and independence, he has lost all three. He has become a slave to his selfishness, stubbornness, and defiance.

True independence—the spirit of Taurus—comes by cultivating self-knowledge, skills and abilities in the art of living, and a healthy relationship with our higher self. Only the person who controls the emotions is free from the consequences of wildness. Only the individual with skills and abilities is free of dependence on society and others. Only the person who has established a connection with the soul is aware of the source of his independence and can use it as a wellspring of motivation.

The bull stands by himself, yet responds to a higher purpose. He is driven by forces greater than himself—but once he has achieved independence, he is not a slave to them. He harnesses them willingly, consciously, and with a sense of responsibility for their expression. This is the challenge of Taurus to each of us. How do we handle the psychological and spiritual energies which impel us to act? Do we respond to them only with our emotions and desires? Or do we strive to control and harness them with the enlightened mind—the mind which is aware of and responds to the light of the soul?

HOW THE FORCES OF TAURUS AFFECT US

Events have a way of unfolding with whirlwind rapidity during Taurus, and the unprepared person is apt to be left gasping, wondering how so much could happen in such a short time.

Obviously, not everyone experiences this whirlwind effect every year during Taurus, but it is surprising how typical this pattern is, year in and year out. And when events do unfold in this way, they may well leave us somewhat dizzy and disoriented. We may even unwittingly compromise our deeper values. But if we have prepared well for Taurus, the whirlwind will not be our undoing; it will simply carry us a step forward on the unfolding path of our destiny.

The average person will react primarily to the forces of Taurus by pursuing his desires, ambitions, and urges with even greater fervor than normal. Immaturity and selfishness will be heightened, until he becomes almost a caricature of pettiness and self-concern. His rallying cry will be, "Don't tread on me," but he will use it, if he can, to run amok over everyone else. He will be like the proverbial bull set loose in the china shop.

If we are motivated primarily by self-centered interests and desires, we should use the time of Taurus to note how our selfishness and willfulness undermine our best interests and alienate us from others. When convinced that selfishness and willfulness do not serve our best interest, we should then adopt a more enlightened motivation for living.

The aspirant will also have a tendency to run amok, but in a slightly different way. The problem here will lie in the tendency to pursue noble causes in self-serving or self-justifying ways. In his eagerness to serve, for example, he will strike out wildly, without discrimination, and devote his energies to counterproductive activities. Or, in his eagerness to grow, he will attach himself to almost anything which claims to promote growth, or be spiritual. In this way, he can get himself into a great deal of mischief.

If we are motivated toward service and self-improvement, therefore, we should take care to make sure that the improvements we seek and the help that we offer are truly in harmony with the best and noblest within us, and not just permutations of our wish life, personal desire for glory, or arrogance.

The advanced person may perceive and be affected by many of these same conditions at the level of mass consciousness, but on the whole, he will find new strength to discover the inner life and serve it effectively during Taurus. It will be a marvelous opportunity to reaffirm his dedication to inner direction, spiritual motivation, and the intent to be helpful. Whereas the average person is motivated almost entirely by personal desires and urges, the advanced person is motivated almost entirely by the forces of spirit and the divine plan. To such a person, Taurus is a time to renew these links and refocus them in dynamic new ways.

Indeed, the advanced person will find a marvelous opportunity for linking his motivation with Hierarchical force.

One of the most productive ways to prepare for Taurus, in fact, is to ask ourself: what would it mean to be motivated by *light?* What would it mean to be driven and guided by the illumination of the soul in each of the major areas of our life?

• To be motivated by light in all decisions we make concerning our work.

• To be motivated by light in the way we treat friends and colleagues.

• To be motivated by light in our personal honor and integrity.

• To be motivated by light in our use of money.

• To be motivated by light in family dealings.

• To be motivated by light in our role as a citizen.

• To be motivated by light in our efforts to serve and support the spiritual life.

If we answer these questions, we will come to understand that the one great way that Taurus affects us, above all other ways, is to spiritualize our motivations. How well we harness the tides of this time will largely determine what happens to us during the rest of the zodiacal year.

In terms of **awareness**, Taurus also has a tremendous impact. The gift of Taurus is the gift of understanding—the capacity not just to know but also to comprehend. The forces of Taurus lead us from the outer to the inner and from the gross to the sublime, thereby lifting the mundane elements of life into greater meaning. This light of understanding can be directed at our work, problems, creative projects, relationships, and individuality. If we are attentive to our hunches and impressions about the meaning of events, we will be rewarded with many new insights. Our blindness will be healed.

In fact, there is real potential for expansions of awareness during Taurus, enabling us to embrace a whole new range of insights. These expansions of consciousness may occur during meditation, in quiet moments of contemplation, or even spontaneously, when we least expect them. Because there is a potential for this kind of expansion, we should give ourself the extra quiet time we need to register subtle insights.

It should not be expected that these expansions of awareness will produce sudden clairvoyance or instant enlightenment, however. True insight is usually quiet, subtle, and easily missed, unless we make the effort to register it. It comes in the form of a deeper appreciation for meaning, stronger convictions about what we are doing, and a clearer comprehension of persistent questions and problems which have plagued us for years.

In this regard, dreams and imagery will be exceptionally strong for many people. Our memories and associative mechanism will also be strengthened; we may find ourself recalling half-forgotten events and decisions from the past and seeing how various memories are linked together in the subconscious. If we dismiss these signals from the past as random remembrances, they will count for little. But if we study them carefully, we can learn a tremendous amount about the way our subconscious is structured—and how this influences our decisions, attitudes, and behavior. We will also be able to see the relationship of these events of the past with the problems and opportunities of the present—and this will help us appreciate that we are generally far more responsible for our current conditions than we usually understand.

Much of this increased awareness will be due to a significant intensification of the activities of the **mind**. The substance of the mental plane itself is stimulated in Taurus. While this will not have any noticeable impact on the average person, it is a tremendous boon to the intelligent person. Any effort to strengthen the mind, by developing new mental skills or focusing our attention more clearly at the level of the mind, will be richly rewarded. Indeed, those who have trained the mind wisely will find Taurus a time of breakthroughs in understanding about self and the world. For others, however, the stimulation of the mind will tend to lead first to a greater sense of contradiction, confusion, and ambivalence. They will be forced to harmonize the possible with the probable, the actual with the potential, and the past with the present—and this can be overwhelming to the person who is unprepared.

The **emotions** will generally be unruly and hard to control. For this very reason, however, Taurus is an excellent time to practice self-discipline and redirect habit patterns. Emotional reactiveness and desire will be at a peak, both in the individual and in mass consciousness. As a result, the average person will spend much of Taurus pursuing whatever loves him or lures him. Taurus is therefore a good time "to get *out* of touch with our feelings!" It is a time for detachment and for viewing the events of life from a mental perspective, not emotionally.

Even if immature emotionalism does overwhelm us from time to time, however, we ought to realize that we can still learn from it, by transforming our immature attitudes or behavior into something more befitting our spiritual nature. This advice, of course, will be lost on anyone who believes that it is a virtue to be in touch with his or her feelings. But such people will be regularly embarrassed by their uncontrolled impulses and self-indulgent behavior during Taurus. They should remember that "he who sows the wind shall reap the whirlwind."

The key to controlling reactiveness is to replace it with a mature capacity to act in harmony with the best and most noble elements within ourself, others, and the events of life. This is the heart of self-determination, and is the reason why Taurus is such an excellent time for all types of mental housecleaning.

In the realm of **self-expression**, the forces of Taurus highlight the unfinished portion of our major life work, encouraging us to review what still needs to be done:

- In our career.
- In our personal growth.
- In building right relationships.
- In expanding the scope of our service.

The key is to look at the work that still remains to be done from the perspective of the soul, not through the eyes of the personality, which has a hundred and one reasons why the work still remains unfinished. The forces of Taurus are direct and straightforward. They penetrate to the heart of an issue and support similar behavior in us. If we will view our unfinished work in this way, looking for how we can complete it and harnessing a stronger motivation to do so, the potential for enlightened self-expression will come alive for us in a whole new way.

THE CHALLENGES OF TAURUS

The power of consciousness to refine that which is crude is very strong during Taurus. It is well known that the forces of Taurus can be impulsive and hard to control; what is often overlooked is that the best way to control them is by refining our sense of purpose and our skills in managing the energies of this time. As we become more interested in the subtle realms and spiritual qualities of life, *and give them the authority to rule*, we refine consciousness and learn to hone the rough edges of impulsiveness.

There are many ways we can respond to the challenges of refinement during Taurus:

• By deepening our interest in the arts and all forms of culture.

• By consciously working to improve our manners.

• By aligning our sense of taste with our values and principles.

• By striving to act with gracefulness and elegance in all that we do.

• By restraining tendencies toward crudeness, selfishness, and tastelessness.

Another important challenge of this time is *spiritual readiness*—the challenge of being prepared for the appearance of spiritual forces. Taurus is a time when "the many are called." But few are chosen, because most are not ready—or willing to cooperate with spirit. The average person might be called only to participate more fully in church, community, or charitable activities. The spiritual aspirant might be called to attain a new understanding of the inner dimensions. The advanced person could be called to a new level of responsiveness to group purpose. But the challenge is the same to all—are we ready to serve and willing to cooperate with the spiritual impulse which has created this opportunity?

The challenge of Taurus to parents is to help their children learn about the nature of motivation and how to harness it. In this regard, they should be alert to the likelihood of rebelliousness in their children, and counteract it with a strong measure of love and goodwill.

The challenge of Taurus in improving human relationships lies in learning to respond to the inner life of our relationships— the bond that connects us with others at the level of the soul.

This presents us with a rich opportunity for sharing and cooperating with others in more significant ways than before. If we strive to understand the ideals we share with others, and the strengths of our inner ties, much can be learned. It is likewise a marvelous time for understanding the inner dimensions of group life.

The challenge to business enterprises is to strengthen their hierarchical organization. Just as Taurus is a good time for the individual to align himself with the wellsprings of motivation, it is likewise an excellent time for groups and businesses to realign themselves hierarchically, so that the power to act and achieve can flow properly from the highest to the lowest levels. Taurus is a time to work from the top down rather than the bottom up, making sure values and policies are being communicated from the very highest level to the lowest.

If we are part of a hierarchical organization, we can use the time of Taurus to define our proper place in the group and work to fulfill our duties. There are always great resources which can be tapped by an individual in hierarchical groups—if the proper skills are developed and used.

The challenge of Taurus in society lies in promoting and supporting the emergence of freedom and liberty in the world. The virtues of human individuality are heightened at this time; the power of Taurus works against tyranny of all kinds. This will be visible on the international scene—but it is likewise important that we find ways to support the principles of freedom and independence in our own life. One of the most significant ways of doing this is to understand the difference between mind control and freedom in human thinking and behavior—between brainwashing and self-determination, between the party line and self-reliance, and between charismatic manipulation and independent thinking.

It should be understood that groups will have a strong impact on the individual in Taurus. Our individual thoughts and beliefs will be strongly influenced by the group minds of the organizations or associations we participate in. Whether it is a business, a church group, or a nation, we can be affected by rigid, narrow, and highly standardized ways of thinking—even while contentedly believing that we are thinking on our own and with great originality. We must take care to make sure our values and sense of purpose reflect genuine spiritual purpose— and are not just warmed over ideas we borrow from the group minds we interact with.

The challenge of Taurus in accelerating our personal growth lies in adequately preparing ourself for the tasks ahead. The major issues in this regard are:

1. Dedicating ourself to be a mature person who does the right thing. The person who is committed only to pursuing his own happiness and acquiring everything he wants will only become more entrapped in materialism. But the person who is interested in the well-being of others and the success of divine intent has a basis for expanding his understanding.

2. Strengthening our values, sense of purpose, and intent to achieve the major goals of our life. Taurus stimulates our desire for enlightened change. But we can respond to this urge at various levels—at the level of personal whims and wishes, at the level of "conventional wisdom," or at the level of our understanding of spiritual purpose. Wishing for a better world does little good. Working in materialistic ways to create a better world may lead us to the brink of disaster. To capitalize on the forces of Taurus, we must be sure to respond to them by integrating our values with an awareness of purpose.

3. Revising habits, priorities, methods, and procedures to better reflect this new sense of direction and motivation. It does no good to pursue new visions with old techniques. We must therefore assess our methodology and make sure it is consistent with the *quality* of our purpose and goals. A tendency to distrust the soul, for instance, would undermine a new determina-

tion to express the ideals of the soul. To give this new determination meaning, therefore, we must first eliminate the tendency to distrust.

As we respond in these ways to the challenges of our own growth, the forces of Taurus will have the opportunity to show us more clearly than ever before the genuine spiritual strengths that we possess—and what we can do with them.

THE PROBLEMS OF TAURUS

Because more people are motivated by selfishness, desire, defensiveness, and ambition than spiritual purpose and unselfish service, the forces of Taurus often seem to generate more problems than blessings. But this is not the fault of Taurus—it is only our own immaturity. Happily, the potential for self-discipline is also greater at this time, and those who seek to control the forces of their human nature and use them wisely can rapidly turn problems and crises into opportunities. The ideal way to approach problems in Taurus is to transmute them as the alchemists of old sought to transmute lead into gold—to transmute desire into aspiration, willfulness into the spiritual will, selfishness into the urge to help, and greed into a thirst for growth, knowledge, and maturity.

In general, the problems of Taurus result from identifying too strongly with the struggle between the personal desire and spiritual duty, thereby generating despair, frustration, and irritability. Because Taurus is an earth sign, there is always a tendency toward inertia and the pursuit of materialistic ends. It is easy to become caught in downward spirals—to let the little we have overwhelm the greatness we can become. It is important not to let this happen, as it is directly contrary to the effort to focus on the best and noblest within us.

Specific problems which tend to arise in Taurus include:

151

1. Impulsiveness. The tendency to blindly follow strong urges without questioning or trying to focus them constructively will be great. This may print out in something as simple as impulse buying—or in the form of heightened sexual urges, strengthened habits and compulsions, and so on. One of the great questions of Taurus is: "Are you the master—or the slave?" Being a master of impulse requires a capacity to focus it constructively and purposefully. Being a slave is easier, but tends to leave many unresolved problems and weaknesses of character.

2. Earthiness. The tendency to be driven by the lowest common denominator or the most mundane goals is likewise heightened. The lure of hedonistic and materialistic pursuits increases. The spiritual aspirant indulges in such pursuits only at his own peril, however, as he risks contamination of his spiritual vision and clear insight, no matter how much he believes he can have both heaven and earth at the same time.

3. The glamour of spirituality. One of the major problems of the spiritual path is an overheated fascination with spiritual concepts, methodologies, beliefs, and achievements. Quite simply, many people get drunk on the fringe elements of the life of spirit. They overdose on the idea of the high rank they think they have obtained, the contacts they have established, the rapture of being loved by God, and other pleasantries of spiritual illusion. All of these glamours tend to increase in Taurus, and it can be very tempting to trade in genuine spiritual values for these "toys" of the spiritual life. But clear thinking and common sense will protect us from this danger.

4. The illusion of remoteness. Others may miss the opportunity to be responsive to new direction in Taurus because they cannot think of spiritual purpose and motivation as applying to themselves. They are overburdened by the illusion of false humility and the remoteness of spirit—the idea that their lives are so worthless or empty that spirit cannot possibly be interested

in them. But this kind of belief creates a barrier of darkness which makes it all the more difficult for the life of spirit to penetrate.

5. A sense of entrapment. There is a strong possibility that we may feel trapped in obligations and responsibilities during Taurus. This may promote rather specious attempts to escape or revise our commitments. But if we are truly obligated in some circumstance, it is only because we willingly took on this obligation in the first place. To handle it maturely, we should try to understand how our original commitment was—and still is—a response to spiritual design. Once we can understand this, it becomes easier to see that this obligation does not really entrap us; it actually gives us an opportunity to grow and become more mature.

6. Guilt. In those who resist the need to reform their habits or the direction of their work, the conscience may become more active than usual, thereby producing strong doses of guilt, and possibly even fear. These feelings may be projected toward others who personify the nagging conscience—or they may just create a general mood of anxiety and apprehension. But it is not really necessary to become bogged down in guilt or fear to work with the changes of Taurus—nor is it desirable. Instead, we should guide our efforts with intelligent love for our noble potential.

7. Arrogance. Habitually positive people may feel a new rush of confidence during Taurus. While there is nothing wrong with a good, healthy dose of confidence, real problems can occur if it is misused to justify plunging forward in the same old, tired ways as before—or to justify continued selfishness, smugness, and egotism.

8. Cynicism. If we rebel against the tendency of Taurus to reveal meaning, we are likely to end up highlighting the shallowness and absence of meaning in our life, thereby creating painful conditions and trauma. The habitual cynic needs to re-

establish points of meaning and value from which he can then view the rest of life.

9. Petulance. Interruptions to our work and interference from others increase during Taurus. It will be tempting to react to these conditions with irritation, impatience, and petulance. But this will only serve to magnify the potency of the interference, not diminish it. If we find ourself becoming reactive in these ways, we should carefully examine the organization of our priorities. There is a strong probability that these interruptions and interferences are actually induced *by our own approach* to our work. If we are self-centered, for example, we will tend to organize our priorities in such a way that we "dare" others to interfere. Reacting to their interference will do nothing but worsen it. The only solution is to change our basic motivation and priorities.

10. Defensiveness. There is always a need to defend or protect our highest values and plans, but this is something which is very easy to overdo. During Taurus, when selfishness and the emotions are stimulated, the temptation becomes quite real. It is therefore important to remain flexible and amicable in our dealings with others, always maintaining a healthy self-respect by acknowledging their perspectives as well.

11. Abrupt and painful reversals. Taurus is often a time of sudden reversals or new branchings of fate. These may be produced by new impulses from our spiritual will, new cycles in established trends, the actions of others, or an unexpected loss of interest on our part. These changes in circumstance become painful only if we identify too closely with them, or delay in making adjustments. If we view these changes as leading us out of old ruts into new experiences, we will harness the power of Taurus well.

12. Backsliding. There is often a revival of old issues during Taurus. If this leads us back to a sense of hope and inspiration, enabling us to renew our interest in growing, it will be benefi-

cial. But in all too many people, it will lead to conditions of backsliding, where they return to comfortable and convenient habits and attitudes from the past, jeopardizing the gains they have made. We must exercise great care not to regress in this way.

13. Untruthfulness. Truth is one of the great archetypal forces of Taurus, but not everyone loves truth. In those who do not, the impulse to discover and honor truth will tend to be perverted. This is because Taurus tends to expose the truth, and those who have something to cover up will be provoked to react defensively. Falsehood, dishonesty, and self-deception will increase. In specific, we should be cautious of making insincere promises.

14. Incompetence. The tendency to slough off and do less than we ought to—to compromise quality and excellence because we are tired or more interested in other issues—will increase. Taurus is above all a time to honor the best and noblest within us, not just in theory, but in all that we do. We should not settle for less than our best!

15. Boldness. We are propelled to act courageously in Taurus, but must take care not to let this lead us into brashness and offensive behavior. Above all, we must take care not to indulge in harsh and excessive criticism of others, lest it cause injury. We should practice moderation and harmony in all comments we make to others.

16. Amorality. The attitude that principles and values do not apply to some phase of life, or life as a whole, is one of the greatest dangers of this time. This is not the same as immorality, which is the deliberate violation of codes and ethics; amorality is more elusive and much easier to rationalize. It leads to a dulling of conscience and the bending of values. It deadens our higher connections.

17. Competitiveness. The need to prove one's worth as a human being may drive some people to fierce levels of competi-

tion. Throughout humanity, there will be more emphasis on playing the games of being the "macho male" or the "seductive female," competing for attention and affection. There may also be aggravated competition at work. Often, these games are played as a means of bolstering a sagging self-image, but it is important not to participate in these games—in Taurus or at any other time. Instead, we should harness the competitive spirit in mature and constructive ways, to build our own skills and capacities and help others build theirs as well.

18. Stagnation. The refusal to take action when action is required would be perhaps the greatest error we could make in Taurus. This is not a time for cowardice and withdrawal. It is a time to "take the bull by the horns" and act creatively on our destiny.

THE OPPORTUNITIES OF TAURUS

The opportunities of Taurus are often like a double-edged sword; while they help us ground our spiritual nature more fully in our mundane activities, we are usually required to modify our human nature to take advantage of them. We cannot assume that we can just "add on" a new idea, attitude, or responsibility while maintaining our old habits and approaches; to seize the opportunities of Taurus, we must be willing to accommodate ourself to the spiritual design and purpose of these opportunities, rather than try to bend them to our personal will! Otherwise, we are just attempting to graft enlightened thinking onto a self-centered base—a hybrid that will not flourish.

Specific opportunities arising in Taurus will be:

1. New projects. Both in our career and in the sphere of spiritual service, new projects and avenues for self-expression will unfold. Fuzzy plans and vague aspirations often become

156

clarified in Taurus, and we see the way before us more fully. We may also discover new and more effective ways to do old work.

2. A sense of fulfillment. Because we are more aware of the purpose of our work, we will be able to appreciate the value of our contributions more clearly, thereby enriching our determination to push on toward our goals.

3. Greater respect for the contributions of others. The same appreciation of value and purpose should lead us to respect the skillful and loving contributions of others, and renew our interest in supporting them and cooperating with them, as appropriate. Many of the opportunities of Taurus emerge out of this respect for others, leading to partnerships and mutual efforts which expand our personal ability to serve.

4. Greater precision in thought and activity. By working to define what we must do and the best way to do it, we clear away the cobwebs of confusion and see more fully what activities are irrelevant and need to be dropped. We streamline our thoughts and actions.

5. Forthrightness. Taurus is a time for plain speaking, honest dealing, and forthrightness. Those who try to be sly and obscure—or who try to peddle baloney—will not fare well. The efforts which succeed best in Taurus are those that go to the heart of the issue and work in a direct way to achieve it.

6. The incubation of new ideas. Taurus stimulates the supraconscious mind in powerful ways. As a result, intuitive and creative inspiration is often sharper and clearer than at other times. This stimulation of the higher mind also means that the opportunities of Taurus frequently come in clusters. Seizing one will open the door to a number of related opportunities. But this will only happen if we are actively using the mind to harness creative ideas as they emerge.

7. The enrichment of life. There is a strong and powerful sense of beauty associated with the forces of Taurus. Any effort

we make to deepen our appreciation of beauty will bring us rewards and help attune us to other spiritual qualities. It is a time for celebrating the richness of divine life and contemplating how we can express beauty in our own life.

8. Spiritual bonds. There can be a subtle but significant increase in our ability to commune with our real friends and fellow travelers on the spiritual path. This may include physical people we know, those we sense at a distance, and even those who dwell only on the inner planes of life. If we participate in this sense of communion, and begin respecting these people as spiritual beings, we can tap some powerful energies of brotherhood.

9. Detachment. The cultivation of the impersonal life—so essential to attunement to spirit—is easier during Taurus than at many other times. The dominant forces encourage us to withdraw our attention from our usual nearsighted preoccupation with events and outer appearances, and become aware of the inner meaning of our experiences.

10. Integration. There is tremendous potential for integrating the multiple levels of our being at this time, so that they all work smoothly together in expressing our inner life. The key to integration in Taurus is to train each aspect of the personality—the mind, the emotions, and the body—to be responsive to the motivating forces of spirit.

11. Self-determination. Taurus gives us the opportunity to gain control of our destiny, by learning to cooperate with the new directions and motivations emerging from spiritual levels. This sign of the zodiac tends to present us with important decisions to make: how we will act, what course we will pursue, and the values we will emphasize. Sometimes, these choices will have to be made in the midst of sudden changes and swiftly unfolding conditions. We must be unafraid to make quick judgments—but these should always be based on the structure of our carefully thought out convictions, principles, and values.

12. Enlightenment. Through the pursuit of self-discovery, we activate the intelligent mind and make it a suitable vehicle for the expression of light. During Taurus, there is an exceptional opportunity to fill the mind with more light than ever before and to see the quality and presence of light within:

- Inspired ideas.
- Other intelligent, compassionate people.
- Spiritual service.
- The forces of light which confront and overpower the forces of darkness.

During Taurus, therefore, let us dwell in light and become an active agent of it.

TUNING INTO THE FORCES OF TAURUS

The inner perspective is very important in Taurus. Even though it is an earth sign, it quickly becomes quite clear that the forces of Taurus are active at all levels of our being. We therefore need to approach the work of tuning into these forces *multidimensionally*—to study them as they embrace, motivate, and influence each level of our awareness.

The key is to examine what we *pay attention to.* And so, we can ask ourself the following questions:

At what level of life are we primarily focused? Spirit, the mind, our emotions, or the body?

From which level do we primarily act? Mentally, emotionally, or physically?

To what elements of life do we primarily pay attention? Our physical needs and concerns? Our emotional needs and concerns? Our mental needs and concerns? Or our spiritual needs, concerns, and directions?

At what levels are the changes of Taurus occurring?

What is our need in each of these areas of change?

159

If, for example, we realize that one of our relationships is changing, we might see that the real changes are occurring at mental levels, as new and more expanded values emerge. Our need, in such a case, would be to adjust the relationship at that level, finding ways to redefine our bond in light of these new priorities and commitments. In the process of doing this, we might discover that our real need was to become motivated by stronger compassion, generosity, or openmindedness.

This type of self-discovery would represent an excellent attunement to and understanding of the forces of Taurus.

The best way to teach in Taurus is by inspiring others to refine their awareness and understanding of life. In this regard, the arts and all forms of culture make excellent teaching tools.

The best way to heal is by finding the spiritual ideal which harmonizes the dualities of our life—the spiritual ideal which enables us to seize the opportunities of the best of times and the worst of times.

The best way to lead is by calling forth the future and accepting it joyfully. The future is to be celebrated as a source of new potential, new power, and new radiance.

And, of course, the trends we set in motion at this time *will* carry us into the future. We can look for definite echoes of the work we do now in Libra and Pisces—Libra because it once again emphasizes the central role of the mind in understanding life, and Pisces because it transmutes desire into the will to sacrifice.

One final point should be made about attuning to the forces of Taurus. Taurus is the time each year of Wesak, a special celebration on the inner planes in which the work of spiritual people everywhere is blessed, strengthened, and renewed. Wesak coincides each year with the full moon of Taurus. It can therefore be quite beneficial to make an extra effort at this time to attune to the highest level of our spiritual nature, seeking to grasp new directions, recognize fuller responsibilities, and adapt ourself to new possibilities. In this way, we can establish greater harmony between our spiritual and human natures, and discover the light that impels the best within us.

A SONG FOR TAURUS

Within a circle of dim light, I see myriad shadows of subtlety and beauty. I rush to embrace them, delighting in their brief pleasure.

The circle of light brightens, and I see that there is ugliness and distortion amid the shadows, as well as beauty. I am repelled, and seek comfort by embracing the shadows of subtlety and beauty more fervently than before.

Again the circle of light brightens, and I discover that there is a form at the center of the circle which is casting all these shadows. I look more closely. The form at the center is *me*.

Hope and grief, delight and despair seize me as I race from shadow to form and then toward the light. I reach out for the light—but my own shadow blocks my way. I move between shadow and light, time after time, in a dance of confusion and frustration.

Finally, a beam of light engulfs me, and I see the shadows retreat before the light. The light grows more intense, flooding my whole awareness, until I stand completely in the light.

And see only the lighted presence which *I am*.

A PARABLE FOR TAURUS

Bulls can be as moody as they look. One in particular became quite sullen, because he did not like his reputation among the other animals. He wanted to be liked, but was feared; he wanted to be respected, but was avoided. He concluded it must be his horns. "It's these horns which make them afraid of me," he thought. "Oh, if only I could be rid of them!" He grew quite desperate and tried to tear them off, ramming the horns against trees and fences, but all he managed to do was give himself a very bad headache.

The moon saw his anguish and spoke to him. "Why are you so upset with your horns?" she inquired.

"They are misshapen and fearful," said the bull.

"Nonsense," cried the moon. "They are shaped like a crescent, just as I am. You carry on the top of your head a very proud heritage—a piece of heaven, come to earth. You should wear it with dignity."

"If it is a piece of heaven, come to earth," rebutted the bull, "why is everyone so afraid of me?"

"Not everyone is," the moon replied quietly. "You exaggerate these fears. The mountains and valleys do not fear you; neither do the stars or the sun. Not even the clouds, as puffy as they are, run from you. Only those who do not see me in the horns on your head fear you."

"Why have you never told me this before?" asked the bull, feeling somewhat better about himself.

"It's something you should have been able to discover on your own," said the moon. "You wear the sign of the moon as a crown—but you are designed to live the life of the bull."

8

Gemini

GEMINI

(May 21 through June 20)

Keynote: The power to relate spirit and form.

Mantra: "The love and wisdom of God draw all things into wholeness."

New moon focus: Nurturing growth.

Full moon focus: Right action.

Rays 2, 3, 4, and 5 dominate.

Primary archetypal forces:

Harmony, nobility, compassion, serenity, adaptability

A Prayer For Gemini:

Heavenly Mother-Father God, the One in Whom we live and move and have our being, we rejoice in Your perfection. Help us to be inspired by the divine perfection and become an agent of Your nurturing love in the world.

May the light of the soul guide us to the center of our life, the source of our actions, and the hidden love which sustains us always. Let the inner direct and the outer conform.

Where conflict has raged, teach us to become a healing force, so that we may reconcile that which has been separated and restore that which has been injured.

Let goodwill rule our actions.

Let harmony rule our attitudes and speech.

Let cooperation rule our thoughts.

And help us find liberation in the dignity of the soul, so that we in turn may help liberate others from the indignities of ignorance, materialism, and selfishness.

164

As in Taurus, the forces of Gemini emphasize the fundamental duality of life. But whereas Taurus highlights the *gap* between opposite extremes, and accentuates conflict, the period of Gemini reveals the *relationship* between them—and the potential to overcome and heal the differences which divide them. This is not to imply that there is no conflict in Gemini, for there can be conflict in any of the signs of the zodiac. It simply suggests that the unique focus of Gemini lies in drawing together that which has been separated.

Gemini can therefore be a time of unparalleled fulfillment—or a time of crushing disappointment. It can be a time for bold new insights—or more confusion than ever. It can be a time of serenity, or worry; of consolidation, or dissipation; of openness and generosity, or criticism and pettiness.

This is not a riddle—it is just the way the forces of Gemini emphasize the duality of any condition, attitude, thought, or event. As the forces of Gemini sweep into our life, they stir up the twin nature of every aspect of consciousness—the inner and the outer, the higher and the lower, the spiritual and the material. As a result, Gemini usually seems to be a time of paradox, surprise, and inconsistency—but it is also a time of great spiritual opportunity. In this interplay between the dualities of life, the power of creativity is generated.

It is therefore not a question of making a choice between the one or the other, but rather a question of building an effective relationship which harnesses both poles of duality for spiritual purpose. This might be the relationship between spirit and form, between heaven and earth, between the promise of a good idea and our opportunities for using it, between our values and our emotions, between our will to act and our physical vitality, between collective and individual need, between two ideologies, between husband and wife, or between friend and foe. The forces of Gemini remind us of the most important relationships we have, showing us:

- Which ones need improvement.
- Which ones best serve our purposes.
- Which ones present us with creative opportunity.

The key to harnessing the forces of Gemini lies in recognizing that the power of the relationship is greater than its individual parts. If we focus too much on the individual parts, or what separates them, we will lose sight of the real work of Gemini. But if we work with sufficient mental discrimination and discernment, and strive always to heal our relationships and make them more creative, we will find the time of Gemini to be one of significant progress.

A good example of this would be in interpersonal relationships, where it is so tempting to define and identify with just our needs and fail to discern the needs of the relationship. The real relationship is the psychological force which has been invested in it. If the relationship is based on distrust, jealousy, competitiveness, selfishness, or resentment, it cannot possibly be a good and healthy one. But if the relationship is based on mutual caring, respect, productivity, and responsibility, it will be solid and strong.

The forces of Gemini work to reveal the healthy potential of our relationships, *if* we will approach them with nurturing love, a creative spirit, and an interest in making them whole. This applies to all of our relationships—our ties with other people, our relationship to our work, our bond with groups, and our relationship with our inner life.

The most important relationship, of course, is the one between the personality and the soul. But just as a child is not always ready to receive the instructions of its parent, the personality is not always willing to accept a full and proper relationship with the soul. And herein lies one of the keys to the nature of Gemini each year. The new forces which are set in motion each year in Aries begin to filter into specific challenges of personal growth by the time of Gemini. *Our relationship with spirit actually changes* to some degree each year in Gemini. If we change with it, and catch the high tide of the emerging new forces, we will do well. But many people are not oriented to this kind of change. For these people, resistance and ambivalence are more common in Gemini than growth.

We should understand that even though the changes which are occurring embrace us at the personal level, they are not limited to this level—or even specifically directed at it. The primary changes, in fact, occur in the archetypal patterns of creation. Since we are governed and influenced by these forces, change sweeps into our life, too. It is as though the mind of God is releasing the force of certain cosmic ideas into the mental plane of the whole planet, penetrating even to the lowest aspects of creation, as well as humanity. Nothing is left untouched by this great showering of light, although most of us can be aware of it only in indirect ways.

In spiritual aspirants, the soul is responsive to this down-pouring of force and seeks to cooperate with it, by also setting in motion new cycles of activity for the personality. The same pattern can be observed in institutions, groups, corporations, and nations. The opportunity of Gemini is to distribute this new force more purposefully through the systems of form, be it the physical activity of a single individual or the contributions of a whole segment of society. For those of us who have worked to develop an organized and alert mind, the period of Gemini leads to enrichment and an expansion of our involvement in life. Both outward and inward growth can be expected.

THE SYMBOLISM OF GEMINI

The word "gemini" means "twins," and the symbol of the sign generally depicts human twins, usually two brothers, intertwined in an embrace. We would like to think it is an embrace of affection, but it is just as likely to be the embrace of conflict.

The conventional symbol therefore emphasizes youth and immaturity, sentimental affection and combat—none of which really captures the essence of Gemini. A more esoterically correct symbol would be two mature brothers—two disciples joined by their work in a common endeavor. In this symbol lies a powerful suggestion for one of the keys to unlocking the forces of Gemini—it is like which attracts like, not opposites.

It is our own maturity that invokes the soul's maturity.

It is our involvement in productive projects which draws in creative inspiration.

It is our participation in growth which draws in new measures of wisdom, goodwill, and strength.

It is the light that we radiate which draws in greater light.

It is the compatibility of two ideas which sets up an interplay between them.

Ideally, we are meant to approach the challenges of Gemini in the spirit of partnership—that we are a partner with the higher self in all that we do. This puts the nature of Gemini at a much higher level than the usual interpretation, which stresses curiosity, fickleness, volatility, the lack of perseverance, expediency, and originality. As we master the lesson of intelligent partnership, then gradually a new lesson will emerge:

We are like the younger brother of the Christ, who can overshadow all we do—if we are in harmony with Him. The Christ is an Elder Brother to us all. As we reach out to embrace Him, He can embrace us.

HOW THE FORCES OF GEMINI AFFECT US

In popular astrology, it is thought that Gemini causes immature people to be scattered or capricious, mature people to be flexible and adaptable. There is certainly an element of truth in this, but the true dynamism of Gemini lies much deeper. Gemini has a gentle but powerful impact on our inner capacities of perception, as though we were rising up to a great height and stretching wide our span of awareness to see the best and the worst of things within ourself, society, and our work.

We are often unaware of this happening at the inner levels, but it does trickle down into our conscious thoughts and feelings one way or another. If we respond wisely, Gemini becomes a marvelous time for nurturing growth and healing in every aspect of our life and every relationship. If we rely on our goodwill and highest values to guide us, we will gain much in wisdom and purity. But if we respond immaturely, by following our feelings, we will probably just heighten our confusion and pettiness—and irritate those around us.

The average person will respond to the forces of Gemini by becoming more resistant to opportunities to grow, to branch out in new directions, or to cooperate with life. He will retreat into moodiness and self-pity, and feel very much "out of sorts" with life. There will be a marked increase in the "if only" syndrome—the tendency to speculate on what might have been "if only" conditions had been different. This type of speculation, of course, deflects attention away from current opportunities and challenges and is just a smokescreen for resistance.

The spiritual aspirant will have a tendency to become somewhat spacy and unfocused. Somehow, the spiritual aspirant always seems to end up with a square peg to put in a round hole. This is not really true, of course, but it often seems to be. The incoming forces of change and growth refocus need and opportunity just enough that the skills and talents the aspirant is accustomed to using simply are not as appropriate as they once were. If the aspirant can adjust quickly to these changes, he will be able to refocus and serve as an agent of healing and nurturing during Gemini. But if he allows himself to identify with the odd feeling of being out of step, he can prolong his confusion.

The advanced person will notice a much sharper definition of the archetypal forces he is working with—to build, to heal, and to serve—but at the same time will also be more aware of the pessimism and resistance of mass consciousness. This will often take the form of envy of spiritual and creative accomplishment, and can be a draining factor on the advanced person, unless compensatory action is taken. Instead of fighting against the force of resistance in mass consciousness, the advanced person must learn to use the force of nurturing love to heal these problems and bless the potential within humanity.

In general, the impact of Gemini will be to emphasize the divisions in our mental household and character, so that we will be inspired to heal and repair them. In a sense, they operate in harmony with one of the Christ's most provocative statements:

"Do not suppose that I have come to bring peace on earth: it is not peace I have come to bring, but a sword. For I have come to set a man against his father, a daughter against her mother, a daughter-in-law against her mother-in-law. A man's enemies will be those of his own household." The last half of this statement is a direct reference to the book of Micah, in which Micah laments the divisions which have arisen within the "household" of his people. "Now is the time of their confusion," he says. "My hope is in the God who will save me." The Christ took the hope of Micah and converted it into a specific instruction: "Anyone who finds his life will lose it; anyone who loses his life for my sake will find it."

By bringing a sword, the forces of Gemini force us to become a peacemaker and learn to harmonize opposing forces. They set our human nature against our spiritual nature, for the purpose of causing us to let go of our intense preoccupation with our human nature—our weaknesses, illusions, and selfishness—and refine our self-expression so it is guided more and more by our spiritual nature. This will influence every aspect of our character.

• Our **motivation** to grow will be strengthened as the forces of Gemini stir up our conscience and values. We will be encouraged to examine ambivalent feelings and subtly destructive impulses and replace them with a more refined expression of our spiritual nature. Our most cherished values will be challenged, forcing us to think them through more carefully and make sure they are rooted in spirit. Even this, however, will not be enough to motivate some people to grow. They will respond by becoming indifferent and jaded. In fact, escapism will increase and many people will be motivated only to find the easiest way out of challenging situations.

• Our **awareness** will be colored by a heightened perception of suffering, both within ourself and within others. Conditions that have been allowed to fester unresolved may become real burdens, like a chronic dull ache in consciousness. This could be even more tiring and wearing than an acute pain or crisis. These aches can only be cured by honestly assessing what we can do to enrich these conditions—and then getting busy and doing it.

• The **mind** will be stimulated so we can see more clearly aspects of our character we have ignored in the past—blind spots, inconsistencies, and deficiencies which must be corrected before we can develop a better relationship with the soul. In addition, our capacity for concrete analysis will be sharpened and our ability to work with symbols and abstractions will be stimulated. The intuition will be more powerful, making possible great leaps of understanding—for those who have developed a good intuitive capacity. It will therefore be an excellent time to be innovative and creative in almost every facet of life: our self-awareness, spiritual attunement, career, domestic relationships, personal interests, and so on. But we should also beware that the narrowness of closed minds will be more noticeable in Gemini—in contrast to the greater opportunity to expand our thinking and perspective.

- The **emotions** will be strongly influenced by fantasy and the wish life. They will also be highly reactive, prone to pointless worry as they churn up frustrations, doubts, fears, and resentments. This turmoil will be beneficial if it catches our attention and encourages us to work to gain better control of the emotions—but will just generate more irritation in our life if we do not. There will be a strong tendency emotionally to second-guess what we are doing and worry about whether or not we are doing it right.

- In the realm of our **self-expression**, the forces of Gemini will encourage us to see the need for new measures of harmony, beauty, and grace in the way we approach the major situations of life. New possibilities of perfection may be revealed to us, and lift our effectiveness to a higher level.

There is always the possibility in Gemini of brief encounters with the phenomenon of "the dark night of the soul," if we let our spiritual nature be eclipsed by the worries, fears, or concerns of the personality. But this is only because there is an equal possibility of real transcendence during Gemini—the opportunity to glimpse more of the inner light and love of spirit than ever before. The latter is far more significant than the former.

THE CHALLENGES OF GEMINI

A fuller measure of the power of spirit will be available to those who use it wisely and benevolently. This is achieved by responding to the authority of the soul. Too many people give authority for their life to their emotions, wishes, and feelings. Others give it to dogma and ideas they have not fully digested. But the wise person establishes the soul as the effective authority in his or her life, and as a result becomes a focal point of spiritual power. In our meditations and spiritual exercises, therefore, we should strive to identify with spirit as our central authority, then focus its power into our life to clear away inconsistencies, distortions, and negativity. In addition, we should make it a daily practice to renew our sense of sanctity or holiness. We may well be challenged to preserve and protect that which is holy, both in our spiritual nature and our human nature alike. We must take care to guard our treasures of intelligence, skill, friendship, and spirituality from all contamination.

The challenge of Gemini to parents is to respond to their children's need for healing and growth. There will be a strong temptation for some parents to judge their children by comparing them with other children, rather than on their own merits. This is just an exercise of vanity on the part of the parents, and is not really helpful to the children involved.

Our relationships in general, of course, represent one of the most significant areas of challenge in Gemini. Instead of just taking them for granted, as we so often do, we should make an extra effort to become familiar with the spiritual qualities which are the raw materials of good relationships:

• Harmony, which we should express as cooperation.
• Goodwill, which we should express as intelligent concern.
• Affection, which we should express as friendship.

Where difficulties exist in relationships, we should honestly evaluate what role we have played in creating them—and correct it. In any relationship, we should endeavor to define its potential strength, then work to cultivate it in active and practical ways.

In the business world, Gemini has a way of producing problems—exposing double standards, a lack of integrity, and so on. To whatever degree our house is not in order, the forces of Gemini will reveal it and encourage reform. It is therefore an excellent time to initiate checks on standards of quality, the conduct of subordinates, and the way our interests are being represented to others, both by internal and external agents.

At a world level, Gemini is an excellent time to initiate new diplomatic overtures, not publicly but on a one-to-one basis, leader to leader. It is an excellent time to build a stronger rapport with key allies, and to work on resolving the nagging problems which separate quarreling groups. As always, however, the ideal of healing should be kept uppermost in mind.

The theme of healing is likewise the major challenge to us in our own growth. We are called at this time to repair and restore whatever has been injured, to reconcile and reunite whatever has been sundered, and to nurture the seed of perfection in ourself and in society. This work of healing will be greatly assisted by a tremendous stimulation of the love nature in anyone who is sincerely seeking to be an agent of healing, but herein lies a key to how well we respond to the challenge of Gemini. Little healing will occur in our life if we just sit back and wait for God to heal our problems. We must involve ourself actively in becoming a healing force in life, not just for our own benefit, but for the benefit of all who need God's wisdom and love.

We must also be sure to pursue *genuine* healing. Far too often, healing is thought of in terms of relieving stressful symptoms, so we are not bothered by them anymore. As a result, the effort to heal frequently becomes little more than an attack on what is wrong or painful. This is not the spirit of Gemini. The healing potential of Gemini is tapped primarily by learning to identify with the health within us and using these resources of health to enrich our consciousness, nurture our maturity, and heal distress. As we build up greater health, that which is unhealthy fades away.

This, in fact, is the reward of meeting the challenges of Gemini wisely: new health, a stronger relationship with the soul, and a greater measure of understanding and light.

THE PROBLEMS OF GEMINI

Gemini has a way of exposing our weaknesses and vulnerabilities, in the hope that we will recognize them and do something to correct them. We become more poignantly aware of our limitations. This is meant to induce growth, but it is all too easy to overreact—to overstate the limitations we face and make the struggle greater than it really is. Getting caught up in reactiveness in this way is the source of many of the problems which tend to arise in Gemini.

Another factor to keep in mind in dealing with problems is that Gemini is a time for adjustment and change, so that we can cooperate more fully with the new trends which are emerging. Some of the problems we face, therefore, arise out of resistance to these changes—resistance in ourself, in others, and in society as a whole.

As a result, Gemini is a good time to be cautious and reserved, to conceal our convictions and reactions from others, and to hold fast to our inner values and quiet confidence. In this way, we protect ourself from becoming unnecessarily embroiled in the problems of others.

Specific problems which often arise in Gemini include:

1. Confusion. The forces of Gemini have a tendency to scatter the focus of our attention, so that we are frequently frustrated and confused. This might be called the "yes, but" syndrome; as soon as we think we have come to a clear conclusion, someone is bound to say, "Yes, but have you considered this other factor?" If someone else does not say it, a voice within our own mind will. This is part of the inclusive nature of these forces, which seek to draw in and harmonize all fragments and parts of any idea, group, activity, or plan. The key is learning that the confusion is only temporary; the more we strive to make sense of the many variables, the more we impose a sense of order and clarity on them.

2. Hypocrisy. The dual nature of Gemini likewise tends to stimulate any duality within ourself, thereby revealing inconsistency and hypocrisy. If we find such problems arising, we should resist the temptation to cover up and pretend that no such inconsistency exists; this would just deepen the problem. Instead, we should honestly face the discrepancy and seek to repair it.

3. Moodiness. Strong sentimental feelings may rise up for no apparent reason, especially in the emotionally oriented. The reservoirs of sadness, anger, and fear in the subconscious may suddenly open up, overwhelming us with tidal waves of strong and uncontrolled emotion. If we have learned the basic lessons of detachment, we will be able to take these sudden bursts of emotion in stride. But if not, we will discover just how extensive our reactiveness is—and how damaging it can be to our dignity and well-being.

4. Exhilaration. Dark moods are not the only forces that may rise up suddenly and uncontrollably; strong surges of excitement and exhilaration can as well. These sudden surges may be strong enough to be embarrassing; in any event, they will upset our poise and common sense, unless we are able to remain centered in our basic values and sense of purpose. In this regard, we also need to be watchful of others who may overreact to what we are doing, and not let their naive or self-serving excitement influence our opinion of ourself.

5. Brooding. Gemini will magnify any tendency we may already have to brood on the past, and this can become a serious diversion from attending to the challenges of the present. For some, this rumination will take the simple form of worry and anxiety, but in others, it will turn more tragic, as they relive old battles and humiliating experiences. Self-pity will increase, and so will needless speculation on what "might have been." At the same time, there will be a tendency to escape into the pleasant memories of the past as a way of avoiding the drabness of the

present. All such tendencies should be avoided. The intelligent way to deal with the past is to see the lessons we learned—or should have learned—and then evaluate how we can benefit from them in the present.

6. Mental gymnastics. There is a tendency for mentally focused people to waste the opportunities of Gemini by becoming absorbed in clever solutions, interesting speculations, and the thrill of mental ingenuity, all the while missing the underlying meaning of what they are doing. Such people limit themselves to the most superficial uses of the mind, pursuing brilliance that signifies nothing.

7. Partisanship. There is a strong tendency to take sides during Gemini and foster an "us versus them" kind of mentality. Obviously, this leads to increased tension and conflict. We need to look beyond our personal needs and rights and consider what is in the best interest of everyone involved.

8. The bartering of affection. The forces of Gemini tend to deepen our affection for others, but immature people often react to this by using affection as emotional coin of the realm—to see what concessions they can win from others in exchange for it. The "you scratch my back and I'll scratch yours" syndrome will be quite strong. True affection, however, is based on goodwill, not the highest bid.

9. Intemperance. "Overkill" is a definite possibility, especially as we encounter situations about which we have strong convictions. We are apt to come on too forcefully, responding to problems with far too much righteous indignation. Our ability to be a constructive influence in halting injustice or promoting reform depends on the reasonableness of our behavior. We can easily undermine the good we might do in Gemini by intemperate action.

10. Dissipation. Those who have a tendency to spread themselves too thin may have a struggle in Gemini, as their usual ability to get by falters. They need to attune themselves

more wisely and prudently to the demands of their activities.

11. Frivolity. Cavalier attitudes and speech may offend others, undermining our dignity and the respect of others for our work and efforts. Practical jokes may be more prevalent, too. But while a light and charming mood is often a great asset, carelessness in how we use humor can easily backfire.

12. Perfectionism. Gemini heightens our capacity to see the ideal of perfection—and also to compare it to the actual conditions with which we must deal. Instead of responding maturely to this realization, there are many people who use the vision of perfection to justify criticizing and condemning imperfection—in themselves, in others, and in society. This can become a definite curse during Gemini. We need to shun condemnation and put our effort into healing that which is imperfect so that it better embodies the ideal.

13. Resentment. Bitterness toward specific events of life, the ways others have treated us, and even our personal limitations may increase during Gemini. But resentment and bitterness are terrible burdens to carry with us; they poison our humanity and alienate us from the life of spirit. Those who feel justified in resentment or bitterness are cruelly deceiving themselves; they need to rise out of this limited perspective and use the healing power of goodwill and compassion to cleanse their systems of these poisons.

14. Bellicosity. Overstatements and hyperbole will be commonplace during Gemini. They should not be given much credence—except to warn us that we are dealing with someone (possibly ourself!) who is given to gross exaggerations.

15. The failure to act. Many of the worst problems of Gemini are sins of omission, rather than sins of commission—the failure to make necessary changes in attitude and thought, the failure to accept new responsibilities, or the failure to honor or defend something we cherish. We must take care not to succumb to moral cowardice or indifference.

16. Jealousy. There will be a strong temptation to compare our lot with that of others, and be envious of what they have— even if we do not fully understand what it is. In particular, many people will be jealous of the achievements of others and the talent of those who have risen to the top of their professions. It should be understood that jealousy and envy are really forms of hatred, and serve no constructive purpose. They demean those who indulge in them.

THE OPPORTUNITIES OF GEMINI

The opportunities of Gemini are generated primarily as we respond to the soul's call to revise our *orientation to life*. If we remain bogged down in our selfishness, pettiness, and difficulties, we will find little opportunity in Gemini. But if we rise above this level and seek to orient ourself to spirit, many rich and significant opportunities can be found.

In a very real sense, we create the opportunities of this time, by the way in which we choose to focus our emphasis, our interest, our attention, and our labors. We either draw to us rich opportunities to express the best within us, or we repel them and attract instead the problems and difficulties which are more in harmony with the worst within us. The choice is ours.

These are the kinds of opportunities we can create during Gemini, if we strive to orient ourself to spirit and act as a healing force in life:

1. Serenity. Outer events and our reactions to them may be distracting, but there is an unusually strong potential for generating peace and poise in our quiet moments of reflection and meditation. One of the great benefits of reorienting ourself to the life of spirit is the opportunity to tap into the serenity and quiet confidence of that level, and use it to look at the chaotic conditions of our life with greater objectivity.

2. Intimacy. The sense of sharing and mutual interplay will be stronger in relationships, bringing about a deeper level of intimacy. But in no relationship will this be more important than in our relationship with spirit. The intimacy of Gemini is not a physical intimacy, but rather the intimacy that develops as we see "face to face" at inner levels—the intimacy of shared values, goodwill, joy, and wisdom.

3. Reconciliation. Where there has been discord and opposition, there is a new opportunity for reconciliation. As we learn the lessons of working with the duality of Gemini, we become more adept at discerning the inner ideals and principles which stabilize our consciousness and permit us to heal differences. This does not happen by accident, of course, but by lifting our problems and divisiveness into the healing light of the soul and seeking to resolve them maturely.

4. A more mature sense of timing. As we strive to reorient ourself to the higher perspective of spirit, and work consciously with the force of harmony, we will find that it gives us a new awareness of the creative uses of timing. We learn that the right action at the wrong time may end up being a wrong action. We also learn to act in harmony with the best time to initiate new activities. In this way, we create "windows" of opportunity for ourself.

5. Improved communication. Gemini sets the stage to communicate with those who need to hear what we can tell them—and to listen to those who are seeking to communicate with us. The forces of Gemini make it easier to transfer our ideas and positions into clear concepts that we can readily express to others. Gemini also helps improve communication between the higher and lower self—and between the conscious and unconscious mind.

6. A greater capacity to learn. Our goal in Gemini should always be to nurture new levels of maturity, practical skills in living, and a greater flexibility of mind. By reviewing difficult

experiences from the past, cleansing them of resentment and regret, seeing the lessons we have learned, and then using them as a foundation for present growth, we can greatly accelerate the progress we make in self-understanding.

7. A greater capacity to serve. Gemini encourages and supports those who involve themselves actively in bringing heaven to earth. We should therefore seek to discover the spiritual significance of the work we do, and how we can use it as an opportunity to serve.

8. A stronger dedication to excellence. Time and again in Gemini, the issues of quality and excellence will arise. If we try to slip by on less than our best effort, we will be nagged by our conscience. But if we strive instead for excellence, seeking always to honor the ideal of perfection, we may be surprised by how often we surpass "our limits" and achieve new measures of competence during this time.

9. Good humor. There is a strong sense of playfulness and good humor associated with the forces of Gemini, and it can be used quite successfully to chase out the sober or grim elements of our disposition. We will also discover that humor can be used by us successfully in healing discord in relationships—and in becoming more comfortable in our relationship with the higher self. If we listen intently enough, we may even hear God giggling from time to time!

10. Nobility. We are something greater than the petty, common elements we so often identify with. As human beings, we have important links to a divine legacy. This means that in the innermost dimensions of our being, we are truly noble. As the forces of Gemini beckon us to reorient ourself to the soul, we inevitably discover the rich measure of nobility which resides within us. One of the great challenges—and opportunities—of Gemini is discovering ways to express this nobility in daily living.

11. Consolidation. Whether in business, our personal life,

or spiritual service, we will be better able to see where efforts are being duplicated and move to eliminate the redundancy. We will also be able to see more clearly how the efforts of others complement our own, thereby encouraging us to forge more active and productive relationships.

12. Becoming an active partner with spirit. Gemini teaches us the practical lessons of becoming an active partner with the spiritual forces within us. It helps us forge a richer alliance with transpersonal powers and intelligences. If we learn to calm our reactiveness and seek the inner life, higher forces will be able to guide us and act through us.

13. The capacity to influence. Those with strong and powerful minds have an unusual influence on others during Gemini. This can be either beneficial or dangerous, depending on what level of thinking we are responsive to. We should therefore make a conscious effort to attune the mind to the highest and most spiritual wavelength possible. And we must make sure that any impact our thinking may have on others around us will be noble and inspiring—not an intrusion on their self-determination.

14. The capacity to care. Gemini stimulates the divine force of love-wisdom, which we express in many ways—goodwill, benevolence, compassion, kindness, and reverence. One of the most practical expressions of love-wisdom is the capacity to care—to care for others, to care about the quality of the work we do, to care for the unfoldment of human civilization, and to care for the plan of God. To care in an enlightened sense means that we respond with goodwill to the best and noblest within the person or aspect of life we care about. We nurture this noble core and help it unfold.

15. An open heart. Above all, Gemini nurtures openness and inclusiveness in our dealings with others, our own potential, and spirit. This may find expression in our life in something as simple as greater hospitality—or in a more powerful

ability to understand others and be a force of healing. The open heart of Gemini is a generous heart, willing to "bear all things, believe all things, hope all things."

TUNING INTO THE FORCES OF GEMINI

Just as relationships between humans are highlighted during Gemini, so also are relationships among ideas, insights, and awareness. Our associative mechanism is probably more active during Gemini than at any other time. As a result, one insight can easily lead to another, which leads in turn to a third, a fourth, a fifth, and so on. It is easy to get completely unraveled in pursuing these kinds of associations, but if we are disciplined and alert to what we are doing, we can profitably use the same process to discover a great deal about the forces of Gemini and how they influence us.

The key is to realize that all of these associations have higher correspondences—roots in the spiritual life. By seeking these higher correspondences, we begin to think in terms of the soul, and this in turn helps us see the scope of our life more clearly. It lets us speculate, for example, on the new trends that are emerging in our life, what their implications for us will be, and how they can be seen in the context of the grand drama of human development.

Then, in examining our own thoughts, feelings, and involvements, we can realize that they, too, have higher correspondences—roots in the spiritual life. And it is at these levels that we are being influenced by the forces of Gemini—and can become attuned to them. If we find ourself confused by a bombardment of ideas regarding a piece of work we are doing, for example, we could just dismiss this as "the confusion of Gemini"—or, we could realize that it is the force of inclusiveness at work, drawing in every relevant idea associated with the project at hand. We are only overwhelmed because we are try-ing to process fifth-dimensional forces in a finite way.

By relating our own experiences and responses to the higher correspondences which shape and guide them in these ways, we can learn a great deal about the nature of Gemini.

In addition, a powerful way of attuning to the forces of Gemini is to seek to respond to the wavelength of goodwill and benevolence.

The way to teach in Gemini is by example—by demonstrat-ing the essence of an ideal and inspiring others to respond to the same ideal on their own.

The way to heal in Gemini is through the use of spiritual principles of integration, transforming mundane elements of life so they become responsive to nobler qualities.

The way to lead in Gemini is by touching the inner qualities of nobility in those who follow and inspiring them to live up to their fullest potential.

If we work harmoniously with the forces of Gemini, we will find we can act with a greater measure of perfection in all that we do. And to the degree that we become aware of areas of our life needing healing, we set the stage for the nurturing activ-ity of Virgo and a more balanced perspective in Libra.

A SONG FOR GEMINI

Two forces meet. In meeting, they are repelled, setting in motion impulse and relationship. As they move through time and space, they etch two arcs. Their movement forms a circle, and they meet again. Once more the forces are repelled, dou-bling back along the circle. Time after time, they trace through memory and possibility their circle of experience, until the circle itself is set in motion, the living presence of a single force.

Two individuals meet. To each, the other seems to block

the way. They embrace and struggle. Both gain the advantage, both lose the advantage. Yet neither wins until they see that they are brothers. Then both are victorious—together.

Two aspirants meet. The one aspires to see the light; the other aspires to taste the full experience of darkness. To each, the other seems the shadow of himself. They battle on the field of mist and illusion, stalking one another in a maze of mirrored reflections, never knowing what is real and what is not, what is self and what is shadow, until their dual aspirations merge and form an unspotted, perfect mirror reflecting the glory of the light—the light which always shines and yet can be both hidden and revealed.

A PARABLE FOR GEMINI

There once were two axes. One was very self-centered, always complaining about how hard life was and trying to get out of work. He bitterly resented having his brains knocked out every day, by being struck time after time against hard wood. When it was time to be sharpened, he almost fainted as his owner spit on him to moisten his edge, and thought it sheer torture to be honed on the whetstone. He would have much preferred to remain dull—and in truth, many of his friends thought he was.

The other axe was very well balanced. He understood his purpose and delighted in being of service to mankind. He knew that an occasional bit of friction and steady use were part of his life, but he accepted these conditions joyfully, rather than complain about them. He styled himself as a "cutting edge" and thought about the homes which were built from the wood he cut, the furniture that was handcrafted, and the people who were warmed by the firewood he had felled. His life was full of satisfaction and a sense of contribution.

It is not hard to guess which axe a teller of parables would choose to fell his trees. But the strange thing is that these two axes belonged to the same woodsman—who used them both every day, without favoring the one over the other.

9

Cancer

CANCER

Keynote: Building a new household of consciousness.

Mantra: "The invisible becomes visible; light takes on form."

New moon focus: Mental housecleaning.

Full moon focus: Breathing spiritual life into our values and convictions.

Rays 3, 4, 6, and 7 dominate.

Primary archetypal forces:
Grace, abundance, order, generosity

A Prayer For Cancer:

Heavenly Mother-Father God, with joy we seek to play our part in Your Divine plan. Guide us as we strive to make the momentum of Your plan the driving force within our life and work.

May our awareness be filled with the light of wisdom, so we can see the path before us more clearly. Let self-deception end.

May our heart be filled with the love that heals isolation, fear, and possessiveness. Let selfishness be replaced by the will to serve.

May our mind be filled with spiritual purpose, so we can see that the opportunities and contributions of our daily life are meant to be the ways we serve Your plan. Let courage and spiritual direction dissolve confusion and indifference.

May the veils of illusion be lifted, so the light of our soul can shine through all that we are and all that we do—and help us liberate all who are trapped in form, including ourself.

The archetypal force of Cancer encourages us to *become involved in living:*

To see the good that we might do, and do it.

To see the talents that we might nurture, and nurture them.

To see the friendships that we might build, and build them.

To see the duties we might embrace, and embrace them.

To see the support of worthwhile endeavors that we might give, and give it.

To see the ways in which we might enrich the quality of our work, the usefulness of our service, and the benevolence of our life—and do so.

Symbolically, it is during Cancer that new life enters the physical plane. Regardless of the literal phase of the zodiac, it is always the force of Cancer which serves as midwife to the emergence of new life—new hope, new potential, new qualities, new understanding, new skills, new projects, and new directions in self-expression. During the actual time of Cancer, therefore, the opportunity for the birth of spirit in form is greatly heightened. In a very real sense, we have the opportunity to be reborn daily—by activating the wisdom, love, and strength of the inner self.

At a cosmic level, the archetypal drive to become more involved in living results in the stimulation of those aspects of the plan of God which are intended to be expressed next. At the individual level, we can most effectively harness this archetypal force by becoming more responsive to the plan of God, by interpreting it wisely, by examining how we can contribute to it in our life, and then by doing so.

It is easy to miss this opportunity, of course, if we happen to believe that we do not know enough about the plan of God to act upon it. This would be a self-deception, however. We have been told a great deal about the plan of God:

• We have been told to "be fruitful and multiply"—to take the talents and skills we have and put them to work in ways

189

which would benefit humanity and enrich civilization.

• We have been told to love the Lord our God with all our heart and soul and mind and strength—to align our body, emotions, mind, and spiritual determination to the light within us, the light of the world.

• We have been told to love our neighbors as ourself—to discover the light and life of spirit within the people with whom we share our labors and loves, within the lesser forms of life with whom we share the planet, and within the world as a whole.

Surely these three commandments encompass enough of our life that we can work to fulfill the plan of God without exhausting the possibilities before us! And as we strive to become more responsive to this plan, we slowly become more aware of how perfectly the whole of life is structured, and how marvelously we fit into this grand structure and play our part. Indeed, becoming aware of the structure of life can be one of the greatest discoveries of Cancer—for those who have the eyes to see:

• The structure of universal law.
• The structure of civilization.
• The structure of business and the economy.
• The structure of the circumstances of life.
• The structure of our subconscious.
• The structure of instinctual patterns.
• The structure of the divine plan.

This structure is not static, like the foundation of a house, however. It is an *abstract* structure and as such, it is a structure of living, moving, and growing energies. One way of thinking of it—although this only captures one facet of its fullness—is to define it in terms of *momentum*. In considering the structure of the economy, for example, it should be easy to see that we must deal primarily with the momentum of economic forces, not its static aspects. And in order to make changes in this structure, we must adjust the flow of the momentum. You cannot change the course of the wind just by shaking the branches of a tree; you have to deal with the forces which set the wind in motion.

Just as Taurus taught us to refine our motivations and make them more spiritual, Cancer can teach us about the momentum of life and how to harness it. And this is important, for even if we act with correct motivation, our efforts may nonetheless be derailed, if the momentum of earlier plans, habits, beliefs, and expectations pushes us in other directions. It is therefore necessary to reconcile our motivations and the momentum of our life and work, making sure both serve spiritual purpose. This is one of the primary challenges of Cancer.

The force of momentum is one of the great sources of power in our life. Much of it is internal—the momentum of established habits, ways of thinking, emotional reactiveness, glamours and illusions, and our own self-image. Some of it is external—the momentum of mass consciousness, the groups we belong to, our profession or industry, and even the forces of the zodiac. Ideally, we can harness this force of momentum and use it to provide power for our own effective self-expression. But many people fall short of the ideal and end up enslaved by the momentum of the past, not the master of it. When this occurs, the force of momentum becomes an obstacle to the life of spirit.

The personality tends to think of obstacles as external—as conditions of life which impose limits on us and keep us from doing or achieving what we would like. But the spiritual person learns that the real obstacles of life are mostly internal—the unchecked and undisciplined momentum of the ways we have thought, felt, believed, and behaved in the past. And if we can learn to neutralize and remove these inner obstacles, we will be able to manage most of the outer ones, too.

If we are alert, the forces of Cancer will lead us to a deeper understanding of the patterns of momentum in our life, the obstacles which block out the light of the soul, and what it will take to overcome these obstacles and redirect our momentum.

For those who are afraid to face and overcome personal limitations and obstacles, Cancer may be an unpleasant time. But for those who are dedicated to the spiritual path, it can be a time of great breakthrough and new understanding.

Through the intelligent review and redirection of momentum, Cancer gives us the opportunity to *focus* the new energies which have been building since Aries into our individual life and work. Some people, of course, think that the forces of the zodiac automatically condition us, but this is true only in the most superficial sense. The manner in which these energies affect us depends entirely upon our personal initiative and self-determination, *because we are the ones who give focus to divine forces!* Goodwill is just an abstract force until we give it expression through generous and helpful acts. Joy is just a divine potential until we give it expression by taking delight in living. Beauty is only a quality in the mind of God, until we find ways to translate it into creative and innovate work. Wisdom is likewise just an abstract force, until we use it to fuel our own understanding of life and act intelligently in pursuing our goals.

In this way, we can see that the drama of Cancer is far more powerful than it seems to be, when assigned the usual characteristics of possessiveness, self-indulgence, protectiveness, materialism, self-sacrifice, and appreciativeness. There is a strong measure of choice and focus in how we use the forces of Cancer that is usually overlooked.

The primary work of Cancer each year is to translate the inner vision which has been emerging since Aries into new approaches and qualities of self-expression for daily work and living, thereby setting in motion subtle adjustments to the momentum of our life. But this is not just a casual process, accomplished by adding a few pleasant feelings to our general outlook. We must see our activities, duties, and relationships as the means by which we bring the light of spirit *into focus* in our daily affairs.

THE SYMBOLISM OF CANCER

The symbolic implications of this sign are rich and multi-faceted. The concrete symbol, of course, is the crab. In a more abstract sense, the forces of Cancer represent something alien which seems to disturb the wholeness of a life expression or activity. This is not always negative in implication, however; indeed, it is usually quite beneficial. A seed is alien to the soil around it and draws strength from the earth, yet grows and flourishes and fulfills both its destiny and that of the soil.

We, too, are "seeds" which are growing, and are often planted in alien conditions in order to develop new skills and talents. Always, we have the choice either to be a destructive or a constructive force. When we are constructive, we will be accepted by our social environment and achieve success; when we are destructive, we will be rejected by our environment and experience defeat and ostracism.

At the same time, we ourself are a complete organism into which "alien seeds" can be planted, primarily through the sub-conscious and unconscious. When these seeds are issues of the soul, they will be productive and ought to be cultivated; when they are not, they will frequently be destructive and ought to be weeded out. Examples of this latter type of "seed" would be the manipulative thoughts of others, poor self-images, bad habits, and fantasies.

The forces of Cancer propel us into new conditions in which we can "plant" our talents, skills, and wisdom. Through these experiences, we gain a sense of selfhood and identity. At the same time, the forces of Cancer also draw us into the sub-conscious, to confront our heritage. Here, we either learn to work with the wholeness of our being—or we try to hide from it, by repressing that which we find.

In this way, we are able to learn something about the dual nature of our humanity: we are finite and limited in what we can do, day by day, but at the same time, we are infinite and unrestricted in our potential. The appearance is finite, but the consciousness and life associated with the appearance is infinite. If we dwell excessively on our finiteness, we can often feel isolated, alien, and alone. But if we understand more of our infinite and immortal nature, we can add significance to all that we do.

Alice Bailey also suggests that an important symbolic aspect of the crab is that it carries its house on its back. She gives as a mantra for Cancer the statement: "I build a lighted house and therein dwell." Having done so, she inquires: "Is the house you are building yet lit? Is it a lighted house? Or is it a dark prison?"

This house that we carry on our back is nothing less than the structure of our momentum. In this house, we must dwell, striving to live as a responsible citizen but conditioned by the way we have built our domicile.

The average person tends to be confined by the limitations of the house he has built.

The spiritual aspirant, by contrast, is hard at work discovering ways to transcend these limits and bring more light into the house. He is converting his house into a mansion and learning to respect the maxim, "In my Father's house, there are many mansions."

The advanced person has learned to build his house wherever he finds the light of God. As a result, it is always lit, because it is built on light, of light, and for the active expression of light. Like the crab, the advanced person takes his house with him, in heart and mind and soul and strength, wherever he goes, whatever he does. It is a temple in which he worships God.

Within the center of the temple, there is a veil, which separates the invisible from the visible. For the person who is truly involved in living, working to fulfill the plan of God, there will often be a parting of the veil during Cancer, producing a deeper

194

insight into the plan. This glimpse could well be misinterpreted, however, unless we remain detached and objective, willing to act with patience in trying to understand what it signifies and how we should respond.

HOW THE FORCES OF CANCER AFFECT US

The primary way the forces of Cancer affect the individual is by stimulating the urge to domesticate the things of the earth, thereby enhancing our self-expression. This means that the forces of this time promote an interest in material goods, the things of the home, and personal comforts. They increase personal possessiveness—not just regarding personal goods, but also regarding friends, philosophies, and even memories and habits. The tendency to cling to and defend that which we feel we own is very strong. But these general traits of Cancer work out in many ways, depending on how we focus them.

For the average person, Cancer is a time when physical things and personal possessions become the center of interest. It is a time of increased greed, selfishness, fear of loss, and envy. Domestic concerns are paramount. The need to defend personal property and security is a strong motivating force. There is also a strong tendency to try to dominate or enslave other people, directly or indirectly.

For the spiritual aspirant, the pull of materialism in Cancer usually outweighs dedication to spirit, and aspiration is set on the shelf in favor of possessiveness. The physical focus of possessiveness will be less pronounced, yet all too often the theme remains the same. He will tend to be immersed in "cultivating his own garden"—and temporarily blinded to the larger issues of life, the garden we all live in. Such concerns as personal independence, status, the subtle influence of others, self-centeredness, and theoretical speculations will consume his interest.

195

The advanced person, however, will endeavor to tame life and refine its expression not for his own convenience, but for the good of humanity. He will act to nurture the spiritual qualities within those he meets, the creative potential within his work, and the liberation of consciousness. In this way, he will liberate himself as well as the people and situations he deals with.

To capture the full potential of Cancer, we should strive to follow the example of the advanced person. Wherever we have been materialistic or self-serving, we should strive to become more enlightened and helpful toward others. The temptation to be self-serving will be strong, but we must not let ourself succumb to it, lest we be trapped by its force.

The great danger of Cancer is to use the emerging new energies *out of focus*—to add power to aspects of our consciousness which ought to be downplayed, not energized. It is obvious that power added to greed will lead to exploitation and the misuse of opportunity. Yet power can also be added to seemingly wholesome endeavors and still backfire, if it is not wisely focused. If our use of the energy is not in harmony with the purpose or spiritual intent of the endeavor, then it will be harmful, no matter how pure our intent. There are many ways the focus of our efforts can be blurred: through carelessness, excessive attention to form rather than purpose, egotism, rigid ideas, and glamorous expectations.

With this in mind, it can be said that while our **motivation** in Cancer ought to be to involve ourself in our work more fully and expand the scope of our responsibilities, in all too many people it will just be a heightened intent to preserve what they have, seek out greater comfort, and take care of personal needs.

Our **awareness**, too, may very well be out of focus. The forces of Cancer can dull awareness, and impinge upon our sensitivity. It is easy to be hypnotized by routine and monotonous aspects of life, until it seems as though we are just walking around in a trance, half-asleep. The antidote to this condition, of course, is to work on a daily basis to awaken the best qualities and talents within ourself. If we are seeking ways to expand our involvement in life, we will be largely immune to the dullness of this time.

The **mind** will be more fascinated than usual with subconscious aspects of problems and the underlying order of things. We should therefore use the mind to build bridges between the intangible and tangible aspects of life. These bridges are constructed of our understanding of how some intangible quality of the inner life can meet the needs of our outer life. The work of the mind in Cancer is to build those bridges on which the inner power of ideas can be transferred into outer expression.

The **emotions**, which are always highly personal, will become even more personalized during Cancer. As a result, most people will become even more entranced in the wish life and the "Peter Pan Department" of their fantasies. The enchantment of personal power, personal knowledge, personal fulfillment, personal struggle (and sacrifice), personal enlightenment, personal ideals, and personal magic will be greatly heightened. There is therefore a great need to practice the impersonal life and emphasize the transcendent values of life over our personal needs.

Probably the greatest impact of Cancer on the unenlightened person is to increase his or her attachments to form—our style, habits, and traditions. The creative person knows that he can be productively involved in form, creating and building with it, without being attached to it. But most people have trouble making this distinction—and the fine line will be blurred all the more during this time. As a result, we should make an extra effort to:

1. Discipline our attachments so they express the ideals of spirit, not entrap us in possessive or materialistic attitudes.

2. Reorient ourself to a spiritual perspective on life, rather than a personal perspective.

In terms of our **self-expression**, the forces of Cancer give us the opportunity to consolidate our efforts and recollect our resources. This in turn can lead to a new and fuller awareness of the purpose of what we are doing—and even to a deeper sense of unity with those who share the same purpose. In this way, we can draw in and collect at a common point the resources we need to succeed in our efforts. At the same time, however, there is a stronger potential than at other times to foolishly allow our energies and resources to be dissipated, by wasting opportunity, the helpfulness of others, and even the offer of money. We should be careful not to engage in practices or activities which drain off time, energy, and money.

THE CHALLENGES OF CANCER

Cancer is a time of receptivity; the great challenge to the spiritual aspirant is to be rightly receptive to the intangible forces of spirit. If we are pessimistic and at odds with ourself, we will not be poised to accept the new issues of spirit. We will fall back on old ways and once more be influenced by the attitudes and beliefs of mass consciousness. We should therefore strive to accept, as fully as we can:
• Our own destiny or fate as noble and purposeful, whether the current events happen to be pleasant or painful. Only as we accept our fate gracefully are we able to work creatively with it.
• Our true nature. We should strive to understand our ties with spirit, and accept them as an important part of our life.
• The help of others, when it is offered.
• The individuality and self-determination of others, especially those close to us.
• New ideas and better ways of approaching life.
Conversely, we should take care *not* to accept:

- The lowest common denominator in taste, values, and conduct.
- Gloominess or the feeling of defeat.
- Crudity or grossness in thought and behavior.
- Laziness or inaction.
- Self-deception and hypocrisy.
- Any tendency to repress or suppress unpleasant memories or ideas.

The challenge of Cancer to parents is to see their role as one requiring a creative investment. Far too many parents interact with their children only at their own convenience; they do not truly cultivate the potential, the talent, and the human richness within their children. Cancer is an ideal time to reflect on how child raising can be a creative enterprise—and on the talents and skills we as a parent are willing and able to invest. "Be ye fruitful and multiply" extends to a lot more than just *producing* children, after all—it also includes finding ways to help our children develop into intelligent, loving, and responsible adults.

The challenge of Cancer in relationships in general involves a number of factors. Cancer is an excellent time to set a healthier tone in relationships and achieve a better understanding of the nature and depth of real friendship. We must go beyond the usual notions of favoritism and partiality, however, and realize that friendship is based on mutual sharing of common ideals, goals, values, and goodwill.

At the same time, we should realize that relationships will not be free of strife during Cancer. In fact, if we let a tendency for self-centeredness overwhelm our relationships, we may find ourself in the midst of a number of battles, drawn along one or more of the following lines:

- The line between being dependent on others and expressing our own individuality.
- The line between soliciting the support of others and developing our own self-sufficiency.

- The line between artificially "maintaining the peace" and achieving true measures of harmony and fairness.

In general, family responsibilities become more important. This can be one's family of birth or marriage or, in the case of the spiritual aspirant, his or her inner family. In this regard, the concept of "inheritance" has powerful implications for the time of Cancer. It can be quite provocative to ponder on the difference between our family inheritances and the birthright or legacy of the soul. In particular, we might ask:

Have I inherited certain qualities or characteristics I might be better off without? How can I change them?

Have I inherited certain strengths and abilities I am not fully applying in life? How can I better use them?

In the business world, Cancer is a propitious time for making investments—not just financial investments, but also investments of time and energy. This is one of the key ways we can work with the archetypal force of abundance. By investing the abundance we have, we make a contribution to human life, multiply the original investment, and make a profit. This is not just good business, but responsible living as well.

Cancer is also an excellent time for business and other enterprises to draw together the resources they need for future activity, and to plan effectively how these resources will be used. It should be kept in mind, in this regard, that one of the great resources of any business is the collective skills and talents of the people working for it.

The same challenge can also be extended to the national and international level, where the task of planning wisely for the use of national resources is quite complex. In general, the work of apportioning resources and making sure support lines are well established is more easily done in Cancer than at other times.

The challenge of Cancer for our personal growth lies in the area of successful mental housecleaning. This is a term used to refer to the process of reviewing, cleansing, and revising our personal habits, attitudes, attachments, and character traits, so that they embody progressively more of the light of spirit. Cancer is an excellent time for all types of mental housecleaning, from the revision of habits to the exercise of greater self-discipline in our thought and speech.

The staging ground for many of the lessons of Cancer is the subconscious. Our own subconscious will be stirred up and become the scene of conflict, as problems from the past well up within us, opposing the new directions we have been trying to establish since Aries. It is not wise to ignore these conflicts or pretend they do not exist. Instead, it is much healthier to pay attention to these conditions and update our attitudes, habits, and commitments, whenever necessary.

There are four basic spiritual lessons to be learned:

1. The lesson of transmuting the need for satisfaction into the willingness to sacrifice. The average person is driven by desire in Cancer and seeks to satisfy his appetites. The spiritual person is motivated by his intention to cooperate with the will and plan of God. He works to make his life more sacred—the true meaning of sacrifice. This is an attitude more than an activity, really; we can practice sacrifice, for example, by being continually attentive to the need to reform our habits, beliefs, memories, and values. The moment we find ourself *clinging* to possessions, longings, prejudices, warm feelings, or indulgences, we can choose to let go of them, so as not to be a slave to them any longer. This is a very practical application of sacrifice.

2. The lesson of transforming sorrow into service. The time of Cancer produces a heightened awareness of the imperfections and hardships of life. The average person will grieve excessively over his small losses or complain bitterly about what he perceives to be wrong. The spiritual person, however, does not waste his time with unproductive complaining, but applies himself instead to serving the needs of humanity—to

doing something which will make the world a better place.

3. The lesson of synergy. Synergy is the close cooperation of two intelligences, forces, people, or groups, bringing unusual advantage to both. Synergy is more than an alliance—it is a close partnership in which each party contributes freely and benefits from the mutual effort in ways that would not be possible working alone. Cancer invites us to learn what it means to establish synergistic relationships with:

• Other people.
• Divine forces.
• Spiritual qualities such as integrity, courage, tolerance, joy, and understanding.
• Our higher self.
• Our opportunities to be innovative and to serve.

4. The lesson of responsibility. Responsibility is the capacity to respond maturely to the ideal for self-expression in any activity or role. It involves fulfilling the commitments we have made and performing the duties which are part of our life, but it is much more than this. Responsibility is the way we involve ourself in life—the way we expand our horizons. It is not necessary to take on new duties to harness the forces of Cancer, but at the very least we should examine our existing commitments and see how we can increase:

• The quality of our work in meeting these commitments.
• The scope of our service or activity—beyond the bare minimum required of us.
• Opportunities for adding new dimensions of spirit to our self-expression through the work we do.

We might also ask ourself how we approach our responsibilities—with a sense of dread and limitation or with a sense of joy and appreciation for the value of this activity?

Esoterically, the challenges of Cancer are summed up in the idea of learning *to sound a proper keynote*—an inner, spiritual chord which sets in motion the proper momentum for self-

202

expression. This keynote is not an actual word or note that is chanted; it is the archetypal essence of a project, relationship, or activity. Cancer is a time to sound the major keynotes of our life. Where we have lost our way, we need to return to the keynote and sound it again. Where we are facing obstacles, we need to regather the forces of the keynote, and sound it again. Where we are initiating new projects, we need to determine the ideal keynote, and sound it loud and clear.

If we learn to sound the major keynotes of our life in this way, we will find that the force of *spiritual* momentum lies in our basic design as a human being. We will also find that the greatest triumph of Cancer lies in fulfilling this fundamental design to the fullest measure.

THE PROBLEMS OF CANCER

Because the forces of Cancer are primarily concerned with creating better expressions of spirit in form, the problems of Cancer tend to arise from the temptation to become too immersed in the world, and forgetful of spirit. Materialism increases during Cancer, and the personality finds it easier to ignore the direction of the soul. But these are not desirable conditions; they merely compound our difficulties and isolate us from our true source of strength, love, and wisdom.

The major problems which trouble us during Cancer include:

1. Superstition. Superstitious thinking of all kinds is magnified during Cancer, causing us to ascribe greater power to people or events than they actually possess. This may create the illusion that we are being overwhelmed by opposition or evil. The fear being generated at present by the anti-nuclear movement is a good example of this phenomenon at work. Huge amounts of uncontrolled anxiety, fear, and hatred are being

poured into mass consciousness, in the name of world safety. The damage being done on a psychic level is far greater than the average person realizes. While it is certainly true that all sane people favor the enlightened curtailment of nuclear arms, sane people also recognize the destructiveness of hysteria, demagoguery, and fear, and use other means to pursue their goals. The manipulation of mass consciousness in these ways is likely to increase during Cancer, however, not lessen.

2. Personal magnetism and charm. Charisma is usually thought to be a positive character asset—and it can be, when used as part of spiritual self-expression. But all too often, people substitute charisma for competence and creativity, trying to achieve their goals on the strength of their personal magnetism alone. During Cancer, we need to take care not to use personal charm to subtly seduce or exploit others against their will—and we must likewise take care not to be subtly influenced by others against our better judgment. The lessons we have learned in discernment, modesty, and enlightened humility may well be put to the test.

3. Confinement. Many people will have a sense of being restricted or limited during Cancer, perhaps by circumstances which keep them from doing what they want, by new rules which take away earlier freedoms, by narrow dogma and fixed ideas, or by the seeming lack of opportunity. Others will create their own confinement, deliberately withdrawing into a shell of defensiveness, prejudice, fear, or inflexibility. In either case, Cancer is not a time when the causes of such restriction can be radically changed, but it is a time when we can adjust our attitudes and priorities so that we do not dwell on the restriction, but rather seek out and find the opportunity within it. Cancer is a time to graciously accept the real limits placed upon us—and to find an enlightened way to deal with them.

4. A sense of emptiness. Those who do not seize the challenge of Cancer to enrich life may well find that their life is

empty of meaning. This may be perceived as heightened loneliness, frustration, or confusion. It is very easy to get caught up in the pursuit of selfishness and ignore our duty to add to life— but selfishness tends to exhaust us and dissipate our energy. Loneliness and emptiness are best corrected by getting busy and becoming a force of helpfulness in the world.

5. Exhibitionism. There can be a strong temptation to "strut our stuff"—to show off our power, charm, wit, brilliance, or talent so others can see it and be impressed. While self-expression is encouraged during Cancer, glitter and style devoid of substance are not. If we pretend to something we are not, we may well be called on to prove our false claim.

6. Self-indulgence. A lot of adults will go around behaving like children during Cancer, as though maturity was a burden to be cast off at every opportunity. The forces of Cancer stimulate all manner of hedonism and personal desire for comfort and security, but if we let ourself become focused in such self-indulgence, we may entirely eclipse the more serious work of providing an adequate focus for the life of spirit.

7. Painful discoveries. Integrity is one of the strongest forces of Cancer, but as we come face to face with the two-edged sword of truth, we may not always appreciate what its cutting edge reveals. Some of the truth we must confront may well be painful or embarrassing. But if we work with a sincere love for integrity and truth, we will build on a solid foundation.

8. Insecurity. The fear of loss, especially the loss of personal possessions, is greatly stimulated during Cancer. The tendency to worry about what we have—or should have—will also be a strong concern. Unless we stay centered in our mature values and perspectives, we may find our generosity of mind, heart, and spirit sorely tested.

9. Treachery. Actions affecting us may well be taken behind our back; some people will use this time to engage in treachery and double crossing. But secrets cannot be well kept

in Cancer, even though secretive behavior does increase. They will leak out and be exposed. In all our affairs, we should strive to act with integrity and in the best interests of everyone involved, lest we become caught in a web of deceit.

10. Aggressiveness. The emotions may run away with us at times. Rudeness and crudeness will be more apparent among people, and selfish people will make less of an effort than usual to camouflage their true nature. It is therefore important to practice self-restraint in the use of emotions and not be reactive to the ill behavior of others.

11. Regimentation. The momentum of mass consciousness is strengthened, and this will tend to lead to instances of groups trying to enforce their will and point of view on individual members—especially those who are beginning to think for themselves. To the degree that individual members of a group are encouraged to respond voluntarily to a spiritual keynote, thereby unifying the group, regimentation can be healthy. But whenever it seeks to rob the individual of his freedom of choice and self-determination, by imposing group standards, it is decidedly unhealthy.

12. Loss of support. There may be times when we feel as though we just stepped into an open manhole—there is nothing to hold us up. Cancer may bring with it sudden changes in fortune and unexpected twists of fate, and if we have put our trust in *things* rather than spiritual principles, we may temporarily have a sense that we have lost stability or support.

13. Intrusion. Those who cherish privacy may find it violated. In some cases, this will be a willful intrusion and should be protested. But in others, the problem is not that someone is invading our privacy, but rather that we have drawn the boundary lines too narrowly. We have invited conflict and set ourself up to miss opportunities.

14. Boredom. This will be a problem for many people, as they become bored with their work, bored with their friends,

and possibly bored with life. The creative person may feel very uncreative. This form of ennui, however, is not something we must succumb to. It is the result of becoming too drugged by the narcotic of materialism. If we turn our attention instead to the beauty, grace, and light of the soul, and dedicate ourself to using these spiritual forces to enrich the quality of our work, relationships, and life, Cancer can be a time of self-renewal.

15. Intolerance. All forms of prejudice, narrowmindedness, and bigotry will increase. It will be tempting to make invalid assumptions which happen to support our selfish interests and resist obvious facts, common sense, inner guidance, and advice from others which run counter to these interests. This, however, will lead to crises in conscience, as we realize we have behaved with blind self-interest and betrayed our ideals.

16. Crystallization. Any area of rigidity or crystallization in thought, feeling, or habit is likely to be shaken until it breaks up. If we are too rigid, we are apt to experience a fair amount of discomfort or anguish. For this reason, adaptability is a good virtue to cultivate, even though it will not be much in evidence. The adaptable person is one who holds to his ideals yet is able to accept and work with new variables and circumstances. In those who are not adaptable, nervousness will be accentuated.

17. Self-deception. It will be very easy to deceive ourself and become trapped in our own blindness, fantasies, and selfishness. In particular, we must be on guard against the temptation to make casual but insincere commitments, to criticize others for our own faults, or to believe the flattery of others.

THE OPPORTUNITIES OF CANCER

The forces of Cancer stimulate our involvement in daily life and encourage us to become more active in expressing the life of spirit within us through our career, our relationships, our family commitments, and the whole of our self-expression. Cancer also stimulates us to refine and upgrade the quality of our involvement, so that what we do becomes more helpful and aligned with divine purpose. In this way, our activities become graced with more wisdom and love and begin to serve as an example of enlightened self-expression. The enlightened person responds to the forces of Cancer by seeing that our domestic and career activities are a meaningful part of our life on earth, and play an important role in our work and progress on the spiritual path.

The major opportunities each year in Cancer include:

1. Abundance. God's life is rich and abundant; if we are attuned to it, we shall not want. Cancer is an excellent time to study the force of abundance underlying all of life, the principles that govern it, how this divine force can be translated into our life, and what we must do to cultivate abundance in our own personality—abundance of ideas, abundance of goodwill, abundance in friendships, and abundance in talents, as well as material abundance. A good drill or exercise for Cancer is to ask ourself daily: "How can I be aware of abundance today? How can I use abundance today to enrich the emotional environment in which I live and move? How can I create abundance today through my physical labors and activities?"

The abundance of genius, in particular, is of special importance, and deserves to be appreciated. The pettiness of mass consciousness will tend to attack genius during this time, because it does not understand it, but the enlightened person should honor it. To the degree that he has genius, he should use it to add to humanity's abundance; if his genius is limited, he should seek to develop it and support it in others.

2. Self-discovery. While Cancer is not especially a time when the intuition is stimulated, it is nonetheless a time when we can discover *new value* in existing character traits such as integrity, courage, and our capacity for dedicated service. It is a

time for discovering our ability to translate noble qualities of character into active expression. In addition, it is a powerful time for all kinds of mental housecleaning—especially in the area of cleansing and repairing pockets of unresolved conflict, selfishness, and inertia. We should also be able to see more clearly the harmfulness of brooding in self-pity and self-resentment, and become more skilled in resisting the conditioning forces of mass consciousness—the enchanting glamours of materialism, power, and sensation, especially as they are focused through religious, economic, and political prejudices.

3. Detachment. This is the process of recognizing that even though we have invested aspects of our consciousness into specific beliefs, concepts, habits, traditions, expectations, relationships, and other ties, we control the investment and can withdraw it if necessary. The vast majority of people are unable to do this, however; having invested psychological energy into an aspect of life, they become so identified with it they cannot withdraw from the attachment. Detachment is cultivated by realizing that we are something more than our attachments; our spiritual nature can indeed control them. By identifying with our spiritual nature, not with our attachments, we gain the same measure of control.

4. Discernment. The ability to see the patterns of purpose and meaning which govern our outer activity, and understand their relevance to our daily affairs, is strengthened at this time— if we take some time to reflect on these patterns. On occasion, this may even afford us some accurate glimpses into the future.

5. Innovation. All kinds of productivity and creative expression are heightened during Cancer, leading to excellent opportunities for innovation—if we are alert to them. This includes innovative ways of solving long-standing problems, innovative approaches to leadership, and innovative programs for learning.

6. The refocusing of our goals. As we seek to act in the

physical world, it is important to review our goals for living and update our plans for reaching them. Unless we have made a constant practice of reassessing our situation in life in this way, we may be surprised how much this refocusing clarifies our understanding of who we are, what we are doing, and how well we are doing it.

7. Leadership. Those who focus new ideas, accept new responsibilities, and seek to enrich the life of humanity often acquire genuine opportunities to lead—even if they are not given the titles and privileges of official leadership. The forces of Cancer promote effective behind-the-scenes leadership. In addition, the ability of leaders to command the attention and cooperation of those being led is strengthened. Care must be taken, however, not to attempt to rule by force, for this will provoke a backlash of resistance and resentment which could undermine the genuine opportunities for leadership at this time.

8. Graciousness. Genuine elegance, charm, and style are enhanced during Cancer, as is our capacity to appreciate gracefulness where we find it. Whenever feasible and appropriate, we should strive to act with as much gracefulness and charm as possible. This goes far beyond mere politeness and good manners and touches the very quality of our character.

9. Efficiency. Cancer promotes pragmatism and efficiency in the way we work and use our time. Routine activities and daily chores may go faster and more smoothly as a result. There will be less waste.

10. Generosity. All acts of generosity will produce favorable results in Cancer, even though the line of least resistance is more oriented toward selfishness than altruism. It is especially important to be generous toward those who depend on us, even if it requires personal sacrifice. Sacrifices of this nature will eventually draw to us much support. The spirit of Cancer is best served by seeing what kind of worthwhile investment we can make in life—through our skills, compassion, financial re-

sources, support, or understanding—and then pursuing this investment.

11. Patience. Right conduct and proper behavior are of great importance. In one sense, some of the developing projects or trends of life are "put on hold" during Cancer, requiring us to deal with daily circumstances with a large measure of patience. Be aware that new opportunities are in the process of ripening, and the time to act will come soon. At present, however, it is time to prepare ourself, especially subconsciously, so that we will be ready to act when the time is full.

12. Recreation. Cancer is an excellent time for relaxation and self-renewal; it is important not to be too intense in what we are doing. There is a danger in becoming overly absorbed in intensity, and thereby trapped in the outer form of routine, competitiveness, and pressure.

TUNING INTO THE FORCES OF CANCER

Cancer is not a time which fosters profound intuitive awareness. This is not to say that those who are already intuitive will suddenly lose their ability; but it does mean that those who receive occasional but meaningful intuitive glimpses into life will find them more rare during this period. As a result, the best way to attune to the forces of Cancer and integrate them into our self-awareness is to put into practice one of the keynotes of this sign, *mastery of the physical plane*.

Mastery of the physical plane is not achieved just by wishing for it; it requires diligent effort. The person who "sleeps" through Cancer will be the master of nothing, not even his dreams; in fact, he will be the slave of everything—his wish life, the hypnotic bondage of mass consciousness, demagogues, his enemies, his bad habits, and fate. To become a master of life, and not a slave, we must awaken ourself to our potential to make a meaningful contribution through our physical activities. In this regard, it can be helpful to ask ourself a number of questions:

1. What investments has the soul made in my life?
2. How well have I responded to these investments?
3. Have I helped them grow and become more abundant, or have I foolishly allowed them to dissipate?
4. What resources of the inner life can I call on to help support these investments?
5. Given my circumstances in life, what does it mean to live an abundant life?
6. What changes would allow me to master the physical conditions of life and achieve abundance?
7. What opportunities of Cancer will help me make these changes?

The way to teach in Cancer is through repetitive drill, building a solid structure of habit. We should not shy away from routine, but learn to use it constructively, as a basis for competence and skill.

The way to heal in Cancer is by repairing that which no longer functions properly. Cancer is a good time to make changes in speech and behavior, so that it can more aptly express the light of spirit.

The way to lead in Cancer is by building a stronger household of light, so that others may see the light shining forth through the windows and doors and be inspired to build a household of light of their own.

The work done in Cancer helps prepare us for challenges later on, in Scorpio and Sagittarius. The gains we make in detaching from mass consciousness now will serve us in good stead in Scorpio, and the success we enjoy in Cancer in focusing the forces of momentum will enable us to refocus our direction in Sagittarius.

A SONG FOR CANCER

A voice cries out in the darkness, chanting: "Worship me, worship me." And the multitudes respond, bowing down and praising the one they hold as God. They paint their bodies in what they suppose to be his image. Yet it is not God. It is only a false idol of physical prowess.

Another voice cries out in the darkness, inviting them: "Worship me, worship me." Again the multitudes respond, kneeling in homage to the one they hold as God. They dance with frenzy in a circle they suppose to be the center of his love. Yet it is not God. It is only a false idol of hypnotic feeling.

A third time a voice cries out in the midst of darkness, tempting them: "Worship me, worship me." And as before, the multitudes respond, singing hymns and offering sacrifices to the altar of the one they hold as God. They celebrate the rituals they suppose to be his law. Yet it is not God. It is only a false idol of mass belief and popular tradition. They worship their own opinions.

At last, however, a light awakens within the darkness—the light of the soul—and reveals the way beyond these false idols of form. Having tired of the gods of darkness, the multitudes follow the light—and learn to worship the one God through the wise and loving acts of heart and soul and mind and strength.

A PARABLE FOR CANCER

Most crabs are no more greedy than any other creature; they need food to sustain themselves, but do not prey on others maliciously. There once was a notorious exception to this rule, however—a crab who was exceedingly grasping and voracious. He could not let anything swim by without attacking it, crushing it in his pincers, and devouring it.

"I *never* let go," he boasted to other crabs.

It was this very attitude which proved to be his undoing. One day he saw a movement in the water and instinctively grabbed for it. But there was actually nothing there—it had just been the movement of light upon the water—and he ended up catching himself instead, with his right claw snapping shut on the left one, even as the left claw clamped on the right.

True to form, he refused to let go, even though they were his own claws. Perhaps he did not realize he had trapped himself, but in any event, he had his prey and was too stubborn to let go of it. He slowly starved, his right pincer locked firmly on the left, and the left still clutching the right.

It was in this pathetic state that he died. As he expired, he cursed Fate for being so cruel.

Fate, sitting on her throne, responded with a groan, wondering how even a greedy crab could be so stupid.

10

Leo

LEO

(July 23 through August 22)

Keynote: Self-determination.

Mantra: "I see the light, I become the light, I send it forth."

New moon focus: The soul rules the personality.

Full moon focus: Fire purifies the personality.

Rays 1, 2, and 5 dominate.

Primary archetypal forces:

Goodwill, wisdom, beauty, dominion, organization

A Prayer For Leo:

Heavenly Mother-Father God, we hear Your call. May the light of Your wisdom pour through us.

Help us understand the nature of our individuality, and what it means to be an agent of light. May our ability to serve Your plan be strengthened.

Help us understand the challenge of self-mastery, and what it means to discipline our human nature. May desire be governed by the will to good.

Help us understand the true meaning of service, and what it means to rededicate ourself to the spiritual presence within us. May selfishness be healed through service to Your plan.

And bless us with the grace to rise out of disappointment and hardship and celebrate with you the joys and triumphs of the lighted way.

There are times when it is appropriate to be quiet and take our cues from the universe, not acting until it acts. Leo, however, is not one of these times. Instead, it is a time for aggressive reform, bold initiatives, the unfoldment of plans, and the fulfillment of aspirations. It is a time to advance projects and move forward on the spiritual path.

The conditions of Leo are characterized by sudden shifts and changes. That which seemed impossible or unthinkable at the start of Leo may suddenly become possible, thinkable. That which seemed a quantum leap ahead of us may suddenly become practical, obtainable. The person who is alert to these changes and shifts and *learns to work with the subtle forces producing them* will be able to move forward dramatically. In this regard, it is an especially powerful time for effective leadership. But it is also a time when we may feel "left behind" or "let down," if we do not work intelligently with these changes.

The forces of Leo stimulate growth and expansion—but they do not discriminate. It may be our opportunities and responsibilities which grow and expand—but it could just as easily be our difficulties and self-deceptions. The key is to make sure that we stimulate our maturity and competence, not our childishness and selfishness.

For those who are stuck in the mud, uninterested in nurturing their own self-improvement, Leo will be an unsettling experience. The force of expansion will be channeled automatically along the lines of least resistance in their character, aggravating existing habits and attitudes. Their problems will be overstated, their potential will be exaggerated, and their egos will be puffed out of proportion to their accomplishments. They will become caricatures of themselves, until even they can see the warts and blemishes which have kept them from growing. Those who habitually complain and badger others to care for them, for example, may find themselves complaining so loudly and bitterly that they suddenly suffer an acute attack of guilty conscience for having abandoned their own responsibility. Those who are exploitive and aggressive will find it all too easy to continue in their bullying ways, until they find themselves in a trap they cannot escape. Those who procrastinate or hang back timidly from a full and active involvement in living may find their lives so impoverished and frustrating that they finally take some initiative of their own.

Yet growth need not be so painful. For those who are dedicated to growth, Leo can be a time of much progress and development. Archetypally, Leo is the time when we integrate the new forces which have been emerging since Aries into our awareness, producing a new measure of self-determination and a clearer understanding of our individuality. If we cooperate consciously with this process, our intention to be the right person and do the right thing can be strengthened enormously during Leo. The principle involved is simple. By nurturing our skills and talents, we work in harmony with the purpose of Leo, and our skills and talents are magnified. By taking stock of our problems and working to reform outdated habits and attitudes, we harness one of the basic characteristics of Leo, and our maturity expands. By acting on plans and striving toward achievement, we respond to the call of Leo, and our accomplishments increase.

In many ways, in fact, Leo can be thought of as the time when we paint our self-portrait—when we redefine who we are and what we stand for. The forces of Leo call us to demonstrate our self-mastery and use it to make a meaningful contribution to life. As a result, the fabric of our own psychology and individuality becomes the primary field of experience during Leo. The conflicts we are apt to confront at this time will be the natural outgrowths of the unresolved struggles within us. The challenges of this time will arise out of the way we have handled responsibility over the last several months and years. The opportunities which come to us will likely be the flowering seeds we have planted in the past. And the manner in which we handle these conflicts, challenges, and opportunities will define who we are at present, and what we are in the process of becoming.

But we must not attempt to paint this self-portrait based on the image we see in the mirror of our personality. We must draw our inspiration from a higher source. The forces of Leo invite us to taste of the inner wellsprings of wisdom and, after quenching our thirst, translate the new measure of wisdom we have acquired into meaningful new dimensions of character and talent. In this way, we transmute knowledge into wisdom—and then express it.

The wisdom of Leo embraces more than just self-knowledge, of course; it also teaches us about the natural forces of life—the rhythms and cycles governing nature and form. Quite often, these natural forces appear to be far greater than our individual capacity to harness them; we seem to be trapped in the limitations of the personality, unable to escape. Yet the secret of Leo is that the design of our selfhood, when fully developed, enables us to tap and harness these natural forces and use them creatively.

Indeed, one of the major characteristics of Leo is that it encourages us to refine our skills in working with these natural forces—the basic skills of gathering them, focusing them intelligently, and then using them to repair and reform imperfect conditions and stimulate and energize that which is mature and productive. If we are alert, we will be able to learn some of these lessons, and thereby be better able to fulfill our responsibilities for personal growth, creativity, business, or service.

In this way, we learn to work with the archetypal essence of Leo, and so our life, resources, and intelligence expand and grow along with the natural forces of the universe. We become an agent of the forces of Leo, a source of light and growth for

219

those around us. This is the basis for all intelligent action in Leo.

After all, the design of our selfhood is to become an agent of light—a channel through which the light of the soul can enter into expression in the earth plane. Becoming this agent of light is always the work of Leo.

THE SYMBOLISM OF LEO

The symbol of Leo is the lion. Traditionally, the lion is thought of in the sense of the king of the jungle, the ruler of his domain. As a result, the forces of this time are often thought to stimulate leadership, dignity, arrogance, pride, domination, and determination.

Esoterically, however, the lion represents the sun, and the sun is itself a symbol rich in implications. It is the sun which illuminates and animates life on earth, and therefore the sun is closely associated with the principles of consciousness. In this context, it can be stated that the lion of Leo represents the principles of selfhood and identity, not just microcosmically but also macrocosmically. As a result, our quest for understanding of identity and self-expression should not be limited just to understanding human nature, but should be enlarged to include the higher implications of selfhood:

• Our roots in spirit. Our true individuality is found in the soul, which is the fount of our wisdom, love, strength, and design for growth and service.

• Our heritage in the community of mankind, which stretches into the distant past and reaches forward to embrace a rich future.

• Our potential to act creatively, thereby adding the archetypal ideals and qualities of the mind of God to our personal consciousness and self-expression.

• Our capacity to be influenced by forces beyond our spiritual self and humanity as a whole. The forces of the zodiac would be examples of these greater forces. Part of discovering our selfhood lies in realizing that we are not designed to be passive victims of these forces, but are meant to learn to work with them wisely.

Awareness of these higher implications of selfhood is achieved by:

1. Becoming more aware of the higher authority of the soul and becoming obedient to it.

2. Becoming more truly self-expressive.

3. Discovering the origins of our personal strength in the greater strength of universal life. To be effective, our personal strength must be able to withstand the heat of great pressure. As long as it is based in the emotions or a finite sense of self, we will not be able to withstand intense pressure. But if our strength is rooted in the intangible strength of spirit, which cannot perish, then we can.

One of the best ways of expressing the symbolism of Leo is by "keeping vigil." The lion is a symbol of the vigil, which is the keeping of watch over that which is sacred and important, protecting it from that which is undesirable. The word "vigil" means "watchman." The lion is the vigil of his kingdom. The soul is the vigil of its domain. The sun is the vigil of its system.

These comments on vigil should not be misinterpreted in the context of paranoia or suspiciousness, which could all too easily be accentuated during Leo. The true spirit of vigil is watchfulness, alertness, and awareness—not just to protect against possible intrusion but also to be sure to seize all meaningful opportunities for self-expression, service, and growth.

The lion also symbolizes the creative potential of Leo—the vast measure of spiritual power which can be tapped if we are willing to work with a mature sense of selfhood, self-discipline, and obedience to the authority of the soul.

HOW THE FORCES OF LEO AFFECT US

Leo invites us to expand our knowledge of the archetypal qualities of life and find ways to harness their power in our work and activities. In order to do this, however, we must be able to *transcend* our ordinary level of thought and feeling and work at higher levels of awareness.

For the average person, the ordinary level of awareness is focused in the baser elements of the personality—self-indulgence, rebelliousness, and desire. These traits will all be aggravated during Leo, in the hope that the average person will be motivated to take the quantum leap beyond them and begin focusing on mature self-expression.

For the spiritual aspirant, the ordinary level of awareness is colored by the duality of his spiritual aspiration and his personal competence and self-esteem. The forces of Leo will emphasize and magnify both poles of this duality, strengthening his will to do good but also enlarging his self-centeredness, pridefulness, and egotism. As he learns to transcend these negative factors and practice enlightened sacrifice, however, he will become more aligned with the plan of God for him.

For the advanced person, the ordinary level of awareness is focused in his obedience to the plan of God and the role he plays in helping fulfill it. In his case, the forces of Leo will magnify the ways in which he limits or obstructs the successful implementation of the plan. He must therefore learn to subordinate his personal plans and agenda to the plan of God for the whole of humanity. He must start serving as an agent of the Hierarchy, not as an agent of himself. This will expand his understanding of stewardship and let him work more effectively as an agent of collective force.

The impact of the forces of Leo on our **motivation** is to increase our will to rule and our will to serve. In some, this will be expressed only in petty ways—to dominate others and serve selfish interests. But it is meant to motivate us to strive for greater self-mastery and a stronger dedication to spiritual service. There is a tremendous reservoir of spiritual potency available to those who would use it for the good of all, and our interest in fulfilling this role increases at this time.

In the realm of **awareness,** the forces of Leo greatly increase our sensitivity or perceptiveness. The range of sensitivity increases as our sense of selfhood develops, and so sensitivity is inseparably involved with the drama of Leo. There are four major areas of sensitivity which are affected at this time:

- Our sensitivity to input from the environment.
- Our sensitivity to the wish life of the personality.
- Our sensitivity to the soul.
- The soul's sensitivity to the plan of God.

This level of sensitivity, obviously, is vastly different from the phenomena of feeling and irritation; it is a highly refined capacity to be aware of and tap the power of the ideals, directions, and forces of varying stimuli.

The **mind** will be primarily affected at this time by becoming more thoughtful and introspective; there is a tremendous capacity (among thinking people) for new measures of discovery, insight, and comprehension. At the same time, however, there is also a greater capacity for mental paralysis and rebellion, as the call of the higher self to make sacrifices is met by a strengthened urge to withdraw and avoid problems. We need to use the mind to understand that Leo is not a time to abandon duty, but always a time to fulfill it.

In the **emotions,** reactiveness and defensiveness will be heightened, leading to increased competitiveness, suspicion, and "looking out for number one." Egomania can be rampant. To overcome these problems, we must strive to cultivate and express a healthy measure of detachment, a sense of fairness, a dash of inspired humility, and a brotherly affection for others.

In terms of **self-expression,** the primary impact of Leo is to create a reversal in perspective. Instead of thinking of self-expression in terms of the personality, we begin to see it more in terms of the soul acting through the personality.

To the earthbound personality, in fact, one of the great characteristics of Leo is that it turns our assumptions about life and the status quo upside down. This can be disconcerting, producing confusion, indecision, and even identity crises. Our relationships may become uncertain, and we may at times find ourself caught in a crossfire of conflict we cannot control.

If we look at these conditions simply from our "upside down" perspective, we are likely to complicate them through our own confused and negative reactions. The temptation to let our emotions, passions, and impulses rule is exceptionally strong—and dangerous. But if we stay centered in our values and principles, and seek to understand the need for a new perspective, we will be able to take the changes of Leo in stride. We will see that even though outer aspects of life do change, our innermost sense of purpose and self-worth does not. The changes merely set the stage for growth and new opportunity.

This means looking at the conditions and new developments of our life, thinking, and habits as the higher self sees them. The forces of Leo encourage us to tap into a higher perspective on life—to begin viewing life from the top down, not the bottom up. This means defining the enlightened purpose at work in any situation, identifying with the forces which are acting to fulfill this purpose, and then learning how we can express these forces in our own life.

THE CHALLENGES OF LEO

One of the most basic issues in refining human individuality is *authority*—how we respond to it, how we express it, and the forces and factors which effectively rule our thinking, feeling, and behavior. The forces of Leo challenge us to learn to use and respond to authority wisely, both individually and collectively. For those who pledge allegiance to the authority of the soul, it will be a time of great triumphs. But for those who let the lower self dominate, Leo may be a time of frustration, confusion, and hardship.

A good way to begin working with the theme of authority is to review what level of authority we most consistently respond to. Do we honor and obey the authority of the higher self, seeking to be ruled by its wisdom, will, and love—in our intentions, thoughts, and feelings? Or do we respond more commonly to the authority of our wishes, immaturity, desires, fantasies, and pride; the authority of traditions and forces in mass consciousness and social pressure; and the authority of childhood conditioning and peer pressure? Only the person who is responsive to the authority of the higher self can truly be considered to be alive, awake, and interacting with life. Most people have yet to discover this basic relationship, however. They are ruled almost entirely by their instincts, emotional reactiveness, blind beliefs, pride, and defensiveness.

Leo has a way of challenging our relationship with authority. If the soul rules, we will be filled with a stronger impulse than ever to cooperate with the unfolding plan of God. The will to good will become more active in our awareness, causing us to become more aware of our potential for assisting in the work of the Christ force. Yet if the lower self rules, we will find that the power of our wishes, desires, and pride is far stronger than we ever imagined—and can easily run wild, out of control. It has the power to crush and flatten, as though it were a steamroller which levels everything in its path.

Confrontations over authority can easily result in identity crises, a common problem in Leo. Issues we thought we had settled, understood, or completed may come unraveled, for one of several reasons:

- We rebel against the imposition of authority.
- We struggle with others for control in some situation.
- The higher self steps in and overrules us.

Another factor which will emerge is the realization of how much our environment and mass consciousness rule our decisions, thoughts, and moods. In many cases, we will discover it was only an illusion that we had control in the first place—we had actually long since lost control to peer pressure and public opinion. Such discoveries will tend to lead to problems of confusion, self-doubt, anxiety, and perhaps even humiliation, a sense of fatalism, a retreat into paranoia, or the attempt to deny that we have lost control.

It is therefore of utmost importance to use techniques of mental housecleaning regularly during Leo, reviewing on a daily basis what forces rule us and whether or not we are able to control the process wisely. Where forces of the personal self or mass consciousness control us, we must work to purify our awareness and values and restore proper authority to the higher self. And in using the forces and qualities of the higher self, we must take care not to distort them or use them carelessly, thereby stimulating undesirable aspects of the lower self.

The challenge to parents, in addition to what they will obviously learn about the right use of authority, is to give their children a good basis for growing. Growth and the expansion of talents and divine qualities do not happen accidentally, as the result of getting older, or by being thrust into an educational setting. It happens by teaching a youngster (or adult, for that matter) to respect the value of growth, to take an interest in growing, and to initiate growth on his or her own. It is the responsibility of parents (not the school, and not a church) to instill this lifelong interest in and dedication to growing and learning—and to remember that the best way to inspire this in children is through the example of our own willingness to grow. The forces of Leo will support any such effort.

The challenge in our relationships is to act with goodwill and a healthy respect for the delicate nature of human consciousness. The impact we have on others—and the impact others have on us—is often far greater than any of us realize. We should therefore take care to make sure our impact is always constructive, enriching, and helpful.

The challenge to both business and government is to make sure they do not become top-heavy and bogged down in extraneous issues. These conditions might be found in something as simple as overworking a good idea to the point of absurdity—or something as insidious as the petty bossiness of bureaucracy in government and many corporations. Leo is a time to avoid wastefulness and trim out all excess wherever it exists—in thinking, reactiveness, personal indulgence, or expenditures.

There will also be a challenge in terms of the use of authority. Leo is an excellent time to set the *tone* of leadership and to inspire those we lead with a greater awareness of the meaning and direction of common goals. It is definitely not a time to bully or to try to lead by fiat, although there will be a strong temptation to do so. The leader needs to respect the individuality of those he or she leads—and seek to stimulate and activate their rich diversity of talent, knowledge, and enthusiasm.

The worst kind of leader in Leo is the person who is madly in love with his own ideas, even though they do not fit reality, and uses the position of leadership to force them on the larger enterprise. Such behavior is guaranteed to lead to disaster.

The challenge of Leo to us in terms of personal growth lies in increasing our strengths of character and self-determination. We need to recognize our strengths of character for what they are, reinforcing them, and then using them in meaningful ways to approach the challenges of life. If we do not strive to work with our strengths of character in this way, we will probably find ourself being intensely preoccupied with self-centered concerns and the effort to protect what we have through defensive-

ness. Instead, we ought to focus on what we do really well—
and do it as consistently as possible.

Our strengths of character, of course, should be defined in
terms of what the soul would consider to be strengths, not what
the personality might view as strength. The capacities to be
aggressive, stubborn, or self-righteous may have the appearance of strength, but they are really just thinly-disguised obnox-
iousness. By contrast, the ability to remain loyal to ideals in the
face of opposition, to express goodwill to those who condemn
us, and to endure trying conditions with gracefulness and
stamina are genuine strengths of character.

Based on this review and refinement of our strengths of
character, we can then work to increase our self-determination.
Self-determination is probably the most central of all character
strengths, and the key to self-mastery. There are four aspects of
self-determination we should seek to build upon:

Expression of personal will. What is the focus of our self-
expression? Are we attempting to make a meaningful contribution to life, or are we just trying to get as much as we can with as
little effort as possible? Are we willing to discipline ourself in
order to achieve our goals, or are we more interested in self-indulgence?

Our self-image. Are we embarrassed by mistakes and fear
what others think of us, or do we respect our strengths, talents,
and capacity to make a worthwhile contribution? Do we
compensate for feelings of inadequacy by putting forth an
image of arrogance, vanity, and egotism, or are we sufficiently
at peace with ourself that we can perceive our limitations and
weaknesses and take action to correct them?

Self-discipline. Are we motivated by impulsiveness,
whim, and emotional reactiveness, or by noble values and purpose? Are we led by our prejudices, fears, and worries, or do
we act in the light of careful planning?

Decision-making. Do we make choices based on the perception of right versus wrong or good versus bad? These are basically emotional choices. Or do we make decisions based on what course of action will be most effective, both in the long and the short term? This is a more mental approach. Making decisions based on the course of action which best serves the plan of God is the spiritual approach.

Defining these basic themes in Leo enables us to act wisely, by constructing a foundation of self-determination upon which we can stand. As much as possible, this definition should be made during the first ten days of Leo. The remainder of Leo should then be spent endeavoring to lift up our awareness, creativity, skills, and character to the next higher level. It is this effort to transcend and begin operating from a higher perspective which will enable us to meet the fundamental challenges of Leo most fully.

THE PROBLEMS OF LEO

The unfocused energy of Leo may at times seem like a "loose cannon," exploding at random. As a result, there will be a definite potential for disruption and a loss of continuity in the activities of life. Some projects may even have to be put on the shelf for awhile, while attention is given elsewhere. Unexpected factors may interrupt our plans—and we may feel as though we have no control over changing conditions.

In some cases, interruptions in our plans may prove helpful in the long run, by giving the seed of success more time to germinate. But this will not always be true. In any event, the important thing is not to magnify the disruption by overreacting to it. Self-discipline, patience, and balance will go a long way in minimizing the disruptive impact of changing conditions.

We may also have the perception that the central problem we have been struggling with for the last several months—whatever that might be—has suddenly grown in magnitude, as though it had become a large boulder blocking our path. But if we keep in mind that it is our perspective on the problem which is growing, more than the problem itself, we can then use this expanded perspective to find a more mature and responsible way of dealing with the problem situation. In this way, we roll the boulder off the path and are able to continue our forward progress.

It is important to keep in mind that most of the problems of Leo arise out of our struggle to define and express our selfhood. All forms of selfishness and self-centeredness tend to increase at this time, as well as self-deception.

The major problems to be dealt with in Leo usually include:

1. Identity crises. Many people identify with relationships, their work, and other conditions of the physical life—rather than their inner values, principles, and divine forces. Then, when one of these conditions of the physical life collapses, as often happens in the changing climate of Leo, an identity crisis is precipitated. The individual is plunged into sharply-focused self-doubt and indecision as to what to do. Yet if we restrain our reactions to these changes and hold fast to our inner principles, we will find the strength to continue. In addition, listening to advice from others may help us regain a balanced perspective.

2. Boldness. Impulsiveness, rashness, arrogance, and aggressiveness are heightened in Leo, and could endanger our ability to reach our goals if left uncontrolled. We should seek to be cooperative, not antagonistic, and channel our extra energy into efforts which support and help others. If it is directed into selfishness and self-aggrandizement, this energy will tend to create conditions of serious imbalance.

3. Carelessness. Indifference to fulfilling our duties in the major responsibilities of our life can seriously endanger the ultimate outcome of our efforts. This may occur in something

as minor as carelessly sending the wrong signals to others, and having our intent misinterpreted, or in something as major as ignoring our obligation to nurture the best within our children, our work, and society.

4. Straining. Becoming too intense in our efforts to reach our goals or fulfill our duties can likewise be a problem in Leo. This does not mean that we should abandon our goals or ignore our duties; it simply means that we should adopt a proper pace as we strive to attain them or fulfill them. The temptation to strain should be replaced by a steady expression of self-respect, dignity, faith, and nobility.

5. Impatience. Irritability and impatience are unusually strong during Leo—especially when we long to take charge of some situation but are thwarted. The slowness, lack of wit, or indifference of others may be unbearable at times. Or, we may become disgusted with our own lack of progress in some area. But irritability and impatience have no power to resolve any problem—they just magnify our discomfort and make it more difficult to manage creative forces. They need to be handled with detachment and understanding.

6. Intolerance. Old prejudices, smallmindedness, short-sightedness, and self-righteousness are all intensified during Leo. Even if we refrain from indulging in intolerance, we may well be abused by others who do not. Slanderous statements and rash actions will abound. Instead of reacting angrily to intolerance, however, it will be more productive to serve as a calming, peacemaking influence—an agent of maturity and wisdom.

7. Passion. The emotions will tend to be fired with passion in Leo—passion for another person, a cause, or our own indignation. Such passion overheats the emotions, however, and obscures our inner vision. In some cases, it may even lead to wildness and a complete loss of control. The practice of dispassion is therefore of great importance. The emotions should be

231

used to nurture goodwill, growth, and maturity—not to inflame our reactiveness to life.

8. Cruelty. The tendency to bully, intimidate, or injure others with sarcastic, cutting criticism may be strong. What we say in unguarded moments may cause us much embarrassment—or we may find ourself the victim of malicious gossip, false accusations, and barbed criticism.

9. Snafus. The tendency to unwittingly foul up arrangements and activities will increase—and lapses in judgment and common sense will compound the problem. We should be especially careful not to make unwarranted assumptions or take things for granted.

10. Excessive curiosity. The temptation to snoop and stick our nose where it does not belong increases in Leo. This will tend to distract us from our true responsibilities—and will probably stir up the resentment of those whose privacy we are invading. The temptation to follow what glitters and satisfy our curiosity will likewise be stronger, but we must remember that this particular road oftens leads to self-deception and unproductive speculation. A healthy measure of discipline and purposefulness will keep us from being overly distracted in these ways.

11. Complacency. Leo energizes self-confidence, and this is basically good. But too much of a good thing is always fraught with danger, and this is especially true of self-confidence. It will be easy to become complacent about our work, our relationships, our duties, and the service we perform, assuming that we do not really have to pay all that much attention to them. If this occurs, we may be lulled into a false sense of security, only to be awakened rather rudely to our neglect at some time in the future.

12. Psychic malpractice. The temptation to play psychic games of manipulation and intimidation will increase. But those who succumb to the temptation will find that it backfires

most unpleasantly. Those who may be the target of such malpractice will find the best remedy for the problem is to reinforce their conviction of the worthiness of their life and goals, and focus their attention in the treasures and resources of spirit.

13. Self-pity. There will be a strong tendency to feel victimized during Leo and indulge in feelings of self-pity. Even when events seem to warrant this feeling, however, we should realize that we always have the option to behave with dignity. We do not have to be a victim. Nor is it healthy to wallow in self-pity. We should discover instead the strength and courage of the soul, and express it.

14. Schisms. The potential for schisms and breaks, in partnerships, groups, and national factions, is stronger now than ever. We should beware the attempt to alienate or isolate, and take action to heal the gap, not let it worsen.

15. Amateurism. The dilettante will steal the show in Leo if he can, but the contribution he makes is superficial at best. We should avoid amateurism and dilettantism, and if we do not know what we are talking about, we should withhold our opinion in deference to those who do. In work situations, we should strive to cultivate a deeper sense of professionalism.

16. Fantasizing. Daydreaming about success will be a favorite pastime of many in Leo. The danger lies in becoming so convinced we can do anything we set our mind to that we fail to take constructive steps to produce success. We should therefore steer clear of touches of megalomania during our reflective moments, and focus instead on pragmatic plans.

THE OPPORTUNITIES OF LEO

Leo is a time when we have the power to bring new life energy from our deepest humanitarian resources into expression in our character and daily activities. There is a tremendous capacity to stimulate and energize the mind, leading to potential growth in our creative talents, our capacity for clear thought, and our use of ideas. To capitalize on this opportunity, however, we must actively seek to tap these inner humanitarian resources—the treasures of spirit—and integrate them into our thinking and behavior. We must be willing to discipline the mind and revise the way we approach life.

The key to seizing the opportunities of Leo will be *thoughtfulness*—seeking always to act from a mature and thoughtful base which understands the larger perspective of the situations we are involved in. The casual or sloppy thinker will make many mistakes in Leo. But the careful thinker, who seeks to understand in full, will be able to see facets of life hidden from others.

For this reason, the ability to discern the *subtle forces* at work in any situation, and cooperate with them, is of special value. The opportunities of Leo are often partially veiled, and unless we are alert to the meaning and significance of events, we will miss the opportunity within them entirely. We should therefore develop the habit of trying to discern what subtle forces are at play in any circumstance, and how we can most intelligently cooperate with them.

Specific opportunities in Leo include:

1. Acting wisely. Acting wisely involves something more than just knowing what needs to be done. It also embraces the capacities to bless, to build, to redeem, and to heal. Unfortunately, we often act *destructively* on what we know. Knowing of a weakness in a friend, we hold it against him—instead of trying to help him overcome it. Knowing of inconsistencies in our own habits and attitudes, we use them to reinforce a poor self-image or sense of inadequacy—rather than striving to reform them. Knowing of imperfections in society, we seek to use them for personal advantage, rather than work to heal them.

Leo does not reward such behavior. The forces of this time

encourage us to take what we know and act wisely upon it—to take what we know of others and blend it with forgiveness and generosity, to take what we know of ourself and express it with nobility and intelligence, and to take what we know of society and work with patience and compassion to improve it. In these ways, we manufacture genuine wisdom, transcend the lower, critical uses of the mind, and learn to act with the full nobility of human thought.

2. Helpfulness. Leo presents us with many opportunities to be helpful toward others. It teaches us the power of the old maxim, "A good deed is its own reward." We have a choice in Leo—to be selfish or openhearted. The person who chooses to be selfish will discover the limitations and traps of self-centeredness—and will be chided by his or her conscience as well. But the person who chooses to be helpful and generous toward others will find that he or she is rewarded with enriched self-esteem and a deeper sense of satisfaction. Generous and helpful acts at this time will also set a powerful example for children— and enhance our reputation in general.

3. Forgiveness. Much healing and cleansing can occur if we are willing to forgive those who have hurt us—and seek forgiveness from those we have injured. Indeed, this is one of the practical ways in which we can discover that *we* can precipitate some of the sudden changes of this time—and become a force for healing and transformation.

4. Fulfillment. There will be a stronger potential for registering joy and a sense of accomplishment as the result of the good we do, work well done, new insights received, and so on. This sense of fulfillment can greatly enrich our efforts to serve, to grow, and to endure in the face of opposition.

5. Creative inspiration. Those who have trained themselves to work with archetypal forces will find a strong burst of new inspiration and deeper understanding of these forces during Leo. In general, all kinds of abstract thought will be stimulated.

6. New awareness. As we reflect on the value of our work and relationships, always striving to discern the higher perspective of the soul, we may well gain a new awareness of the plans of the inner being. Active meditation will be exceptionally fruitful in establishing a stronger relationship with the higher self.

7. The rediscovery of power, confidence, and ideas. Our doubts, fears, and lack of ambition tend to obscure many elements of our human and spiritual potential. The forces of Leo work in the opposite direction, unveiling to us what has been hidden by our limitations. If we are able to muster sufficient courage to express this power and confidence and act upon these ideas, we will progress rapidly in Leo.

8. Self-mastery. While the forces of Cancer promote mastery of the physical plane (form), the forces of Leo foster mastery of our selfhood (consciousness). Leo encourages us to heal and repair areas of weakness or conflict, so that we are able to think and act more effectively. If we have been working persistently and maturely toward correcting specific problems in habit or attitude, we can expect a breakthrough during Leo, leading to a new appreciation of who we are and what we are capable of doing in life.

9. Celebration of the majesty of life. Spiritual aspirants often become so absorbed in their problems, and the problems of the world, that they forget that joy is a natural spiritual state and should be cultivated as the tone for spiritual growth and work. The forces of Leo promote a sense of the true grandeur and majesty of life. If we are responsive to this, we can greatly enrich our own capacity to express joy—and will find ourself at times lifted up to celebrate the noble elements of life with God.

10. The heralding of new directions in life. A herald is a servant of a king who proclaims major new developments. The forces of Leo are often heralds of the soul, revealing to us new directions in life and how best to pursue them. They summon us

to respond at a higher and more mature level to the rich potential the soul has prepared for us.

11. The ability to triumph over seemingly impossible odds. We have the opportunity to tune into the courage of the higher self and take bold action which will produce remarkable results. In many ways, in fact, it will seem as though it is high tide for us. New projects which we launch will have a great chance of success. We must take care not to get carried away with unfounded or excessive optimism, but all in all it will be a good time to begin new projects or invest new energy in bringing existing projects to fulfillment.

12. Spiritual aid. Assistance from the inner planes and the spiritual forces of life will be more tangible now in our efforts to serve, but if we expect to benefit from this help, we must be ready to assist others wherever needed, and play our part in the work of mankind.

13. Responsibility. Psychological "ownership" for our obligations and commitments is something to recognize and fulfill in Leo. If we have volunteered to help with a certain project, or been assigned a duty at work, we should realize that we have a proprietary interest in completing it intelligently and thoroughly. There is a driving momentum in Leo which pushes things toward completion and resolution. If we participate intelligently in the projects and activities of our life, aiming for practical accomplishments, we will be well supported by the forces of this time.

In the same way, it is important to recognize "ownership" of our responsibility for personal growth. It is time to stop blaming childhood events and society for that which hinders us and get to work solving our anger, fear, sadness, or whatever it is that bothers us.

14. Psychic ability. Our psychic capacities are stirred up in Leo. This may result in a higher level of creative inspiration or a greater clarity of psychic perception, for people who have de-

veloped skills in these areas, or simply in more vivid dreams than usual. For people with many unresolved problems, this could result in nightmares and broken sleep, but for the majority, this stimulation of the associative mechanism of the mind will provide new insights and self-awareness.

Many of the dreams we remember may well touch the collective subconscious of humanity, leading us to a deeper appreciation of the mythology of our own culture, if we pursue them. Indeed, if we take an active interest in interpreting these dreams and psychic clues, we may be able to trace certain ideas or elements of our growth back to their source.

15. The appreciation of beauty. Beauty runs through all creation, and human self-expression is no exception. Leo is therefore an excellent time to cultivate beauty in our own creative expression—and to admire it both in nature and in the creations of humanity. Our admiration of beauty should lead us to an appreciation of the inner elements of beauty—especially the beauty of the human character.

16. Spiritual maturity. Nothing blesses our life, and the life of those around us, more in Leo than the dedication to act and think always with the noblest and most mature levels of our consciousness:

- To give help wherever it is needed.
- To nurture growth and understanding in others.
- To fulfill our responsibilities.
- To set an example of wisdom and goodwill for others.
- To lead with a strong sense of enlightened purpose.
- To work creatively.
- To cooperate with the genius of others.
- To serve the plan and design of the soul.

17. Love. The greatest discovery we can make in Leo, however, is our capacity to love. The spiritual quality of love is the divine force which nurtures that which it has created. It sees its duties clearly, and cares for them without reservation. It helps,

it serves, it supports, it guides. Love helps us see the value of what we do and what we aspire to; it enriches all that we do with meaning and significance. It gives us the motivation to discipline our efforts so that they are truly helpful. In Leo, therefore, let us learn to love with wisdom and dedicate ourself to the expression of goodwill, not criticism; of trust, not suspicion; of cooperation, not alienation; and of caring, not selfishness.

Let us love God with all our heart and mind and soul and strength. Let us love the people we deal with as we ought to love ourself. And let us love ourself and our noble destiny even as God loves us.

TUNING INTO THE FORCES OF LEO

One of the most provocative ways of tuning into the forces of Leo is to create a *personal myth* which embodies the essence of our self-expression. A myth is a symbolic story which portrays the archetypal forces at work in a situation and how they interact; in this case, it would portray the major lessons, duties, and forces which influence and shape our individual self-expression. Both the song and the parable of each sign would be examples of myths describing the nature of the forces of the zodiac in the abstract; a personal myth would be similar, but would describe our own individuality as it emerges out of our experiences and character development. A good personal myth embraces the past, the present, and the future—and casts the odyssey of our life in heroic terms.

Some might be tempted to think that such an assignment is just an exercise in fantasy and self-deception, and it could be. But it will not be if we develop our myth as a way of understanding how the soul views our life and activities—and the creative forces which go into making us who we are.

As we reflect on our personal myth, write it out, and apply it to our life, we contact many of the strongest forces of Leo.

The way to teach in Leo is by building an awareness of the unseen. In esoteric circles, this would mean becoming more aware of the subtle forces of life and how they influence us. In more conventional circles, it means reading imaginative fiction, studying mythology, and working with abstract symbols which suggest that there is more to life than literal fact.

The way to heal in Leo is through transformation. The advanced healer will find a rich opportunity in directly contacting spiritual fires and using them as the basic resource of healing.

The way to lead in Leo is by setting an enlightened example of handling our responsibilities.

The work of Leo helps prepare us for the challenges of other signs later on, most notably Virgo, the very next sign, and Aquarius. In many ways, Virgo picks up and reinforces key themes of Leo such as personal responsibility. Aquarius will give fuller expression to the helpfulness initiated in Leo, transforming it into spiritual stewardship.

A SONG FOR LEO

The sleeper wakes and beholds a vision of fire.

"Now I know who I am," he whispers to himself.

"No," replies an unseen voice, "now you know what you must become."

"I feel I am this fire already," the sleeper says. Too late, he realizes the folly of his words. The fire rushes through his veins. He burns with the fire of desire, then falls asleep again.

The sleeper wakes and beholds a vision of fire.

"Now I know who I am," he whispers to himself.

"No," replies the unseen voice, "now you know what you must become."

240

"I know I am this fire already," the sleeper says. Too late, he recognizes the error of his words. The fire races through his brain. He burns with the fire of arrogance, then falls asleep again.

The sleeper wakes and beholds a vision of fire.

"The fire is the will of God. It burns within the heart of everything alive. Yet it does not harm me, for I have no desire except to serve the will of God. I have no arrogance, only the urge to serve. Now I know what I must become."

"And by knowing that," replies the unseen voice, "you know at last who you are."

A PARABLE FOR LEO

Many primitive tribes believe that if a man kills an animal and eats of its heart, he will inherit the strengths and virtues embodied in the beast. So it was, in the ancient beginnings of time, that a party of native tribesmen set out one day to hunt the lion. Each man was filled with the anticipation of being the one who would kill the lion and become kingly in heart and strength.

On and on they marched, set on triumph, until they arrived at a grassy knoll frequented by the lions. The men hid in the bushes and waited until their prey arrived. Even then, they did not move, waiting for the lion to lie down in the sun and sleep. Then they sprang forward, hurling their spears through the air. The lion was killed before he could move.

The tribesmen returned to the village victorious, rejoicing in their kill. Yet not a one of them was transformed by the death of the lion; not a one of them became kingly or virtuous.

High in the heavens, however, a transformation did occur. A new constellation of stars was formed, the constellation of the lion. Ever since, the spirit of the lion has governed the transformation of men.

11

Virgo

VIRGO

(August 23 through September 22)

Keynote: Acceptance of duty.

Mantra: "I guard the light within me and nurture its
expression on earth."

New moon focus: Seizing opportunity.

Full moon focus: Stewardship.

Rays 2, 4, and 6 dominate.

Primary archetypal forces:

Compassion, harmony, charitableness, joy, devotion

A Prayer For Virgo:

O heavenly Mother-Father God, we seek to become more
responsive to the light of our soul, and to renew our dedication
to serving as an agent of Your healing power.

May divine strength be added to our own limited strength,
so that we may act more effectively.

May divine light be added to our limited understanding, so
that we may understand in full.

May divine love fill us with greater devotion, so that we
may serve Your plan more consistently.

Help us express the light of the soul in all our thoughts and
efforts, so that we will be successful in bringing the presence of
heaven to earth through our life.

Our talents and abilities are a major focal point during Virgo, serving either as a channel through which divine force can enter our life or as a barrier which eclipses the light of spirit. Those who have wisely nurtured their skills and abilities—especially the skills of the life of spirit—will find their resources and opportunities enhanced. But those who have failed to develop their talents or find new uses for them may encounter restricted circumstances, or even lose what they have gained in the past.

This will be most readily observable in the business world, where the development of talent is generally rewarded with new opportunity or position—and where the effort to cling to the status quo usually ends in being passed by. But it also applies to the life of spirit and our interaction with the treasures of spirit. As we gain new understanding, do we find ways to express it in our life? As we tap new resources of joy or peace, do we use them to enrich our self-expression? As we tap the compassion of spirit, do we learn to treat others with the same measure of benevolence and goodwill? As we are helped, do we take what we have learned and use it to help others?

If we have been in the habit of reinvesting the treasures of spirit and talents of the inner life in productive and effective ways, Virgo will be a time of remarkable opportunity for growth. But if we have tended to use spiritual forces only for our personal comfort and enrichment, Virgo may be a time of frustration and grief.

The importance of talents and abilities at this time is a natural extension of one of the most basic patterns of Virgo: the creation of the seed. Esoterically, spirit enters form via the forces of Virgo, only to be obscured in the denseness of matter. But the light of spirit remains active as a seed within the darkness. It germinates and gradually the whole of the form becomes more responsive to the impulse of spirit.

Actually, the seed is a powerful symbol for the nature of the energies of Virgo. A seed planted in the ground is completely dependent on "its outside conditions"—the soil, adequate water, and the warmth of the sun—yet there is also a living force within it that draws vitality from these environmental factors, thereby germinating the seed and causing it to grow.

In the same way, our use of talent and ability, both mundane and spiritual, can be a seed that we plant in Virgo, dynamically drawing to it the opportunity and assistance which will nurture and activate our plans and aspirations. But we must be careful to plant a mature and enlightened seed. Those who plant the seed of selfishness, through their pursuit of personal wants and desires, may find themselves reaping a crop of embarrassment, as their true nature is exposed. Those who habitually indulge themselves at the expense of others may find "the soil" less fertile than it has been before.

The forces of Virgo emphasize the basic duality of our life—our involvement in the life of matter on the one hand and our need to be responsive to spirit on the other. For some, this will produce conflict, as they become more poignantly aware of the difference between their human and spiritual natures. But for others, especially those on the spiritual path, the duality will not be a source of conflict, but rather an opportunity for effective partnership.

Those who work daily with the talents and treasures of spirit know it is possible—and desirable—to harmonize the spiritual and mundane elements of life, and express them together. Such people will be in tune with the forces of Virgo; in fact, it might be said that it is this capacity to harmonize the inner and outer conditions of life that germinates the seed.

In the human, this force of harmony works through the awakened, intelligent mind. As we learn to love intelligently the rich potential in ourself and in the circumstances of life, we begin responding to the inner patterns and designs which hold the key to our opportunities for growth and creativity. These, in turn, nurture the seed of our potential and cause it to grow, expanding the scope of our involvement in all aspects of life.

There are four major forces which characterize the archetypal impulse of Virgo to nurture growth. These are:

1. Efficiency. The law of economy is particularly active at this time, both individually and universally. Wastefulness, prodigality, and inefficiency will be exposed. Virgo is not a time for flashy excesses, but rather a time for moderation and self-restraint. The person who can work quietly, in response to noble purpose, will accomplish much. But those who are scattered and disorganized in the way they approach the challenges of life will accomplish little.

2. Purity. The intangible is far more significant in Virgo than the tangible, and the forces of mood and opinion which play such an important role in setting the quality of our life can be easily affected. In the individual, for example, a mood of grimness, guilt, or anger might pollute and render useless a noble intention to help others. This can seriously endanger our attempts to germinate new seeds of talent. So it is important to learn the lesson of purity and control our moods and opinions so we do not contaminate our activities and plans. Virgo presents us with an unparalleled opportunity for working with the essence of archetypal forces and using it to refine the quality of our immediate environment.

3. Responsiveness. The mind can be a powerful tool during Virgo, if we focus it primarily in responding intelligently to spiritual direction. This requires using it actively to discern spiritual ideals, refine values, and apply these values to all that we do, with self-discipline and common sense.

4. Helpfulness. The unique character of Virgo is its capacity to heal and nurture the best within developing situations. We can best harness this quality by striving to be a positive, constructive force of helpfulness in our own sphere of activity.

Indeed, the true creative work of this time lies not so much in what we build or produce physically as in the seeds, skills, and abilities we add to the rich "soil" of our character. And this is determined, to a large degree, by how we respond when we have the opportunity to help, when given the chance to lead, and when given the chance to correct mistakes made in the past.

THE SYMBOLISM OF VIRGO

The symbol of Virgo is the virgin, who is able to give birth to a god because she has reached a complete state of purity. Esoterically, the state of "virginity" is not one of never having succumbed to temptation, for no man or woman alive has completely avoided temptation. Indeed, it is part of man's destiny to experience life. But, having been entrapped by temptation, the virgin consciousness is one which has cleansed and purified its awareness, so that the Christ within can manifest. In this respect, each human being, man or woman, should strive to be a virgin—which means expressing the forces of Virgo as they are designed to be used.

In practical terms, therefore, we should ask ourself: "What am I giving birth to?" There should always be something new within us that we are nurturing—carrying to term, so it can be given birth at the proper time. What is it? Is it something divine and godlike—a new expression of love, a greater capacity to forgive, new creative ideas, or a healthier self-image? Or is it something selfish and impure? Proceeding in this way, we should review all new issues of life emerging within us, and make sure that, as much as possible, we are giving birth to something creative, worthwhile, and divine.

Then, we should consider the forces within us which might rebel against this new child of consciousness. What subconscious forces will try to block this new issue and prevent its birth? These might be old habits, tendencies to be lazy or careless, or just the force of resistance. Whatever we find, it should be neutralized and eliminated through the use of proper mental housecleaning techniques.

Giving birth is always an event which opens the way to the future—to new involvement in life, new creativity, and new growth—and this is just as true of the birth of new life within us as it is with physical birth. We should therefore consider the purpose of carrying this new life to term, and giving birth to it—as well as how we will protect and preserve it and help it grow.

Above all, Virgo is a time for *celebrating* and rejoicing in the birth of new elements of divinity within us and within our life. Those who respond only to the conventional characteristics of Virgo, however—worry, nervousness, introversion, dependability, fussiness, and passiveness—are likely to miss the richness of this time.

HOW THE FORCES OF VIRGO AFFECT US

Leo tends to be plagued by an epidemic of self-centeredness. Far too many people, including spiritual aspirants, allow themselves to be overwhelmed by self-pity and excessive focus on their problems. Fortunately, Leo is followed each year by Virgo, and this allows us to get out the mop and clean up whatever mess we may have created in Leo. And the forces of Virgo are well suited to break whatever spell of self-concern we may have cast upon ourself. In order to show us how we have strayed from our intentions, these forces will lead us back to "square one" and remind us of our true goals, responsibilities, and commitments. They will encourage us to review the progress we have made toward our goals, where we have lost sight of them, and what mid-course adjustments we need to make to get back on target.

As a result, we should view Virgo as a time for introspection, contemplation, and review of who we are, where we are heading, what we have achieved, and what we can do to improve the effectiveness of our efforts. It is also a time for purifying and healing habits and approaches to life that have gotten out of control. For many of us, the purpose of this review will be to remind us that our divine nature has a vital investment in our welfare and behavior, and that it does not fail us, even at those times when we believe we have been abandoned. We, in turn, are accountable for the way we honor the opportunities this divine nature arranges for us—as well as the way we use our talent, face crises, and fulfill our duties.

One of the ways the soul will help us conduct this review is to make some conditions or thoughts seem just slightly jarring or discordant, as in a movie where the spoken words are not quite "in synch" with the actors' lips. During Virgo, for example, we may find that our acts are not quite in alignment with our conscience, that our performance is not quite in alignment with our commitments, or that our promises are not quite in alignment with our intentions. Wherever we detect conditions somewhat out of alignment with what they ought to be, we should take it as a summons to restore proper alignment and harmony. We should therefore ask ourself:

Just what is out of alignment?

What would proper alignment be?

What adjustments must I make in the way I am approaching this situation?

Sometimes, we will find the key to proper alignment lies in our *dedication*. Virgo is not necessarily a time when we dedicate ourself to new causes or ideals, but it is a time when it is appropriate to review and reenergize the strength of our dedication. Virgo will frequently reveal areas of life in which our dedication has become sterile, misdirected, or ineffective.

The average person, of course, does not make any effort to examine his life. He has never left "square one," so there is no way he can return to it and evaluate how well he is progressing.

For such a person, Virgo will be a time of confusion and unrest, as the inner forces try to stir up a conscience which is under-developed and a sense of duty that has never been recognized. There will be a tendency for such people to reflect at least briefly on the emptiness of their lives, but it may not be enough of an impetus to impel them into constructive alternatives. Virgo is more likely to stimulate reactionary attitudes in such people, not progress.

The spiritual aspirant will be able to rise above this problem and work more effectively with the forces of Virgo. Where the forces of Leo may have caused the aspirant to forsake his dedication to spirit, at least to some degree, the forces of Virgo reawaken his aspiration, faith, and devotion. This inspires him to cooperate intelligently with the impulse to review life and realign to his inner nature, thereby becoming more fully aware than before of the ongoing patterns and cycles of duty, limitation, and opportunity operating in his life. In fact, he may be able to see how some of these cycles are starting all over again, not as a closed loop of repeated problems, but as a fresh opportunity to apply the wisdom, goodwill, and strength gained in the past to a *new approach* to relationships, work, and other activities.

Out of this insight, the aspirant should be able to distill the power he needs to nurture and heal the patterns of life which have indeed recycled more hardship and misery than enjoyment and triumph. Virgo encourages us to evolve and find new measures of power, insight, and goodwill within ourself, leading to a deeper appreciation of our capacity to grow in meditation, daily life, the way we manage our problems, and the way we seize our opportunities.

The advanced person is stimulated in much the same way, but works to break up and heal the repetitive cycles of selfishness, grimness, and pessimism in mass consciousness, more than in himself. He strives to create an enriched environment in which the whole of humanity can prosper, grow, and mature.

The effect of Virgo on our **motivation** is to renew our aspiration and encourage our devotion. In the ordinary person, this might just increase the wish life and a desire for the comforts of home. But in the spiritual aspirant, it represents a wonderful new surge of idealism and heartfelt devotion. We should strive to saturate all that we do with this motivation.

The effect of Virgo on our **awareness** is to reawaken us to a recognition of the inner quality and force of our life. We will be prompted to look at our talents in a new and different light, to revive our interest in growth, and to reenergize all of our activities. As a result, we will become aware of where our efforts have been inadequate, enabling us to refocus our interest and revive stagnant projects.

At the level of the **mind**, the forces of Virgo will stir up a greater attunement to the ideals of life, thereby enhancing our discernment. In the aspirant, this should lead to fresh insights and realizations of the power of these ideals and what it means to express them. In the person who lacks commitment to the inner life, however, it may only produce a retreat into nihilism—the denial of meaning and the significance of ideals.

At the level of the **emotions**, the forces of Virgo will stir up our receptivity to impulse and our capacity to nurture life. In the aspirant, this makes Virgo an excellent time to build faith in divine life and train the emotions to become agents for the expression of goodwill, affection, compassion, and forgiveness. But in the ordinary person, the potential for emotional turmoil will greatly increase, as even more emphasis than usual is placed on feeling, reactiveness, and a highly-personalized focus.

In our **self-expression**, the forces of Virgo stir up abrupt changes in the trends and patterns of living, as both good and bad karma fall due. Established trends may suddenly reverse themselves, and the routines of life may be uprooted. It may even be a time when the proverbial straw breaks the camel's back, resulting in a good deal of disruption in our physical circumstances—unless we are oriented toward the quest for meaning.

Since the majority of people are focused primarily in their emotions, emotional turmoil is likely to be the most common focus for struggle in Virgo. The key to not being drawn into this emotional turmoil is to handle emotional situations, positive or negative, from a mental orientation—with detachment, intelligence, and a sense of meaning.

But how is meaning established? There are actually two levels of meaning to consider in Virgo—the universal and the personal. The universal meaning of an idea, circumstance, event, or quality is what it means to the divine plan or to humanity as a whole. The personal meaning is what it means to us—and how we intend to apply it to our life. If both the universal and the personal meanings of our duties, insights, aspirations, and values are the same, then we know we are in harmony with the emerging divine forces—and are oriented toward applying them in our life. But if they do not agree, then we are still selfish, separative, and focused in our emotions, and the forces of Virgo will emphasize and magnify these conditions.

A large part of the work of Virgo is to help us practice *right receptivity* to divine forces and ideals—to align our thoughts, feelings, and acts with the archetypal patterns of life. Right receptivity involves a great deal more than just believing in God or contemplating the perfection of divine life, however; it is an active state of learning to think, feel, and act *in step with* divine rhythms, laws, and directions. It involves integrating the qualities and forces of spirit into a practical and purposeful expression in daily life.

It is therefore of great importance to understand how the forces of Virgo affect us and how we are meant to respond to them.

THE CHALLENGES OF VIRGO

Virgo challenges us to make needed adjustments in attitude. Our attitudes are primarily emotional in nature, and govern the way in which we habitually view ourself, life, and other people. Ideally, our attitudes should be governed by our *principles* and *values*—the mental correspondence to attitudes. If we value hard work, for example, then our emotional attitude toward our labors and creative projects should be one of enthusiasm, enjoyment, and satisfaction. In most people, however, the attitudes which rule their emotional reactiveness to life are *not* linked to any higher correspondence. They may say they value work, but their attitude belies the truth—they approach work as though it were a drudgery, a source of stress, and something to avoid if at all possible.

Virgo encourages us to update our attitudes and align them with our perspectives, values, and spiritual principles, not just individually but also collectively. In the business world, for example, morale will be even more volatile than usual and easily contaminated by negative factors. Morale is nothing more than the collective attitude of a group of workers toward their work; the great challenge of management in Virgo is to inspire their employees to adjust their morale in healthy and positive ways, and not let it sag into chaos.

Some people, of course, assume their attitudes are determined by the quality of life around them, but this is a self-deception. We choose what we like and dislike and how we approach life, and this means that we have control over our emotions—if we choose to exercise it. Virgo challenges us to do so. In the early days of the sign, therefore, we are likely to register increased confusion and indecision, as we encounter attitudes which need updating. If we work with the spirit of Virgo, however, this confusion will not endure for long.

An important key is to refine our use of detachment in the

way we approach life. Detachment is the capacity to interact with life impersonally, from a perspective of knowing who we are and what we are trying to accomplish. The attached person defines his life in terms of who he knows, what he owns, what he likes and dislikes, and what has happened to him. The detached person has possessions, friends, likes and dislikes, and memories just as the attached person does, but is not controlled by them. He identifies with the force of spirit within him and seeks to act in life, not react.

Detachment gives us the capacity to view our attitudes objectively and see which ones are helpful to us, and which ones are limiting and restrictive. It also gives us the ability to focus at a mental level, energize our principles and values, and use the power of these convictions to regain control of our attitudes.

Some of the key attitudes to work on in Virgo are:

• Our attitudes toward our possessions. The forces of Virgo are conventionally thought to promote possessiveness, but the divine purpose of this sign is actually antagonistic to it—be it possessiveness of material goods and money, possessiveness of children, spouses, and friends, and even possessiveness of ideas and beliefs. We need to replace possessive attitudes with a stronger respect for the individuality of others, a stronger devotion to the treasures of spirit, and a healthier openmindedness about ideas.

• Our attitudes toward ourself. Many people put everything that happens into a context of how it affects *them*, always emphasizing the personal element. In Virgo, people who continue to personalize life will find conditions extremely confusing, because the conditions will just not make sense in terms of themselves alone. It is therefore important to cultivate a more universal perspective, a sense of kinship with life, and an awareness of brotherhood.

• Our attitudes toward our work. Work is one of the most central elements of life, but many people maintain very negative attitudes about the work they do, their employer, and what work means to them. We need to begin viewing work as the principal way in which we make a contribution to the life of humanity—and understand that it is a key part of the destiny through which our soul expresses itself. Instead of despising our work, or resenting the need to work, therefore, we should embrace its active, living elements.

• Our attitudes toward others. In no area do our attitudes usually get us into more trouble than in dealing with others. In most cases, we react emotionally to relatively minor and insignificant traits in friends, relatives, and colleagues, then build our attitudes on these reactions—not a mature appreciation of their kindness, goodwill, or friendship. We need to replace these very limiting attitudes with ones that emphasize the good and healthy aspects of our relationships.

• Our attitude toward growth. In most people, the only attitude toward growth is resistance—a strong dislike for any suggestion that we ought to grow. This is true even in most spiritual aspirants. It needs to be replaced by an attitude which invokes and embraces new opportunities to grow and become a more mature person.

• Our attitude toward spirit. Most of us view God and the life of spirit as something "up there," remote, and unconcerned with us. We pray to it occasionally when we have a need, and worship it when it is convenient. But we do not really believe we can have much of a relationship with spirit. This attitude very much needs replacing, so that we begin to view ourself as a companion of the soul. We need to see that spirit is involved in our life "down here" and is a constant and vital part of our self-expression.

The challenge of Virgo to parents is to take their role as parents seriously. In a very real sense, the forces of Virgo sum up the whole responsibility of parenting, and so this is an excellent time to reflect on and renew our dedication to being a mature parent. The spirit of Virgo indirectly asks each parent a series of questions:

- What are your duties as a parent?
- How well do you fulfill these duties?
- What are you seeking to magnify in your children?
- What are you magnifying that you should not be?

The challenge of Virgo in improving our relationships is to be a healing force. Conflicts and disappointments may well arise in some of our relationships, and it therefore behooves us to take our relationships seriously, tending, nurturing, and cultivating the noble potential of our friendships, business associations, and family ties. The conflicts or problems which may arise will demand great skill and restraint to manage properly. This is not a time for arguing, issuing demands or ultimatums, or being contentious. It is a time for holding fast to the spiritual ideal served by the relationship, for nurturing this ideal, and for changing our attitudes so that we better express it.

The challenge of Virgo to business is to improve morale, as already described, and to look for ways to expand the involvement of the business in community life. Business people need to pause and realize that their product or service is a contribution to human life. If it was not, it would not be supported for the long term. The business world also needs to spend more time appreciating its obligations to the community. Where these obligations are ignored, conflict will arise. But where they are accepted and honored, new opportunities will develop.

The challenge of Virgo at the level of society is to cultivate healthier attitudes toward self-sufficiency, the value of cooperation among nations, and the ties we share with all peoples. The fervor of nationalism is likely to increase, but its limits need to be seen for what they are—fanaticism and chauvinism—and replaced by a healthier goodwill which embraces all nations.

In terms of our growth, the challenge of Virgo is to recognize the great importance of growth in our life. The aspect of love which nurtures growth is one of the great archetypal forces of Virgo; it is therefore almost a duty of Virgo to nurture growth toward divine ideals—in ourself, in others, in projects, and in society. In this regard, it is not enough just to honor growth and talk about it; we must actively support it, encourage it, reward it, and make it possible.

We should nurture the good in every situation, and help it grow.

We should heal imperfection wherever we encounter it, in ourself and in society, so that new growth can then occur.

We should enrich the work we do with nobility, love, joy, and harmony, so that its impact is expanded.

We should enlarge our sense of duty.

We should add meaning to our acts and activities, so that they reflect the growth of spirit.

These are the challenges of Virgo.

THE PROBLEMS OF VIRGO

The conditions of life can often seem limiting in Virgo, and the way we perceive them will determine to a large extent how well we respond to the problems of this time. If we resent the limitations we encounter and blame them on something or someone else, we will probably become trapped in them, unable to accomplish very much. But if we see these limitations more as a concrete focus which lets us learn a specific lesson, perform a certain task, or fulfill an important obligation, we should be able to manage the problems of Virgo quite successfully. Actually, the limitations of Virgo are more illusion than reality, because they are almost always the limitations of our own *assumptions* and *projections* about these conditions, rather than insurmountable obstacles. Sometimes, in fact, the limitations are merely the result of becoming stuck in one facet of a larger cycle. If we can understand the larger pattern, we may be able to break through the problem and move forward again.

Specific problems to be alert for during Virgo include:

1. Temptation. All forms of temptation become more attractive during Virgo, but the most seductive of all is the temptation to indulge long-standing character weaknesses. It will be very easy to rationalize such behavior and convince ourself that we are only "doing our own thing," but such self-deception undermines our self-respect and damages our character. It will lead eventually to embarrassment, possibly even disgrace. Virgo is an excellent time for the practice of self-restraint.

2. Pushiness. The desire nature is heightened in Virgo, leading us to pursue our personal urges more aggressively than at other times. Many people will pay even less attention than usual to common courtesy and respect for others. But this kind of behavior will limit the impact they can have, trapping them in their own desires and trivial pursuits.

3. Naivete. Simpleminded approaches to complex challenges of living will seem to abound. This will range all the way from innocence to gullibility. The antidote for this problem is to strive always to meet the challenges of life with competence, common sense, and a healthy respect for genuine intelligence.

4. Indifference. Carelessness and inaccuracy in our work habits, speech, and appearance can easily be aggravated during Virgo, if we do not make an extra effort to discipline ourself. There will be a subtle tendency to slip into indifference about the quality of our work, the impact of our comments on others, and the impression we convey. This in turn may irritate others and compound our difficulties.

5. Self-pity. It can be very attractive to some people to view themselves as victims of life, and this reaction to disappointment may become almost epidemic in Virgo. There will be a strong tendency to blame those we work for, our friends, the government, and society in general for our failures, inade-

quacies, and problems. But this is just another form of self-deceit, and it focuses us excessively in our disappointments, thereby obscuring our potential. We need to spend our time creating seeds of goodwill, wisdom, and opportunity in Virgo—not seeds which will yield additional harvests of failure!

6. Fatal assumptions. We may find that various assumptions we have made in the past are not accurate assessments; in some cases, in fact, they may be leading us perilously close to serious error. Theory and speculation of all kinds are tested by the forces of Virgo, and those which do not pass the test need to be discarded.

7. Permissiveness. There will be a strong tendency to indulge the inferior ideas, behavior, and proposals of others at this time, even though we can see the harmful effect they will have if left unchecked. It is therefore a time in which moral courage is a great asset—and moral cowardice is a liability. It is a time for standing up and exposing propaganda, prejudice, and self-serving philosophies for what they are.

8. The "free lunch" syndrome. The prospect of getting something for nothing will be even more attractive than usual to many people, and not just in mundane ways. There will be a stronger tendency than usual to long for short cuts to fame, success, or enlightenment. There will also be a tendency to seek miraculous resolutions to our problems, expecting God—or the government—to do our work for us. Yet such longing for a free lunch undercuts our own individuality and competence.

9. Superficiality. The effort to zero in on details may be overdone, resulting in thoughts and actions which are too shallow, narrow, and superficial. This tendency may appear in some as a lack of imagination, in others as an insistence on plodding along in old patterns of thought and habit, and in still others as a lack of depth in motives and what they do. While we need to be practical, we must take care to remain broadminded, flexible, innovative, and responsive to inner meaning.

10. Resentment. Reactiveness is stirred up in Virgo, and this can easily lead to resentment toward the real and imagined problems of life. We may resent what others expect us to do, the way others treat us, the sacrifices we must make, the restrictive conditions of our life, or anything else which upsets us. But resentment is distinctly harmful to our health. We need to see that it leads us into a cycle of ill will which will repeat itself over and over again until we learn to express goodwill and benevolence.

11. Anxiety. Those who are prone to worry will find this tendency much stronger in Virgo, poisoning their enjoyment of life. But even those who are not usually worriers may find themselves indulging in moments of anxiety as they review the lack of progress they have made toward their goals or look to the future and see the ground they must yet cover. Fortunately, the opportunities arising in Virgo tend to keep us focused in the present, but we do need to cultivate a measure of poise and detachment so we do not drown in a sea of worry.

12. Fear of the unknown. Ambivalence, unfocused plans, vaguely defined principles, and free-floating feelings can produce a sense of agitation and fear of the unknown during Virgo. We can easily convince ourself that something which is indefinite and not fully worked out in every detail is too risky or threatening to pursue.

13. Mockery. The values and ethics of the person with strong convictions may be mocked or ridiculed by unthinking people who are threatened by them. But there is no need to react strongly in the face of such ridicule, for anyone who mocks something that is worthwhile is ultimately seen as foolish and vain. Silence is often the best protection for our values.

14. Stagnation and repression. While Virgo does stimulate our potential for growth, the conservative nature of the time may also provoke resistance to it. And so it often seems that conditions stagnate during Virgo, or even regress. Yet generally

it is found that these areas of our life "died" some time ago, and we are only now recognizing it. This is especially true if we have been self-centered and focused in pettiness and personal concerns. In such cases, we will probably spend most of Virgo being defensive and reactive, rather than taking firm steps toward renewing the stagnant areas of our life.

15. Suspicion. It is very easy at this time to harbor dark suspicions about the motives and acts of others. We need to understand, however, that suspiciousness poisons our relationships and obscures our own capacity to respond to the good in others.

16. Competitiveness. There are often tests of strength in Virgo between the personality and the soul, between the individual and mass consciousness, between competing companies or groups, and between competing individuals. We must understand that the one who wins such tests of strength is not always the true victor. The ideal of Virgo is to nurture cooperation, not competition.

17. Isolation. Virgo promotes a sense of individual responsibility and dedication to doing the work only we can do. Yet this can put unnecessary emphasis on the idea of "standing alone," to the point where we become isolated, uncooperative, antisocial, or withdrawn from active life. This is not healthy. Loners and shy people should make an extra effort to pursue practical activities and involve themselves in social interaction.

18. Neglect of ideals. There is a very strong tendency in Virgo to turn our back on our ideals and "sell our soul" to the highest bidder for material advantage. This will tend to induce a strong reaction from our conscience, however, and could lead to a major crisis or confrontation between our spiritual and human natures.

19. The feeling of pressure. There may be times when "emotional tidal waves" sweep through our awareness, especially the feeling of being overwhelmed by pressure. Detachment will be especially important at these times, lest we lose perspec-

tive and forget who we are and what we are trying to accomplish. Peer pressure and the demand for conformity will be heightened. There may also be a sense that the Fates control our destiny, but it is more likely that the experiences which come to us are the result of our own attitudes and habits of behavior. Nonetheless, there is the potential in Virgo for some rather bizarre events and twists of fate.

THE OPPORTUNITIES OF VIRGO

Virgo promotes a fuller awareness of our spiritual nature and the plans of the soul. This may result in new mystical insights into our divine nature and work on earth. More commonly, however, this fuller awareness is achieved by struggling to overcome one of the more serious barriers or obstacles to spirit in our life. To succeed in this struggle, we must see what the truly important issues of life are, renew our dedication to the life of spirit, and revitalize our whole approach to living.

What we do with the opportunities of Virgo will depend on how well we have created a coherent and intelligent framework of values, convictions, and commitments. If we have such a framework, it will be relatively easy to review the progress we have made in life, see the obstacles obscuring the life of spirit, and determine what adjustments are needed. But if we do not, we will have no idea what to do next, and will miss the opportunities which arise.

Another valuable tool for capitalizing on the opportunities of Virgo will be the mental capacity for recognizing the subtleties of life and refining our tastes, beliefs, and values to better reflect these subtle realities. These subtleties will be especially relevant to understanding the motives of others, decisions affecting our work, and our relationship with the soul.

The major opportunities of Virgo include:

1. Idealism. The forces of Virgo are best harnessed by increasing our awareness of and responsiveness to the ideals and treasures of spirit. As we confront a wide variety of issues, we are meant to relate them to the ideals of spirit and try to understand them from the soul's perspective. In this way, we refine our values and priorities and discover what it means to honor and express these ideals in practical ways. Any effort to contemplate and implement these ideals will be rewarded in Virgo.

2. Forthrightness. We may find that we are surrounded by incompetent people, or people who stand for inferior ideas. While Virgo is a time to act quietly and with self-discipline, this does not mean standing by silently while inferior people trample on our ideas and make counterproductive proposals. The courage to honor our ideals and convictions and protect that which is noble, right, and worthwhile is a great asset during Virgo. And if we do honor our highest ideals forthrightly, it will open up significant new opportunities of self-expression.

3. Conflict management. Most people view conflict as a problem, but it can also be an opportunity, if we learn to manage it well and use it as a venue for change, new growth, and constructive activity. Because of the importance of acting quietly and peacefully in Virgo, we are encouraged to refine our skills of conflict management. The question to pose to ourself is: how do we resolve and process inner conflict? Do we carry it with us until we can find an outlet for blowing off steam? Do we blame it on others? Or do we respond to it by determining which elements in our character are in conflict, then using the superior elements of spirit to transform the inferior elements of our human nature?

4. Brilliance. The well-trained mind that is harnessed by spirit may well produce a series of brilliant insights and ideas during Virgo. But the mind that is trapped by the dullness of materialism will tend to be confused and unfocused.

5. Respect and reverence. Virgo fosters a deeper level of

respect—respect for our own talents and achievements, respect for the goodness and talent of others, and reverence for the order, intelligence, goodwill, and beauty of life. We can enrich our character in significant ways by taking this opportunity to deepen our respect and reverence.

6. Self-reliance.   The self-centered tendency to expect everyone else to help us solve our problems and reach our goals will not be supported by the forces of Virgo, which systematically influence us to develop a genuine capacity for self-reliance. In this way, we detach from false assumptions about how others are holding us back, and we see that the real issue lies in the skill with which we move toward our goal.

7. Energizing the personality. There will be times in Virgo when we seem to suffer from a personal energy crisis. At these times, we need to realign ourself with the strength and enthusiasm of the inner being and focus new vitality into our mind and emotions, reenergizing them so we can proceed with constructive work and activity. If we do, we may create conditions which enable the higher self to nurture the personality in unusually powerful ways.

8. Charitable work. Virgo encourages a charitable concern for the collective needs of mankind. It prompts us to look at our own life and see what we can do, in a practical and direct manner, to make a constructive contribution to the well-being of humanity. In this way, we learn what it actually means to join with other men and women of goodwill to help redeem the life of humanity.

9. Quiet confidence. While the challenges of Virgo can be intense, there is an inner capacity for poise and tranquillity which can be developed, if we have learned some of the basic practices of detachment. This quiet confidence emerges out of the realization that while the work we must do is far from done, it is successfully and intelligently launched, and the momentum which has carried us thus far will certainly give us the strength

we need to continue on to completion. And so, because we are confident in the value of what we have done, we face the future with equal faith and tranquility.

10. Self-healing. Virgo is an excellent time to become a better friend with our subconscious. Sometimes, in our eagerness to reform bad habits, we begin to view the subconscious as an enemy, or at least an unruly brat. This can be a most unhealthy attitude. The subconscious is a valuable part of our being and should be treated as a loyal friend. Even though certain aspects of it undoubtedly need reforming, we must appreciate that it also contains all of the patterns of our talents, skills, and good qualities. We need to nurture a wise and mature relationship with the subconscious.

11. Mental experimentation. There is a certain flexibility in Virgo which promotes an air of experimentation—not an uncontrolled environment, but the freedom to try different approaches, modes, and methods. We should actively use the mind to explore the different possibilities of the various options presented.

12. Forgiveness. Virgo is a good time to forgive others and to seek their forgiveness for harm or injury we may have caused. Forgiveness is not a process of forgetting or repressing harm that has been done, but one of neutralizing the hostility, bitterness, and grudges we have built up in reaction to this harm. It has a tremendous ability to heal and rejoin.

13. An expanded sense of duty. The willingness to take on difficult assignments, new experiments, and greater challenges—even if they involve personal sacrifice—in order to get a job done or serve a noble purpose is a tremendous asset in Virgo. It opens new doors for service and opportunity, and demonstrates that we can be trusted with new assignments and duties.

14. Pride in our work. Many people think pride is a sin, but it is really vanity which is the sin, not pride. It is a virtue to take

pride in excellence and the expression of skill or talent; it is noble to strive to do better work than we have in the past, and to take joy in our achievement when we do! We should strive to give our customers, our employer, or our clients *more* than they expect or require. We should strive to teach our children *more* than they need. And it is right and proper to delight in these accomplishments.

15. Stewardship. The steward is one who recognizes his responsibility to help all life on the planet grow—and seizes opportunities within his sphere to do so. The light of spirit shines best in Virgo through our individual efforts to nurture growth, enrich the quality of life, and add elements of spirit to our activities and projects. As much as possible, this activity should take us beyond the bounds of our personal life and involve us in honoring our ties of kinship and brotherhood, by serving the needs of others.

16. Compassion. Above all, Virgo is a time to respond to the spiritual ideal of compassion and knead it into our character and self-expression. This is done first and foremost by developing the mothering aspect within us to nurture the seeds of greatness within ourself, others, and our work. But it includes much more than helpfulness alone.

Where we have been critical, compassion inspires us to discover that there is more to the person, situation, or dilemma than the elements we have criticized; there is an inner purpose or latent seed of nobility we can love, respect, and nurture.

Where we have been angry, compassion helps us understand that our anger has not solved any problem—it has just compounded the situations which incited our anger in the first place. Compassion teaches us to forgive and to put our energies not into anger but into constructive activity.

Where we have been selfish, compassion teaches us to seek out those who need support and find ways to help them grow in mind and heart and spirit.

Compassion is more than the absence of anger; it is the presence of divine goodwill, focused in service and helpfulness. It is the ideal to strive to honor and express during Virgo.

TUNING INTO THE FORCES OF VIRGO

Because the forces of Virgo lead from the mundane to the sublime, one of the best ways to tune into them is by paying attention to the symbolic meaning of ordinary events. In many cases, the tangible signs of the events of life will be our surest guide to discovering and tapping the forces of this time.

In fact, these outer signs of life may almost represent a catechism for the spiritual path, asking us:

Whither do you journey?
From where did you start?
Where are you heading?
With whom do you travel?
What strengths lead you on?
What signs show you the way?
What obstacles bar your progress?
Why do you let them hinder you?
What do you give to life as you journey on your way?
In what manner do you tread the path?

The answer to these questions will be multidimensional in nature, for the path leads us not only through our destiny on the physical plane, but emotionally, mentally, and spiritually as well. And as we respond to this catechism, we will become more aware of the forces of Virgo, the light within us, and how this light enables us to see the path before us more clearly.

The way to teach in Virgo is by nurturing the inner capacity to grow—by focusing attention on high and noble ideals and building a true devotion to expressing them.

The way to heal in Virgo is by focusing the transforming

power of the appropriate ideal into the distressed condition, reawakening the seed of perfection within it.

The way to lead is by opening the eyes of others to the power of divine ideals, teaching them to follow these ideals.

The work which is done in Virgo will reappear as a powerful basis for self-expression and service in Aquarius, and will in fact sow the seeds for the new wave of direction and focus which will emerge next year in Aries. It is therefore of great importance to work intelligently with the forces of this time.

A SONG FOR VIRGO

Forced into exile, the empress sings a lamentation. She has lost her land, her people, her crown, and her glory. All that remains is the royal cloak she wears. She stands alone, bereft.

But even though the cloak trembles, the empress does not weep, for she knows it is woven of the finest threads—majesty, grace, wisdom, tenderness, compassion, patience, joy, integrity, goodwill, reverence, and strength. It has withstood the demands of rulership, and now will endure the rigors of exile.

"I have lost all except this cloak," she says, "but I shall not lose the opportunity before me.

"Knowing what it means to be bereft, I shall nurture the life of this land of exile, and help it prosper.

"Knowing what it means to cry, I shall dry the tears of those who suffer, and help them find new joy.

"Knowing what it means to be condemned, I shall rebuild the good which others have thoughtlessly destroyed.

"Knowing what it means to be eclipsed, I shall fill the people of this land with hope. Today, it is the kingdom of my exile, but tomorrow it shall be a kingdom of light."

An empress still, she walks into the future, restoring the land, the people, the crown, and the glory that are hers by right.

A PARABLE FOR VIRGO

A woman was tending the flowers in her garden when a fierce squall blew in from the ocean, threatening destruction. The woman was afraid that her young flowers, over which she had labored so lovingly, would be uprooted by the storm. She rose and went to meet it.

"I beg you to go around, Storm, so as not to damage these flowers in my care," she said.

"What does that matter to me?" came the reply. "I am Storm. I blow wherever I please. Your garden is no exception."

"But these are not just ordinary flowers," the woman explained. "I have cultivated them with the greatest of care. When they were still seeds in the soil, I invoked the strength of the earth to instill them with the will to grow. As they began to break through the surface of the dirt, I prayed that the warmth of the sun would fill them with aspiration. As they grew, I blessed them with the majesty of the mountains and nurtured them with beauty, love, and joy. In the evenings, I sang in harmony with the breeze blowing through the trees. And as I watered them, I taught them to worship the rainfall, for their very existence depended on it. Would you destroy life which has been nourished with a measure of your own spirit?"

Storm was touched by the woman's eloquent plea. "I cannot go around, yet you need not be afraid for your flowers."

The woman stepped back and Storm rushed on. But as it entered her garden, it abruptly became quiet and serene. The storm stayed there the whole of the afternoon, raining softly and lovingly upon the flowers. At dusk, it regathered itself and went thundering on its way once more.

From that day forth, the flowers in the woman's garden appeared almost angelic. And the rain that fell upon them was always gentle.

12

Libra

LIBRA

Keynote: The enlightened mind must rule.

Mantra: "I listen to the word of God, and strive to understand. Then I build."

New moon focus: Insight into divine order.

Full moon focus: Restoration of the plan.

Rays 3, 5, and 7 dominate.

Primary archetypal forces:
Peace, order, justice, truth, mercy, beatitude

A Prayer For Libra:

O heavenly Mother-Father God, the power that can restore all things to a state of divine balance, help us understand the nature of Your plan for humanity, so we can shape our plans to reflect and embody Yours.

Give us the wisdom to comprehend the part that we can play, as individuals and as a part of humanity, in establishing peace on earth, goodwill toward all men and women.

Give us the love to cherish the noble works of civilization and the divine ideal of brotherhood.

And give us the strength to unite that which has been torn asunder, restoring balance.

Libra is a time of *intersection*—a time when two or more differing paths of destiny cross, when separate themes of life merge and become one, or when the past and future seem to meet. This condition can produce an unusual kind of conflict, if we fail to understand that it is part of a larger pattern. But it can just as easily lead to an unusual level of balance, if we are able to realize that differing elements which have always belonged together have finally come together and been united. Balance, in fact, is the great key to the forces of Libra.

The highest level of intersection in Libra, of course, would be the unification of the soul and the personality as partners with common goals and purposes. But there are other ways in which the intersecting forces of Libra work out as well:

Mentally, the intersection of two or more ideas can produce either new conflict or new understanding, depending on how we handle it. Wherever ideas and ideologies have been at war, either within our own mind or in society, the battle is likely to intensify. But if we refuse to be drawn into such conflict, and seek to perceive the larger issues in the background, we can see the seeds of balance within differing ideas, and thereby better understand them.

Emotionally, our self-interest will be juxtaposed with our responsibilities more vividly than usual. Through the choice we make at this time, we will tend to tip the scales either in favor of honoring or betraying our values and deepest convictions.

Physically, coincidences will be more noticeable, as unlikely events occur in tandem with one another. More importantly, however, various lines of destiny in our life that we have always regarded as unrelated may suddenly emerge as closely connected with one another. Or, our self-interests and the best interests of others may suddenly seem to coincide, where they never did before. A good example would be the boss and employee who recognize that their interests really are the same and that it is, indeed, best for both of them to work cooperatively.

273

In *relationships,* our respect for our friends may very well deepen in Libra, as we see more clearly the common themes we share. But by the same token, our antipathy for our enemies may likewise deepen, unless we can see that enmity is counterproductive and poisons the quality of our life as well as the life of our enemy.

Relationships are one of the most important of all intersections in Libra. While Gemini is the sign most directly involved in shaping the *quality* of relationships, Libra is the one most directly involved in determining the structure of relationships.

In the all-important relationship between the personality and the soul, the potential for intersection during Libra lies in our capacity to balance force:

• In discovering the unique strength the soul can give us for exercising dominion over our personal world, thereby demonstrating the power of the intangible elements of life to control and direct the tangible conditions of life.

• In discovering the ability of the personality to refocus its understanding at a higher level and harness its human and spiritual potential more effectively, thereby demonstrating the power of the human mind to expand and become responsive to spirit.

• In discovering the special relationship between the opportunities and events of daily life and the larger patterns we know of as the plan of the soul and the plan of God, thereby demonstrating the essential intelligence of life and the dynamic basis of balance.

In practical terms, this means that the forces of Libra will focus our attention on the ordinary ways we can express force, and whether they are in balance or out of balance with the forces of the soul. If, for example, we are self-centered and think that the world exists to serve us, this force of self-centeredness will be emphasized to the point where we can clearly see that it is in conflict with the soul. But if we are generous and seek to do good in the world, this, too, will be emphasized, so that we can more easily see that it strikes a resonant chord in the life of the soul. Our efforts to be generous and helpful will be strengthened from within.

When the forces of the personality are in harmony with the forces of the soul, they figuratively form a cross. Archetypally, the four major factors forming the cross in Libra are:

1. Balance. The forces of Libra work to promote balance. This is not a philosophical concept of equilibrium, however, but a very active principle of living. The way to achieve balance in Libra is to repair damage which has been done, work toward new expressions of ideals, and perfect that which has been inadequate. To work effectively with others, or with the environment, or with the opportunities which come to us, we will have to be in balance with them—and in balance with the ideals we seek to serve. Any aspect of life which is out of balance simply will not work in Libra. It will produce irritation, opposition, or a lack of cooperation, until the imbalance is healed.

2. Intelligence. The forces of Libra stimulate the mind and the principle of intelligence. Through the mature use of intelligence, we can understand the many factors involved in a situation, and what will be required to bring them into effective balance. The great example of the influence of intelligence on human life is *civilization*, which is really the demonstration of the creative use of ideals.

3. Order. Libra acquaints us with the principles and workings of the universe. It is a time for learning cosmic principles, divine law and justice, and the orderly way growth unfolds. It is a good time for working to achieve greater organization, especially in the conduct of business or groups.

4. Building. There is a strong emphasis in Libra on constructive activity and building upon the foundations which have been laid, by our past activities, by the good works of others, and by civilization. The person who indulges in laziness

or destructiveness will miss many good opportunities in Libra. But the individual who approaches life with a "building consciousness" will fare well.

For the average person, the opportunity to build will lie in his work and assignments—making a contribution to a larger building effort.

For the aspirant, the opportunity will lie in putting together and coordinating effective group work, so that heaven can be brought to earth.

For the advanced person, the opportunity to build will lie in constructing systems of ideas that will inspire and sustain new trends in human consciousness, creativity, and philosophy.

THE SYMBOLISM OF LIBRA

The symbol of Libra is the scales, indicating that the energies of Libra move toward a condition of balance. In the human being, balance is achieved through the process of making correct decisions, evaluations, and judgments. In government, it is attained by passing laws that gradually correct situations that are out of balance; in society, it is achieved by inaugurating essential reforms.

Proper judgments and evaluations cannot be made without a well-trained mind—a mind which is dedicated to human unfoldment. When knowledge is not consecrated to constructive achievement, it becomes unbalanced. There are many examples of this in the world today. In the search for solutions to technological problems, the ecology has been unwittingly harmed. In response, corrections have been advanced which would protect the ecology, but at the price of harming the economy. In both cases, knowledge is out of balance; what is needed is a capacity to view the needs of both the ecology and the economy. Both are divine expressions; neither can be abused without serious consequences. Balance can be attained only by promoting a coordinated growth of both.

Mature judgment is very much a hallmark of the work of Libra. The judgments we will have to make, therefore, should be mental, not emotional—even if these judgments primarily affect the emotions. When judgments become emotional, our capacity to evaluate degenerates into harsh criticism, doubt, denial, and prejudice. These tendencies should be restrained.

The problems of relationships, for example, are often "solved" in unbalanced ways—by one person "winning out" over the other. The better way is to strike a balance between the legitimate needs and resources of both parties. Often, this balance can only be found in terms of the future, not the past. Instead of trying to balance out past grievances, in other words, it is often healthier to strike a balance which helps both parties fill their current and future needs.

In each of these cases, the scales continue to move up and down until balance is achieved. If the solution we try is too radical, it throws the scales even further out of balance. But if we use our intelligence, sense of fair play, and goodwill to establish true order, the scales will come into balance, and our genuine growth and creative labors can proceed.

HOW THE FORCES OF LIBRA AFFECT US

There may be times in Libra when we seem to be a pawn pushed capriciously through the experiences of life by larger forces—family, work, government, society, and perhaps even fate itself. As a result, we may feel overwhelmed and unsure of where to turn next. In most cases, however, this would be little more than a retreat from personal responsibility into fatalism. This problem can be largely eliminated by striving to comprehend the pattern of our life.

What, after all, is the difference between being a pawn and a master of one's own fate? The major difference is *active intelligence*—a pawn is swept along by larger forces, whereas a self-directed person harnesses the larger forces and uses them creatively. The one who has mastered his or her use of intelligence is able to see that the force of momentum that sweeps through our life is really just the culmination of our own past. We have set in motion various forces which bring to us the problems, opportunities, challenges, restrictions, and good fortune we face today.

In general, to the degree that we approach the events of Libra intelligently, the effect of its forces will be positive. If we do not ponder intelligently on the events of this time, however, we will largely stumble through Libra as though in a haze.

The average person, in fact, will just drift through Libra, not making any effort to achieve balance or use the mind. He will be affected by the forces as though he were a buoy bobbing on the surface of the ocean.

The spiritual aspirant is generally one who is striving to approach life intelligently, yet still has not mastered all of the lessons of balance and common sense. The folly of previous indiscretions or lack of involvement in life may well come back to haunt him. Or there could be a crunch in his conscience, as his own ambivalence and hypocrisy are thrown in his face.

The advanced person, however, will find that his judgment is even sharper and clearer than usual, and he has an expanded ability to embrace larger ideas. There will be opportunities to work directly with the forces of order, justice, and balance.

The effect of the forces of Libra on our **motivation** is to stimulate a more profound sense of justice or fairness. We will be motivated to correct injustices wherever we find them, to treat other people fairly, and to try to impose a higher level of order in our life. And we will understand more fully that intelligence is a necessary part of the spiritual life.

The effect of the forces of Libra on our **awareness** will be to stimulate our memory, so we can better understand the relation of the past to the present and see the ongoing continuity of our habits, intelligence, evolution, and talent. In part, we will be encouraged to review certain trends from the past, to see where imbalances still exist and how they can be corrected. But there is more involved than this alone. We can help ourself immensely, for example, by recalling sources of strength and guidance we have successfully relied on in the past. It is also a good idea to be alert to the intuitive importance of memories which spontaneously arise in our awareness to remind us not to repeat a past mistake, or to remember a lesson learned long ago. We may also achieve a sudden new understanding of what patterns from the past meant to us—and what they mean now.

The primary influence of the forces of Libra, of course, is at the level of the **mind,** where they stir up our intelligence and capacity to reason. If we are not a thinking person, Libra is a good time to exercise the mind and develop our mental muscles. If we already are a thinking person, we will find that the forces of Libra lead us to higher levels than we normally tap, and help us discover inner peace.

For those who remain focused **emotionally,** however, the forces of Libra will seem rather sterile. These people will tend to lose their sense of direction—not because it is missing or on vacation, but because they have always interpreted it emotionally. With the strong emphasis of Libra on balance, thinking, and understanding, the person who *feels* his way through life may not know exactly how to proceed.

As for the focus of our **self-expression,** the forces of Libra will tend to encourage us to work toward reconciling the actual conditions of our life with the ideals we grasped during Virgo. Instead of just reacting to the imperfection and disorder of the world, in other words, we will be inspired to see that we have the option to take action in practical ways to correct these distortions.

THE CHALLENGES OF LIBRA

One of the great purposes of Libra is to give us the opportunity to take stock of the forces and energies already at work in the situations of our life and determine how to balance them so they better express the ideal. During Libra more than at any other time, the forces of the zodiac are best understood through our own actions and responses, individually and collectively. The microcosm holds the key to the macrocosm, at least as it affects us. It is as though Libra is a time for making mid-course adjustments in our handling of the forces released in Aries. This does not in any way belittle the opportunity of Libra, however, for the skill with which we make these adjustments will determine, to a large degree, how well we respond to the tests of Scorpio, just around the corner.

Libra is therefore an excellent time to invest in good ideas, advance our plans and commitments, and work to reform conditions which would obstruct the manifestation of these plans.

By investing in good ideas, we honor and express the divine forces which are already at work in our life.

By advancing our plans and commitments, we harness the momentum of these divine forces for eventual achievement.

By working to reform situations and conditions which would obstruct the manifestation of our ideas and plans, we protect our efforts from inner weaknesses, outer opposition, and the distortions of ignorance.

What many people do not realize is that there is a tremendous potential for backlash during Libra, both individually and in society as a whole. The new divine forces which have been subtly influencing us now for half a year have finally been registered, and the forces of resistance are moving to oppose them. But in most cases, this backlash will not erupt in violent confrontations. It tends to be far more subtle, manifesting primarily as indirect pressure from family, friends, colleagues, and our own subconscious—the quiet suggestion that the new ideas and directions we are working with just are not worthwhile.

In general, the whole of mass consciousness will be stirred up. But because most people are unaware of the influences of mass consciousness on their thinking, feeling, and behavior, they will miss the real significance of this time. Only those who are able to work wisely and consciously at the mental level will be fully in step with the potential of Libra.

Because of the activity in mass consciousness, the great challenge of Libra is its opportunity for enlightened men and women to help reform and redirect the basic assumptions, beliefs, and convictions of humanity as a whole. Any thinking person can respond to this challenge, by carefully thinking through the key issues of growth confronting humanity and then promoting an enlightened view of them whenever appropriate. But the greatest challenge lies in working to enlighten the structure of human thinking directly.

The great danger of Libra, in this regard, is to fall victim to the pervasive attitudes of mass consciousness and allow them to drag down our standards to the lowest common denominator. In general, we must take care not to let the power of our thinking be diluted by any of the group minds we may belong to.

The challenge of Libra to parents is to stimulate the thinking and intelligence of their children. It is also important to teach children how easily the mind can be hypnotized or brainwashed by unscrupulous people for their own ends, and what can be done to build up sufficient self-determination so this cannot occur. Libra is likewise an excellent time to teach children the basic lessons of fair play and to help them cultivate a sense of responsibility.

The challenge of Libra in improving relationships is to make sure that the structure of our bonds with others is well built and nourished. Many of the problems which develop in relationships arise from an improper structure. A boss, for example, may expect an employee to do something which has not been properly explained to the worker. Or we may enter into a relationship with expectations which the other person has no interest in fulfilling. Libra is an excellent time to review our relationships and define exactly what each one is designed to accomplish and fulfill—and how well this function is understood and appreciated by those involved.

The challenge of Libra in business is the challenge of effective management. Are the resources of the enterprise well coordinated and effectively utilized? Are the needs of the present time being properly addressed? Are the opportunities of the marketplace being tapped?

The period of Libra is also an excellent time for negotiation. Whenever possible, the goal of negotiating should be to reach agreement, rather than compromise—a true intersection of common interests. Quite often, there are more areas of agreement than disputing parties realize. Once they get past the bombast of partisan rhetoric, and carefully examine the common goals, similar values, and parallel principles of both sides, they may be amazed by how closely their interests coincide. As long as they struggle to compromise on the details, however, they may never discover their common base of agreement.

The challenge to society in Libra is the confrontation with fascism, which is really the prototypical confrontation with the forces of darkness. Conflicts between totalitarian groups and the people they seek to control will heighten, as the people realize that the allegiance they are forced to give is not a sound investment in the public good. The ruling cliques, in turn, will sense they are losing control and try to tighten their grip. This pattern of conflict will be visible throughout society, in nations, companies, families, and social groups, as those who are used to dominating others find their fascist tactics challenged.

This challenge is tied to the whole problem of our individual susceptibility to the pressures and influences of mass consciousness and its agents. There is a strong temptation in Libra to conform to group standards and deny our individuality and personal convictions—but it is a temptation we need to resist.

As for the way the forces of Libra challenge us to grow, perhaps the most powerful challenge of this time is to become a "master builder"—a person who builds in the worlds of form in such a way that he unveils the presence and glory of God. It does not matter whether we build with bricks or boards or ideas or services—the principles are the same.

Individually, we are challenged to build an effective and enlightened self-expression, using the talents and abilities we have been given. Collectively, we are challenged to build civilization. In each case, we are meant to build not for our personal glory, not even for our national glory, but for the glory of God. There is much to learn in order to be this master builder. We need to learn to work with an understanding of the archetypal forces of life; we need to learn how to harness these archetypal patterns for the needs of the moment. We need to learn to plan effectively, so we can translate these plans into manifestation; and we need to learn to build in the world of form with such style and grace that we capture the essence of light.

It is a great assignment, to be a master builder—and the heart of the challenge of Libra.

THE PROBLEMS OF LIBRA

Most of the problems of Libra derive from the failure to respond to inner purpose. Where we have drifted and allowed ourself to react emotionally to circumstances, or to follow our basest passions and desires, we will find that we must bear the consequences. Most of our problems will not be *new* ones—they will just be the backlash of our previous acts, individually or collectively. To the degree that we continue to deal with these situations as we have in the past, we will aggravate them. But to the degree that we see the role we have played in generating these problems, and act with a new sense of balance, we can overcome and heal many of them.

In Libra more than any other sign we can readily see that our problems are not caused by the configuration of the stars, but by our own selfishness, reactiveness, and irresponsibility. Instead of waiting for others to clean up their acts and solve our problems for us—or waiting for the planets to play musical chairs and produce a more favorable configuration—it is important to squarely face the ways we have generated and compounded our problems, and take action to restore order and fairness.

If we do not take this kind of initiative, however, there is an excellent chance of becoming so attuned to our problems and hardships that we develop a "problem consciousness"—such an intense awareness of what is wrong with our life that it saturates our thinking, attitudes, and plans. This is a very unhealthy state of mind and feeling—an obsession with our problems.

Unfortunately, a parallel type of condition often arises in mass consciousness during Libra, making us all vulnerable to what might be called the "diseases" of mass consciousness. These are not diseases of the physical body, but of the emotions and the mind—primarily the emotions. They infest whole cultural groups, subtly changing the moods and perspectives of the members of these groups. Because these diseases are spread at invisible levels, they are not recognized by most people. But they are highly contagious, and deeply infectious. Some of the ones most highly communicable during Libra are:

• *Separativeness*, which estranges the members of a particular group from the mainstream of human society. It heightens the sense that the group is special or has unique needs or rights. The impact of separativeness on the individual is that it cuts him off from contact with the higher self.

284

- *Nihilism*, the belief that there is no meaning or purpose to life. This has been a growing force in the body of human thought, and blackens the lives of many good people with pessimism, cynicism, and despair.
- *Pettiness*, which drugs us into believing that the most petty and insignificant elements of life are actually quite important, thereby causing us to turn our attention away from the expression of our spiritual ideals. This disease could also be called "trivial pursuit."
- *Fear*, especially the fear of catastrophe, which stirs up the reactive elements of the emotions to such a fever point that we are distracted from our intention to act as a building force in life. The fear of economic ruin, the fear of nuclear holocaust, and the fear of major earth changes are a few of the epidemics of fear which paralyze human thinking.

Because of the heightened vulnerability to such diseased conditions in mass consciousness, Libra is definitely not the time to let others do our thinking for us—or to "buy into" someone else's system of thought. It is a time to stretch the mind's capacity to make sense of life. The byword of Libra should be "common sense."

Specific problems which tend to arise in Libra include:

1. Disappointment. A busy life is filled with its share of mistakes, as well as successes and achievements. We do not make any more mistakes than usual in Libra, but we are apt to recognize the mistakes we have made in the past—and their consequences—more poignantly than at other times. Unless we have a healthy capacity to accept mistakes and learn from them, this could unduly plunge us into disappointment and self-criticism. This will be especially true if we discover that we have no one to blame for these mistakes except ourself.

2. Assigning blame. The tendency to blame others, society, or fate for our troubles will be unusually great—but it is just as silly now as at any other time. Sometimes, our own careless-

ness or poor judgment is augmented by the incompetence or interference of others, but it is counterproductive to become angry with them or make them responsible for our own failings. This only weakens our own ability to act effectively in the future.

3. Betrayal. There is a strong temptation to betray what we value and claim to serve. This may be very obvious, as in the case of failing to fulfill a responsibility we have pledged to honor, or it may be more subtle, as in becoming angry with someone else in the name of spiritual righteousness, not realizing that spiritual righteousness is best honored with compassion and understanding, not anger. If we find we have betrayed a value or ideal we meant to honor, the best course of action is to carefully evaluate what it means to honor it properly—and then do so.

4. A loss of dignity. Excessive pride and false dignity will tend to be tweaked during Libra—by others and by life itself. If we have puffed ourself up out of proportion, we need to take the inevitable deflation with good humor and realize that the joke is on us. In any instance where our pride, dignity, or nobility is threatened, we can best respond to this threat by staying focused in the real and important issues, not being distracted by trivial or personal concerns.

5. Stagnation. Libra can be a time of "doing little"—a time of spinning our wheels and accomplishing hardly anything at all. This is almost always because we are waiting for life to hand us opportunity on a silver platter, rather than carefully assessing where we can best make a contribution—and then getting busy and making it. Those who are not actively investing their skills, talents, and goodwill in meaningful ways will indeed find Libra passing by with little accomplished. But those who by habit seek to enrich life—through the work they do, their friendships, their responsibilities, and their opportunities to serve—will find Libra a very productive time.

6. Narrowmindedness. There may be a temptation to think in narrow, legalistic ways—reducing complex issues to black and white terms, judging purely by the rules, and demanding a strict accounting of behavior. The failure to see problems in a broader context or to blend goodwill and compassion with our understanding of issues may doom us to a whole new cycle of difficulty, until we learn what it really means to think.

7. The "ivory tower" syndrome. Theory is fine, but there is often a temptation to cling to theories which do not match reality—or to use a theory in wholly impractical ways. Whether the theory is a cosmic principle or just a speculation about life, it is not worth anything to us unless it helps us make sense of the practical choices we must make in daily living.

8. Gossip. Malicious tongues will wag even more sharply than usual during Libra, producing gossip, rumor, and criticism. But indulgence in gossip and criticism stirs up the basest elements within us, and makes it almost impossible to respond to the nobility and dignity within us—or anyone else. We should therefore carefully avoid the temptation to participate in gossip, rumor, or slander.

9. Prejudice. While the tendency of Libra to juxtapose differing elements is meant to lead to greater balance, in those who resist growth this same tendency heightens prejudice and stereotypical thinking. In addition, the capacity to form self-serving opinions will be greater, leading to hypocrisy and rationalizations. It is therefore important to exercise restraint in passing judgments on others without knowing all the facts.

10. Mental intoxication. Libra can be a time of new insight and understanding, and this is generally healthy. But there can be danger in becoming drunk on the power of new ideas—or swept away by such exuberance that we overestimate our talents, opportunities, influence, and achievements.

11. Indifference. If we have experienced intense struggle

during recent months, we may be tempted to achieve Libra's ideal state of balance simply by adopting an "I don't care" attitude. But apathy and indifference is never a healthy solution to problems. Instead, we must cultivate a genuine state of detachment which enables us to continue to care about who we are, what we are doing, and the well-being of society, without being devastated by hardship, opposition, or our own personal weaknesses.

12. Misunderstandings. We should be careful in what we say, lest our words be misunderstood or even used against us. The greatest area of potential misunderstanding lies in joking, as people without a sense of humor will take offense at comments which were only meant to be amusing. We should therefore strive for balance in what we say to others.

13. The urge to play. Recreation is an important way in which the personality recharges itself and revitalizes its capacity to act, but like any aspect of life, it can be overdone. During Libra, the urge to play and indulge in pleasant, even hedonistic pastimes will be heightened. If we are not careful, this urge to play could lead us to abandon our adult responsibilities and return to an earlier stage of development, where play was more appropriate. If we are unable to maintain a healthy balance between responsible activity and recreation during Libra, we may miss valuable opportunities to grow and serve.

14. Denial of ideals. Some people will even be tempted to deny the value of spirit at this time, substituting materialistic values for spiritual ones, rejecting the guidance of the soul in a fit of pride, or treating others in inhumane ways. We should take special care not to *curse* life or any aspect of it, by condemning, damning, or blighting others with anger, hostility, or intimidation.

15. Lust. There is a basic drive for acquisition in Libra which may print out as lust, theft, or even vampirism. It is not necessary to grasp in order to acquire, however. Wisdom, for

example, can be acquired without depriving anyone else the same access to it. This is true at emotional and physical levels as well, if we just take the time to understand it.

THE OPPORTUNITIES OF LIBRA

The intelligent comprehension of life is the one great opportunity from which all other opportunities in Libra derive. As we learn to direct our life as an intelligent person who accepts responsibility for his conduct, we tap a rich reserve of opportunity at all levels. Conversely, the tendency to blame others for our lack of achievement, or believe ourself to be a victim of fate, actually inhibits our capacity to attract opportunity.

The forces of Libra stimulate our intelligence and every aspect of the mind, both intuitively and intellectually. The best way to harness this extra power of the mind is to strive for balance between our use of intuition and the intellect. One of the best ways to do this is to focus our mind on understanding the archetypal patterns or forces of life, their structure, and how we relate to this structure. In this way, we can better understand the structure of our own character, how it is nurtured psychologically, and what we can do to build a more effective and enlightened character.

For this reason, one of the best ways to focus the mind in Libra is to look for evidence that the Law of Correspondences is active in our life. This law states that "as within, so without." In other words, our inward beliefs, attitudes, and values eventually become apparent in our outer behavior and the events of life. As we discover the actual correspondence between inner values and outer behavior, we will begin to see how much control we have on the quality and direction of our life, and how vital it is to regulate this control through a well-trained mind.

For those who are already mentally focused, there is an

unusual opportunity to tune directly into the matrix of thought which is the plan of God for humanity. This matrix is similar to the one described in the novel *Glory Road* by Robert Heinlein. It contains the true history of the human race, knowledge of the forces currently shaping human activity, and the plan for future human development.

Due to the stimulation of the mind, Libra is an especially fertile time for meditating. Contact with the higher mind and its guidance will come more easily. Old barriers will be at their weakest. It will be possible to work effectively to integrate the past with the present, the higher with the lower, and our ideals with our actual expression and thoughts.

The imagination and all creative abilities are likewise stimulated. For those who do not make an effort to discipline the mind, however, the flashes of insight which occur may be so fleeting and hard to hold onto that they disappear even more quickly than they arrive. It is therefore important to be alert to and prepared to receive intuitive and creative inspiration.

Other opportunities of Libra include:

1. Invocation. Our ability to call forth the resources and assistance of spirit to help us in meeting the challenges of daily living will be repeatedly tested during Libra. This presents us with an excellent opportunity, therefore, to refine our skills of invocation, planning, and self-expression.

2. Spiritualizing our values. The forces of Libra help us find the true center of our being—the focal point where all things are held in balance. By reconsidering our personal values and principles in the light of our spiritual values and purposes, we can make significant progress in building a stronger, more spiritual character.

3. The power of example. We will tend to learn from the examples of others and teach by the example we set in Libra, whether the examples be good, bad, or indifferent. Much intuition and inspiration, for instance, will come via example, as

we draw ideas from nature, the actions of others, and the inter-action of groups. There will also be much we can learn from "object lessons," which are opportunities to learn from the mistakes and experiments of others.

Given this factor, one of the creative challenges of Libra will be to seek out excellent examples of nobility, service, compassion, and similar qualities, so that we may be inspired by the best possible examples, not demeaning ones. And by the same token, we should strive more than ever to set a good example in the way we treat others, our attitudes toward work, our use of money, service, and our dedication to personal growth.

4. Thoroughness. The ability to think things "all the way through"—to see the flaws, benefits, and consequences of any proposal—will be at a peak. This capacity will serve us well as we review past events and what we should be doing now.

5. Cheerfulness. Libra lets the sun shine figuratively into our life. In most people, this will simply mean that a sunny disposition will be easier to sustain. Some may even feel exhilarated at times. In the spiritual aspirant, however, there is a higher correspondence to cheerfulness: the capacity to view life from a more inclusive perspective. There is a real opportunity in Libra to tap the joy that is the basic mood of the soul.

6. Wholesomeness. Libra promotes a return to wholesome values and attitudes, and rejects attitudes which degrade or cheapen life. For some, the insights of Libra may even represent a turning point in appreciating the fundamental benevolence of life. All too many people act in life as though the universe were a hostile place. This kind of attitude estranges them from the benevolence and mercy of God's love. Anything we can do to cultivate our love of God during Libra will be rewarded.

7. Competence. Skill, pride in the work we do, and the capacity to act effectively are all highlighted during Libra, giving us a marvelous opportunity to get busy and do what we are designed to do. Doubts and inhibitions will decrease, enab-

ling us to mobilize our power to act more freely and without excessive fear of criticism or failure. In addition, the spiritual aspirant will be able to see more clearly the role he or she is meant to play in the unfoldment of the plan of God.

8. Vitality. The energy available to us for working with creative ideas and useful projects will be stronger than usual. If we make the effort to harness it and integrate it into our thoughts and daily activities, we should be able to sustain this greater measure of vigor.

9. Friendliness. Libra creates a climate in which it is easier to cultivate more effective social relationships. We are drawn to others and are able to appreciate how our interests intersect with theirs, thereby creating a basis for relationship. In addition, our potential for charm, graciousness, and other social skills increases. While some people will express these social skills only at superficial levels, in many people they will emerge from a deep and profound level, greatly enriching their friendships.

10. The resolution of old conflicts. If we tap the central issues of long-standing conflicts, and act with intelligence and goodwill, there is a remarkable opportunity in Libra to restore balance to situations which have been greatly imbalanced. And there is great wisdom in working to heal old conflicts in this way, since it will clean the slate and keep these old problems from throwing new plans and projects out of balance before they even take shape.

11. Citizenship. The forces of Libra tend to stimulate our involvement in community affairs and the fulfillment of our duties as citizens. They also help us become aware that we are citizens of the planet and the whole of divine creation, and have responsibilities and duties to fulfill in this regard as well.

12. Civilization. The ideal role model for Libra is the individual who cherishes humanity and works toward the fulfillment of its potential. There is a strong call to honor the ideals of

human civilization and to celebrate its achievements. Indeed, those who love humanity and respect the role they play in its development will find Libra to be a time of great progress.

13. Clarity. Libra is a time to strive for lucidity in thinking, self-expression, and writing. Lucidity implies a level of clarity which reveals *light*.

14. Justice. Our awareness of the order of life and its inherent fairness will be increased. We should respond to this impulse by seeking to put our own affairs in order, and by striving to treat others with a sense of fairness.

15. Mercy. Sometimes, in the quest for justice, we forget that justice must be blended with mercy. Mercy is the divine quality which encourages reform; it lifts justice out of the realm of punishment and insures that a lesson will be learned. It is useful in Libra to take time to learn the expression of mercy, and use it both in reviewing our own mistakes and in dealing with others who have wronged us or been troublemakers.

16. Truthfulness. As we seek to understand the ideals and archetypal patterns of divine life, we need to cultivate a stronger capacity to be true to these ideals in all we do. This means training the mind to think with objectivity and act with integrity. If we learn to be truthful in this sense, then we can look forward to a new understanding of recent trends, opportunities, and possibilities for a refined self-image.

17. Peace. Perhaps the greatest opportunity of Libra is the chance to cultivate a genuine sense of inner peace. This inner peace is not just a state of quiet rest, however; it is the capacity to be involved in great outer activity, even chaos, and yet be so in tune with inner measures of harmony, serenity, and order that the outer unrest does not disturb our inner balance. We become, in fact, a *peacemaker*, as the maturity and poise of the soul saturates the personality and intersects with its needs.

We should all strive to be peacemakers of this caliber during Libra—and throughout all twelve signs of the zodiac.

TUNING INTO THE FORCES OF LIBRA

An excellent meditative technique for Libra is *contemplation*. Contemplation is usually thought to be a passive basking in ideals and qualities, but it is potentially far more powerful. It means "laying out the foundations of the temple," and as a meditative technique, it involves translating the force of an archetypal quality into designs, structures, and specific plans for expressing this quality on earth, through our work. In this sense, our work becomes a temple in which we worship God.

One of the best ways to use contemplation in Libra is to reflect on the major themes of our self-expression and evaluate how well we have laid out a foundation for our temple. A theme of self-expression could be the expression of joy, beauty, goodwill, compassion, scientific discovery, wisdom, order, or any other divine quality.

Unfortunately, the themes of living for many people are negative. These people cannot be happy unless they spend at least two hours a day complaining about everything that is wrong, or putting others down, or pursuing their private hedonistic pleasures, or engaging in fierce competitiveness. Their "temple" is nothing but a slaughterhouse.

Such antihuman themes are always out of balance with the spiritual qualities of divine life, and keep the people who pursue them perpetually out of balance as well. But the enlightened themes of self-expression which are based on the spiritual qualities of life are, by nature, *in balance*. As we contemplate them and integrate them into our thoughts, feelings, and behavior, we bring our self-expression into greater balance as well.

A second way to use the power of contemplation to tune into the forces of Libra is to ask ourself the following questions:

In what ways am I currently able to bring the light of spirit into the world and express it?

Am I able to continue expressing this light during times of

crisis and difficulty? Or do I allow the light to be eclipsed?

How well do I express this light during times of pleasure?

In what ways can I be more consistent in expressing the light of the soul in all that I do?

The way to teach in Libra is by stimulating the mind to think, training it in both intellectual and intuitive skills.

The way to heal in Libra is by working to establish conditions of peace and balance—in particular, to create a balanced relationship between the higher self and the personality.

The way to lead in Libra is by encouraging a deeper sense of personal responsibility and accountability.

The careful definition and balancing of the themes of life in Libra helps us face the challenges of Capricorn and Aquarius successfully. Yet the actual impact of Libra varies from year to year, depending on what needs to be balanced. As a result, there is always a measure of surprise and unpredictability. We should expect the unexpected, and meet it with the best within us.

A SONG FOR LIBRA

The word is sent forth and order established. The network of woven light becomes the fabric on which the reflection of manifestation is seen.

Force, direction, motion, and momentum are measured and weighed. The nadir and zenith are breached, substance penetrated. The farthest reaches of the emanation are envisioned. Within the play of light and shadow, many centers of force are found.

The outer, having seen its source, embraces it. The light, having seen its reflection, draws it back into itself. The word, having heard its echo, sounds forth a higher note. The lines of force merge, establishing a new center, which holds all other centers in its radiance.

A PARABLE FOR LIBRA

Thinking it would be educational, a woman had her young son accompany her on a trip to a jewelry store. She showed him all the displays of precious stones and jewelry, and explained something about each kind. The boy had never before seen so many diamonds, so much gold, or so many finely crafted items of adornment, and was fascinated by their beauty and radiance. To one so young, it seemed as though all the riches of the earth had been collected in the cases of this one store.

But what amazed the mother was that the boy, after seeing all these magnificent gems, became more attracted to a pair of scales. It was not an exceptional pair of scales, but they held the boy's fascination in a curious way. The jeweler, seeing the lad's interest, took delight in showing him how the scales were used.

"I can put a diamond in the pan on this side of the scales," the old gentleman said, "and these weights in the other pan. Now, I know the value of the weights, so I can determine how heavy the diamond is by measuring it against them. When the number of weights in the right pan brings the pan containing the diamond into perfect balance, I add up the value of the weights.

"Of course, I wouldn't have to use weights. I could weigh the diamond against the weight of this gold ring, or my watch, or even the coins in your pocket. That would not tell me precisely how much any of these objects weighs, but it would tell me which is the heaviest and which is the lightest."

"That's neat," said the boy. "But tell me: do you always use the scales to weigh one thing *against* another? Do you ever use them to balance the one side *with* the other?"

His mother, embarrassed by the boy's impertinence, said, "Well, that's quite enough! Come along, and stop troubling the jeweler." But the jeweler, recovering from his initial surprise, smiled. "No, Madam. Let the boy stay awhile, to teach me more about the proper value of my jewels."

13

Scorpio

SCORPIO

Keynote: Communion with our spiritual strength.

Mantra: "I radiate the light of goodwill."

New moon focus: Strengthening our values.

Full moon focus: Dispelling self-deception and glamour,
in ourself and in the world.

Rays 4 and 6 dominate.

Primary archetypal forces:
Responsibility, temperance, strength, nobility, goodwill

A Prayer For Scorpio:

O heavenly Mother-Father God, let there be light, to help us understand the ways of spirit and roll away the boulder of selfishness in our lives.

Where fear rules, let strength and order be sovereign.

Where ambition rules, let the desire to serve reign.

Where resentment rules, let understanding dominate.

Where passion rules, let dispassion and detachment triumph.

Where conflict rules, let goodwill build harmonious relationships.

Lead us from frustration to peace, from despair to hope, from sadness to joy, and from doubt to faith. And help us recognize our spiritual path and duty, so that we may serve with joy and wisdom, triumph in the face of adversity, and bring the life of heaven to earth.

Scorpio brings us face to face with ourself, as though we were looking in a mirror which was incapable of reflecting our self-deceptions, cover-ups, and pretenses, and could only reflect our character as it truly is—its strengths, flaws, virtues, deficiencies, talents, egotism, potential, temptations, and its ideal design for growth and achievement.

It will do this by stirring up within us the twin forces of our idealism on the one hand and our self-centeredness on the other. If we are honest with ourself and dedicated to our growth as an individual, the resulting interplay in our consciousness will give us a much better understanding of who we are and what we ought to be doing. But if we are the kind of person who would prefer to continue acting out our self-deceptions and pretensions, we will probably miss the real opportunity of Scorpio and retreat into even greater self-centeredness.

We should not be surprised if the forces of Scorpio stir up sleeping problems and even induce crises in our life, because conflict between unreconciled forces is one of the strongest characteristics of Scorpio. The question to ask is not "Why is this happening to me," but rather "How can I most intelligently respond?" If we respond by panicking and retreating into defensiveness, we will guarantee another cycle of hardship and conflict. But if we respond by seizing the opportunity to grow in maturity, strength, and dedication, Scorpio will be a time when we move forward boldly in fulfilling our destiny.

The new forces which have been building since Aries challenge and test the old and established forces of habit, character, and belief during Scorpio. This will therefore be a time in which we demonstrate either our responsiveness to spirit and its new directions—or our commitment to the status quo.

The impulse to grow is one of the great forces which shape the quality of experiences in Scorpio. Those who cooperate with it wisely will find this to be a time of new insight and wisdom, greater control of our emotional expression, and a new capacity to act effectively. Those who do not cooperate—or even rebel against it—will find Scorpio to be a time of confusion, hurt feelings, irritation, and conflict.

What does it mean to cooperate intelligently with the impulse to grow? It means:

• Honoring the commitments and obligations we have taken on in life as completely as possible, seeking to expand them if we can. In this way, we express the archetypal quality of *responsibility*.

• Looking for repeated patterns of immaturity and conflict in our behavior and taking steps to transform or heal them. In particular, we should strive to overcome any tendencies toward selfish behavior and self-centered priorities. In this way, we express the archetypal force of *temperance*.

• Aligning ourself with the power of the higher self, and using this strength to help us meet the tests of this time. In this way, we express the archetypal quality of *strength*.

• Honoring our highest potential as a human being by taking steps to improve the quality of our self-image and tap the treasures of spirit. In this way, we express the archetypal quality of *nobility*.

• Taking steps to become a force of helpfulness in our work, family, and community. In this way, we express the archetypal quality of *goodwill*.

Scorpio, of course, is famous for being a time of testing, although the average person overdramatizes this and puts far too much emphasis on the negative aspects of these tests. The tests of Scorpio are usually quite subtle; they tend to test the strength of our convictions, aspirations, and good intentions, more than our actual performance or behavior in specific situations. We might be tempted, for example, to approach a problem at work in a self-serving, self-indulgent way, rather than acting for the good of the company. If we recognize the temptation for what it is and respond with proper self-control and dignity, we will pass the test and open doors to fresh opportunity. But if we succumb, the doors will close once again.

It must be remembered, in this regard, that tests are designed to be passed. They demonstrate to us, and the higher self, whether or not we are ready for a new round of growth.

As might be expected, therefore, Scorpio not only presents us with tests, but also the means to pass them, if we respond with intelligence and a willingness to grow. The tests of Scorpio are almost all tests of our spiritual discrimination—our ability to differentiate between duty on the one hand and temptation on the other. All of these tests emerge out of the fundamental disparity which exists between the soul and the personality—between the higher and the lower, the good and the evil, the noble and the selfish. But even while the forces of Scorpio stir up this disparity, they also stimulate and strengthen our capacity to *integrate* the higher with the lower, so that the lower is transformed and better able to serve the purposes of the higher.

For this reason, a good exercise for Scorpio would be a daily meditative effort to integrate some aspect of the higher self—its temperance, strength, joy, wisdom, or goodwill—into our active self-expression. By taking daily action in this way, *we* create the pattern in which the tests of Scorpio arise.

Scorpio is meant to be a time when we rise above our material focus and prepare for a fuller involvement with spirit. It encourages us to leave behind our childish ways and realize what it means to be a spiritual adult, both in thought and deed.

THE SYMBOLISM OF SCORPIO

The symbol of Scorpio is the scorpion, whose bite causes death. Death is one of the primary archetypal forces of Scorpio. Due to the fear and misunderstanding associated with death in the minds of most people, it may prove difficult to grasp the rich opportunities of this particular archetypal force. But it should be kept in mind that all archetypal forces are benevolent and constructive. Only our negative distortions of them make them destructive at times.

Esoterically, death is just a necessary prelude to *rebirth.* Death must sometimes occur at the level of form so that consciousness can be reborn in a new and more powerful way. Scorpio, in other words, is really a sign of the triumph of consciousness over death—the triumph of consciousness over the old and worn out habits and traditions which prevent new ideas and spiritual forces from entering into our life.

The real threat of Scorpio, therefore, is not death, but any attitude which leads to acceptance of the way things are—be it contentment or despair. Such acceptance is the prelude to stagnation. And when this happens, the soul has no option but to jolt us rather rudely—to reawaken us. The jolt can seem like a scorpion's bite. But it produces rebirth, not death.

In Scorpio, we must put to death our illusions, our tattered ideas, and our destructive habits. The best way of doing this is simply to let them die, by turning our attention away from them and giving birth to the genuine qualities of human life. As we nurture the qualities of love, goodwill, compassion, dignity, courage, and trust, our illusions slowly atrophy and dissolve.

But it is important to give these things a proper burial—and make sure they stay buried.

The individual who learns to work correctly with the archetypal force of death, and begins to see death as a necessary part of daily experience, becomes aware of the great joy with which the soul approaches this activity—whether it is initiating the death of one phase of life, the death of a bad habit, or the end of a physical lifetime. Death represents a release from limitations and is the culmination of a cycle of growth, opportunity, or destiny. It is for this reason that the esoteric symbol for Scorpio is the eagle, representing the liberated consciousness. We should strive to understand Scorpio in these terms, not in the conventional terms of aggression, distrust, sensuality, jealousy, determination, and rebellion.

As Paul said, "I die daily." We need to learn to die daily, too, and understand how this enriches our life enormously. A greater understanding of the power of death is one of the secrets of the forces of Scorpio.

HOW THE FORCES OF SCORPIO AFFECT US

There may be times in Scorpio when we seem to be lost in a labyrinth or maze, unsure of which way to turn next—perhaps even unsure of where we are heading. We will take paths which turn into blind alleys and impassable obstacles. Sometimes, the walls of the labyrinth may even seem to shift, so that the path to the center is no longer the same as before. If this happens, it can be very frustrating, but it is important not to allow ourself to be irritated. The labyrinths of Scorpio can be successfully solved.

The walls of the labyrinth appear to be made of environmental pressures, external conditions of life, and the demands of others—all of which may become so intensified they leave us bewildered. But these factors are *not* what create the impression of being caught in a maze. The labyrinth's walls are actually our own tendencies to create illusions and succumb to temptation.

There are many ways we give into temptation. At times, it happens by sliding back into older patterns of behavior. At other times, it occurs by exaggerating unstable or antagonistic conditions and overreacting to them. But whatever the source of our capacity to be tempted, the forces of Scorpio will tend to stir it up. Time and again, we will find ourself in situations where we must quickly choose how to respond to a particular challenge. If we choose to align ourself with the ideals and wisdom of the higher self, we will tap the inner strength to cope with this challenge successfully. But if we abandon our ideals and choose defensiveness, impulsiveness, and skepticism instead, we will find ourself once again lost in the labyrinth.

The labyrinthine forces of Scorpio will present us with different kinds of temptation, depending upon our level of development:

The average person will be tempted simply to plunge further into the darkness of the materialistic life. The person who has been habitually angry, for example, will be tempted to be angrier than ever; the person who has been hostile by nature will be tempted to become even more hateful or malicious. Such people need to learn that there are alternatives to these materialistic approaches to life, and that they do have the strength within them to resist their temptation and begin acting in a more mature and compassionate way.

The spiritual aspirant will be tempted by the illusions and glamours of his aspiration. The aspirant is a person who is aware of both the soul and the personality—and the gap between them. But he does not know the soul in full, and so he is vulnerable to misconceptions about the life of spirit and what being a spiritual person actually means. These misconceptions often limit his efforts greatly—even though he does not fully realize it. So the forces of Scorpio magnify them and endeavor to demonstrate to him how limiting his beliefs are. He passes the test if he can see through the illusion and become more aware of the true nature of spirit.

The advanced person tends to be tempted by the forces of darkness themselves. This does *not* mean that Satan appears on his doorstep and tries to sell him an "insurance" policy; the temptation is far more subtle than that! It comes more in the guise of discouragement with the work being done, a temptation to reject the needs of humanity out of contempt, or an acceptance of certain free floating attitudes in mass consciousness as normal.

It might be said that the temptations of the average person in Scorpio occur at a conscious level, the temptations of the aspirant occur in the subconscious, and the temptations of the advanced person occur at unconscious levels.

The effect of these tests and temptations on our **motivation** will be to increase either our escapism or our dedication to growth. We need to see the pointlessness of looking for an easy way out—or someone to blame—and realize that there is much we can learn in Scorpio if we simply face the tests of this time and act with goodwill and nobility.

The effect of these tests and temptations on our **awareness** will be to shine light on dark corners which have previously remained hidden, deliberately or otherwise. As a result, Scorpio is an excellent time for introspection and self-examination. Life becomes a mirror in which we can study our own character.

The effect on the **mind** depends on our response to being tested. In those who let the emotions control the mind, the effect of Scorpio will be to increase their tendency to rationalize shortcomings and excuse lapses in good behavior, on the grounds that everyone else is doing it, too! There may also be heightened problems of distrust and cynicism. But in those who control the emotions with the mind, and seek to serve spirit, the mind will be greatly expanded by an inflow of new intuition.

The effect on the **emotions** will be to heighten reactiveness and a sense of threat or insult. We may be taunted by criticism or ridicule about our lack of strength or competence, or seduced into neglecting our responsibilities in favor of pursuing a more frivolous approach to life. We may even be tempted to present a misleading image of ourself to others—or to misrepresent a commitment or an idea. To avoid this temptation, we must choose to be true to our highest self, not our feelings, and to respond with compassion to ridicule, with a sense of duty to any urge to goof off, and with self-restraint to the urge to mislead others.

The effect of Scorpio on our **self-expression** is to involve us in conflict. Other people will be more argumentative, aggressive, or domineering than usual. If we react in kind, by being argumentative, aggressive, and domineering ourself, we will be giving into temptation. If we let our life be sucked into a whirlpool of conflict by our reactions to it, we will be giving into temptation. But if we choose to respond to the ideals of the higher self and act with the archetypal forces of patience, tolerance, and justice, we can overcome the temptation.

To find our way successfully through this labyrinth of temptation and rationalization, we must understand that the events and challenges of Scorpio are primarily a projection of our own nature. Only when we change the fundamental pattern of our character and approach to life will the way to the heart of the maze become clear. But this means that Scorpio presents us with a powerful opportunity for self-examination and self-awareness—if we are able to identify with our inner nature and understand that it *is* more powerful than our self-deceptions, habits, prejudices, fears, and limited thoughts.

If we make the effort to solve the labyrinth, instead of just reacting immaturely to the events and challenges that arise, our relationship with the higher self will become more clear and obvious than ever. Scorpio is not just a time of temptation and testing; even more importantly, it is a time for transformation and transcendence. Caught in the blind alleys of the labyrinth, we may not always be able to see which way to turn. But the higher self is able to look at the conditions of our life as a single whole, and knows the qualities of character, skill, and wisdom that we need in order to restore order and meaning to what we do. If we will therefore identify with our spiritual nature and view the labyrinth from this perspective, we will tap the added strength we need to overcome our difficulties and *resolve* them, once and for all.

The sword of the life of spirit is tempered in the furnace of Scorpio and emerges stronger and more powerful from the experience. But does the person who must wield the sword emerge from Scorpio equally well tempered, and able to handle the new responsibilities of the time?

This is the question Scorpio insists that we answer.

THE CHALLENGES OF SCORPIO

Our values are one of the prime characteristics of our inner life. The person who has not yet discovered the richness of the inner life generally has few values. As a result, he is entirely reactive to what happens to him in life and is easily manipulated by others. He does not know who he is, what he believes, what he is willing to work for, and what he ought to cherish and protect. But the person who has examined his life and formulated values is able to take action which will lead to new opportunities, growth, and achievement.

Scorpio challenges us to develop and refine our values, as a primary way of building a better relationship with our spiritual strength. Where we have allowed delusions, rationalizations, and bad habits to usurp our judgment, we should recognize this pattern and reform it. Where we have become mesmerized by the difficulties and obstacles of life, we should break out of our trance and reestablish proper priorities. We should strive to understand what we value and what will bring us into harmony with the forces, ideals, and virtues we respect.

In pursuing this self-examination, it is of great importance not to succumb to the temptation to settle for lower standards of conduct and lesser values. The forces of Scorpio encourage us to rise to our greatest potential, not compromise or sell out. If we demean our values, we likewise demean our own self-worth. We need to grasp the dynamic power of establishing and maintaining the highest possible—the most spiritual—values and standards for self-conduct.

The challenge of Scorpio to parents is to strive to act with *consistency* in the expression of love and guidance, realizing that the tests of Scorpio affect children as well as adults. Parents must play the role of the higher self for their children, and one of the greatest requirements of Scorpio is to be a steady, reliable source of compassion, understanding, and support.

It is also a good idea to spend time helping children learn how to examine their lives and develop strong, spiritual values.

In addition, Scorpio is an excellent time to stimulate the imagination of young children through the use of symbols. This can be done nicely through the use of fairy tales and similar literature. The parent should avoid appealing to the baser elements of the child's imagination, however, and seek to teach him or her that the invisible dimensions of life are sources of wisdom, love and strength.

The challenge of Scorpio in relationships is to establish new avenues for cooperation. This can be done by acting consistently on the wavelength of goodwill and trust. Even though conflict may threaten some relationships, it is important to see the opportunities we have for reconciliation and forgiveness, if we act with enlightened values. We should also look for ways to inject new creativity and meaning into those relationships which are already solid and healthy.

The challenge of Scorpio in the business world will be to find ways to increase productivity. The forces of Scorpio do tend to stimulate our ambition to attain our goals, but we must work wisely and with moderation to insure that this ambition is properly directed. Any attempt to increase productivity through threat or anger will backfire. Instead, we must seek to build a stronger dedication or devotion to efficient work. It is especially important to show appreciation for increased productivity, through suitable rewards.

Above all, the business community must take care not to fear change at this time, but reach out to embrace it. The forces of Scorpio promote intelligent change whether or not we cooperate with it; to the degree that we initiate change on our own, we will work well with the opportunities of this time.

The challenge of Scorpio to society is to foster the sense of community, which is one of Scorpio's strongest characteristics. Just as individuals are meant to refine their values during Scorpio, nations and groups are also meant to grapple with the central issues of their needs and ideals and formulate new and stronger values. This puts a special burden on leaders, who must serve as focal points through which the ideals and new directions of a nation or group must flow. They are often caught in the middle of the conflicts and crises which promote the new definition of values, and are then blamed unfairly by their followers for being responsible for them.

The challenge of Scorpio to our personal growth is an extension of this concept of community. Nothing stimulates our individual growth at this time more than expanding our participation in the meaningful groups we belong to. For some, the challenge will be to develop a deeper level of cooperation with co-workers and family members. For others, it will mean a deeper sense of involvement in community and nation. For a few, it will mean greater responsiveness to the struggles of humanity as a whole.

Understanding this, we should expect that self-serving, independent action during Scorpio will most likely backfire, thereby encouraging us to see the larger scope of our work and the role we play in the world. We may begin to realize, for instance, that our own efforts are just not enough for the task that lies ahead, so we turn to others for assistance. Or, we may discover that fierce independence—the "don't tread on me" approach to life—can be more of a burden than a blessing, and that we need to blend our independence with a healthy ability to respect others, cooperate with them, and serve mutual interests.

Our "community" can be our family, the city we live in, the

company we work for, a religious denomination, a professional group, our nation, or even humanity as a whole. Whatever the group, however, we need to take time to define how we fit into this community, what contribution we make, the benefits and problems we share as part of it, and the responsibilities we accept through this participation. Then, we should integrate the needs and ideals of this larger group with our own needs, talents, and sense of identity.

Some people, of course, feel that participation in groups leads to a loss of independence and individuality. But this illusion can be overcome, if we understand that the actual force of unity within any group lies at the level of values and principles, not physical membership. To the degree that we recognize that the values and principles of a group strengthen and preserve our own, we establish a basis for enlightened cooperation and harmony. We integrate with the actual force of unity, and learn something about the true harmony which links all of us together at the level of the soul.

The ideal harmony within any human group is a reflection of a spiritual state in which the talents and wisdom of a great number of people are perfectly blended to serve not only the needs of each person but also the needs of the whole. And in this ideal harmony, we can tap the power of unity and learn to express it ourself. Indeed, harnessing this power of unity is the ultimate challenge of Scorpio.

THE PROBLEMS OF SCORPIO

Opposite lines of force in our life tend to be precipitated into definite realities during Scorpio, producing conflicts, crises, and tension. Ideally, we are meant to see the potential for growth and forward progress in these circumstances and confront them with maturity, wisdom, and resourcefulness. If we do, we can harness the power which has produced these crises, and benefit greatly from them.

Unfortunately, the average person reacts to conflict, crisis, and tension emotionally, seeing the circumstances which embody them as something negative and harmful. He becomes afraid and tries to run away, and thereby loses the advantage he might otherwise gain. Because of this typical reaction, Scorpio has come to be feared by people who do not understand it.

The obstacles we encounter on the path before us are of our own making. It is fruitless to blame others, even though others may be involved; it is foolish to blame life or God. Instead, we must confront our problems in the spirit of self-discovery. Why have we chosen this path? How have our own attitudes and acts created these conflicts and crises? What must we learn to overcome them? How can we use these challenges constructively?

The mature person knows there is tremendous opportunity in every crisis and faces his problems squarely. He quiets his reactiveness and aligns himself with the wisdom and love of his higher self, acting to resolve his difficulties with enlightenment. He places his emphasis on solutions much more than on suffering, on triumph much more than on tribulation.

The more pronounced problems of Scorpio tend to include:

1. Egotism. The burst of elation and pride which tends to accompany egotistical actions can give us the feeling that we know what we are doing and are on the road to success—but it is a false feeling not grounded in the real substance of success. Such egotism inevitably will create a great deal of mischief.

2. Defensiveness. When egotism falters, it usually turns into defensiveness, as an effort is made to protect our personal position, even if it is wrong. We should therefore make a conscious effort throughout Scorpio not to indulge in mere defensiveness when more courageous and innovative action is called for—and to recognize defensiveness when it arises in others.

3. Self-serving assumptions. The tendency to assume that

our ideas are best, that others agree with our stands on issues, or that others share our motives can be especially strong—and very dangerous. This is a time to listen to and understand what others are actually saying—not to our own projections and desires. It is also a time to weigh the probable results of our ideas and not take for granted that they will succeed.

4. Irritability. Scorpio dredges up hidden corners of conscience, in ourself and in others. This tends to put us on edge, and we will be more prone than usual to overreact to small things. Habitual cynics and paranoids will in particular have a terrible time.

5. Panic. At times, the tendency of Scorpio to magnify our perceptions of our problems and challenges may become so acute that we suddenly become overwhelmed by them, inducing crisis and perhaps even panic. We must realize that panic is an emotional reaction to our perception of difficulty. In most cases, it is not justified by the actual circumstances—and is never constructive. The person who is vulnerable to panic is the one who has not done very much thinking or reflecting on who he is, the roots of his problems, or ways to resolve them. He is caught off guard and reacts emotionally without thinking. The tendency to panic will be observable at both individual and collective levels in Scorpio.

6. Militancy. People will be more prone to making demands and issuing ultimatums at this time, rather than addressing the actual issues involved and trying to deal with other people as human beings.

7. Despair. If we discover that we have failed to sustain or honor our ideals—or someone else points it out for us—the force of this realization may send us into a state of despair. This may then prompt us to find a way to atone for our failure—yet try as we might, we carry a sense of guilt with us. The only way to really heal this kind of despair is to achieve a better integration between our ideals and our performance in life—to contact and

direct the force of our ideals into our character to cleanse away our guilt and then begin expressing the ideal we meant to serve all along.

8. Dead ends. Some people will find that their efforts to grow, earn promotions at work, or achieve some personal goal have become blocked, with no further progress possible until old methods or attitudes are abandoned and new ones cultivated. In some cases, it will be necessary to transcend our personal focus and begin working more consciously as part of a team. But whatever changes must be made, we must understand that no dead end is a permanent barrier to the expression of our talent, wisdom, and goodwill.

9. Overloading. Especially in leaders, there will be a tendency to push people beyond their capacity, by demanding too much or building up too much pressure to meet deadlines and goals. In some cases, this may become destructive. A far better alternative is to teach people how to increase their own drive and expand their capacity, and encourage them to do so.

10. Passiveness. Those who do not like the push and shove of aggressiveness may well decide that the hassles of this time just are not worth the effort. As a result, they will either give into the intimidation of others or try to walk away from the pressures. It should be clearly understood, however, that trying to avoid the confrontations which arise in Scorpio is *the worst of all possible choices,* as it may cause us to lose what we would otherwise gain. While the personality may be timid and reluctant to stand up to a confrontation, it must be understood that courage and strength are qualities of the soul. It is right and proper to call on this courage and strength during moments of confrontation—not to put others in their place, but to give us the wisdom and ability to work toward a just solution.

11. Frivolousness. The way in which we present ourself and our ideas is a major theme of Scorpio. This may pose a problem for those who tend to shoot from the hip or act without think-

ing. In particular, there is a strong tendency to respond to life too cavalierly. But if we treat life as a joke, we will soon find that we are the butt of it, debasing only ourself. There are many subtle ways frivolousness can sabotage our self-expression: we may take our responsibilities too lightly, be too humorous when we need to be serious, or be so caught up in outer appearances that we miss the inner significance of what is happening. The best antidote for frivolousness is to look for the inner value of events and situations, and respond to it.

12. Sexual intolerance. One of the major areas of divisiveness in Scorpio is the issue of sexuality. Differing points of view regarding sex are apt to collide at this time and generate friction. To handle these conflicts wisely, it is important to look beyond the outer issues and see the real conflict—which is seldom just about sex. These issues must be approached with understanding and tolerance, or the conflict will simply continue.

13. Sadism. The temptation to inflict pain can be stronger at this time, especially in subtle ways, where we may be tempted to embarrass others or behave cruelly at psychological levels. But we must realize that sadism and cruelty kill the good and noble within ourself as well as in others. We should therefore make the effort to cultivate a deeper measure of compassion and respect for others.

14. Envy. Jealousy and envy are basically expressions of intense desire—the desire to have something other people have but we do not. They are destructive forces, because they obscure our relationship with the higher self, which should be seen as the source of all good things in our life. We should take care not to envy what others have, or feed the jealousy others may direct at us. Instead, we should learn to appreciate the accomplishments of others, and carry our accomplishments with dignity.

15. Resistance. Stubbornness, rebelliousness, and disobedience will be heightened. It will be very easy to see only that side of an issue which is most favorable to our own personal inter-

ests. We should therefore strive to view the situations of Scorpio with an open mind. And one of the great tests of Scorpio is how we handle resistance when we encounter it in others. In particular, it will be a common test for parents, teachers, and employers.

THE OPPORTUNITIES OF SCORPIO

The great opportunity of Scorpio is to achieve a higher measure of selfhood—a better understanding of who we are, what we can accomplish, and why it is important. This understanding of selfhood should never be reduced to selfishness—a great danger in Scorpio—but set forth as a central value of spiritual living.

In this regard, the forces of Scorpio pick up on work that was begun in Leo, and add to it. Basically, the forces of Scorpio challenge us to do the most we can. If we are selfish by nature, we will end up becoming, at this time, the most passionate, most anxious, most resentful, most proud, most critical, and most aggressive we can be. But if we are spiritually oriented, we will find Scorpio to be a time when we can be the most productive, the most intelligent, the most loving, the most joyful, the most inspired, the most patient, and the most helpful we can be.

The opportunities of Scorpio include:

1. Improved communications. It will be easier than usual to communicate with others on all levels. In particular, it will be more productive than usual to discuss the meaning of events and to make plans for the future. It is an excellent time to increase our respect for the values and talents of others, and it is also a good time to increase communication between the personality and the higher self. But whether we are communicating with others or the higher self, we should make sure that we are communicating something worthwhile—and not just complaining

315

or indulging in hurt feelings. Engaging in self-pity is *not* a way of capitalizing on this opportunity!

2. Leadership. As long as we do not succumb to the temptation to be coercive and dogmatic, the time of Scorpio is a favorable one for developing leadership skills and using them. It is a good time for demonstrating our strengths, principles, and vision, especially in the face of changing conditions and challenges. If we respond to these challenges with firmness, steadfastness, and a strong sense of purpose, we will attract the help and responsiveness of others.

3. Nobility. The forces of Scorpio summon us to respond to the nobility within ourself and within others, and to find ways to express it in our life. We should therefore take time to reinforce our values and noblest convictions, and not allow anything to degrade or debase them. It is the strength of this inner nobility which gives us the power to triumph over temptations.

4. Blessing. The strength of our inner nobility is also a rich source of blessing and healing. Our higher self knows the struggle and pain of our life, and stands ready to help. It seeks to bless the potential of each aspect of our life, but for this blessing to be fully effective, we must open our heart to it. In Scorpio, blessed are they that stand fast in their inner nobility, for they shall be liberated from oppression.

5. Faith. Few qualities of the spiritual life connect us more powerfully to the strength and resources of the higher self than our faith in its wisdom, love, and power. When lost in the labyrinth of the tests of Scorpio, it is faith and a strong and abiding love of God that will carry us through and help us penetrate to the center of the maze.

6. Helpfulness. The forces of Scorpio do not just stir up problems; far more importantly, they stir up our idealism and a humanitarian urge to be a constructive influence in life. The average person will respond to this impulse by being more inclined to help out at work and in family situations. The aspirant

will respond by renewing and expanding the scope of his service to mankind. The advanced person will respond by discovering new implications in the creative work he is engaged in, and pursuing these implications to their fullest degree.

7. A renewed sense of purpose. Scorpio has a way of lifting us out of our personalized views of life and giving us an awareness of the purposes which motivate and guide humanity as a whole. This, in turn, should give us a deeper appreciation for the value of the ordinary events of our daily life, as well as for those great events which occasionally shape the whole of humanity. Aspirants may also gain a glimpse of the archetypal levels of these purposes.

8. Self-restraint. Most people view self-restraint as a negative process of self-denial, but this is not really the case. The person who has learned to work with spiritual force knows that great care and precision must be taken in handling it. The ability to harness spiritual force with self-restraint is therefore an exercise of joy and achievement, not self-denial. This lesson will be reinforced time and again in Scorpio, as those who fail to exercise self-restraint get their fingers burnt, while those who act with discipline achieve success.

9. Joy. The challenges of Scorpio encourage us to align with the life of the higher self, and one of the great blessings of the inner life is its strong presence of joy. This joy should never be confused with superficial silliness or artificial happiness; it is a deep and profound ability to delight in the benevolence of life. If we are alert to joy during Scorpio, we will be able to discover it in the attitudes of others as well as our own inner being. And if we strive to express this deep and mature joy in our life, we will find it has a powerful healing effect that liberates us from some of the grimness and reactiveness that pollutes human living.

10. Harmony. As we lessen the gap between our higher and lower selves, we discover the power of harmony and how to use it. We become a force of harmony in life, not discord. And we

discover the real power of Scorpio, which is not the power to tempt and to test, as so many believe. Temptations and tests do arise, but only so we can discover our ability to express harmony and find the power of unity. The real power of Scorpio is its ability to reveal to us the ideals and spiritual forces which will lead us intelligently and constructively into our own future, as we learn to work with them.

11. Humility. There is a marvelous opportunity for inspired humility—the knowledge that we are dependent upon vast and benevolent divine forces, yet we are designed to express them in noble and creative ways. Humility establishes a proper, reverential rapport with God and divine forces; it magnifies the nobility of our innermost humanity without overstating it or creating vanity. The true demonstration of humility is the constant expression of thankfulness and gratitude for the blessings and abundance of God's life.

12. Creativity. For those who succeed in awakening dormant areas of consciousness, there may be unexpected gifts, both of the outer and the inner planes. One of these gifts might well be increased creative inspiration—in fact, a whole series of renewed bursts of creative activity.

13. Communion with our spiritual strengths. Scorpio provides us with a rich opportunity to discover the presence of spirit within our innermost self. The key to this discovery is striving to honor the presence of spirit in all that we do, and learning to call upon it and rely upon it when we need extra strength to face the tests and challenges of this time. In this regard, it is useful to remember that tests are meant to stretch us to the utmost of our ability—to give us no option but to go beyond what we know and try to work at a higher level. We are *meant* to call on spirit at these times and discover just what levels of strength and love are there, waiting for us to tap them. And we are meant to get into the habit of communing with these inner, spiritual strengths on a regular basis.

318

TUNING INTO THE FORCES OF SCORPIO

One of the best ways of tuning into the forces of Scorpio is to meditate on the symbol of The Path. This symbol represents the link that is made by the spiritual aspirant between heaven and earth, between the soul and the personality, as the evolution of talent, self-expression, and service develops. Each aspirant creates his own path, made of his dedication, aspiration, talents, good works, relationships, and destiny. For long eons, the path is not clearly marked or followed; it wanders through life aimlessly. But as service becomes more and more a central feature of the life of the aspirant, the path becomes clearer, more definite. It guides the aspirant—and it also serves to inspire others to pursue the path of growth and loving service as well.

Archetypally, the path that the whole of humanity is treading is the Noble Middle Path described by the Buddha—the path of light which leads us into our heart of hearts, the Christ light.

By meditating on the path and determining how well we are able to recognize and follow it in our own life, we can become aware of most of the primary forces of Scorpio. We can make this exercise even more powerful by taking any theme of our life and asking ourself:

What am I doing here?

What am I doing that I should not be doing?

What should I be doing that I currently am not doing?

In what way does this help me tread the path of loving service?

Who is there to help me pursue the path before me?

The way to teach in Scorpio is by direct inspiration—by establishing a bond of rapport which enables both the teacher and the student to commune.

The way to heal in Scorpio is by eliminating the obstructions and hindrances which created the disease or distress in the first place.

The way to lead is by demonstrating a steady devotion to the ideals of spirit, and by tapping the power of unity which draws all members of the group together.

The work done in Scorpio will be echoed later on in Aquarius and at the beginning of the next cycle of the zodiac in Aries, when the lessons learned now will be translated into permanent aspects of consciousness.

A SONG FOR SCORPIO

The lines of battle are drawn, and the dual forces engage each other in struggle, the higher with the lower.

A pawn is caught in their conflict and must endure long cycles of confusion and destruction. As it attempts to move forward, it is captured by the lower and pledges loyalty to it. The battle renews, with the pawn striving against the upper.

During interludes of stability, the pawn wonders, "Who is my enemy, who is my friend?" He perceives virtue in the upper but continues to honor his loyalty to the lower. The struggle renews many times.

The veils of darkness and deception must be rent nine times before the pawn recognizes, at last, an inner reality which has always been loyal to the upper. The pawn is released from his captivity to the lower and joins the upper—his friend; indeed, his homeland.

A PARABLE FOR SCORPIO

While asleep, a man dreamed he was stung by a scorpion. As the venom spread throughout his veins, he was overwhelmed by light. When he awoke, he found himself physically paralyzed, even though the experience had been only a dream.

Because he had been a very active man, being a paralytic radically altered his whole style of life. He had to conduct his business from his home, by correspondence. He could not travel as he once had; his life became a "fixed point." He had to rely on friends to do many of the physical tasks he once had delighted in. But he coped admirably and continued living successfully.

Years later, he was asked by a business associate if he was bitter about his paralysis.

"Bitter?" he responded. "At first, I suppose I was—until I saw that bitterness and fear are the only things which truly paralyze a man. Soon, I came to realize that even though my body was paralyzed, my mind and spirit were not. And so I've been able to live a full and active life."

"But you are confined to your home!"

"Ah, but that has helped me discover a fuller world than I ever knew before. Because I have had to rely on friends, I have discovered a world of cooperation and affection I had never appreciated. Because I cannot move physically, I have discovered how to move in a world of goodwill and generosity I had ignored. And because I cannot travel, I have discovered a vast inner world of exotic ideas and wonderful insights I had never imagined.

"The sting of the scorpion is not so bad, my friend. It has cheated me of nothing—and has led me to chart worlds within myself I never knew existed."

14

Sagittarius

SAGITTARIUS

(November 23 through December 21)

Keynote: Finding the higher way.

Mantra: "With my soul as guide, I seek, I know,
and then I act."

New moon focus: The willingness to change and reform.

Full moon focus: Grounding our spiritual ideals in daily life.

Rays 2, 3, 4, 5, and 6 dominate

Primary archetypal forces:

Dignity, dedication, compassion, authority, hope, reverence

A Prayer For Sagittarius:

O heavenly Mother-Father God, help us pursue our goals of daily living in harmony with Your will and plan.

May the light of the soul bring illumination.

May the mind reveal this light to all who seek it.

May we respond with acceptance and understanding, and be guided by the soul, even as we walk the ways of men.

Give us the strength to transform our ambitions and desires into a stronger aspiration to serve Your plan, so that we may tread the spiritual path and play our part in the work of humanity.

"The bite of the scorpion" during Scorpio has stirred up many issues and presented us with many challenges. The attitude with which we approach the time of Sagittarius will depend to a large degree on how severely we have reacted at the personality level to the events of Scorpio—and how successfully we have viewed them from the perspective of the higher self. Ideally, Sagittarius is a time of *rediscovery*—a time when we renew our aspiration and rechart the direction in which we are heading in life. Yet in no way is it a time to yearn to return to the "comfortable" life of the past. It is a time to harvest the wisdom of our past experiences, integrate the talent and strength and understanding we have acquired, and invest them in a thorough overhaul of the personality, so we can push forward into the future, along the course the soul has set for us.

The archetypal forces of Sagittarius impel spiritual aspiration in the life of the personality through the illumination of the mind. It is therefore an excellent time to review the decisions we have recently made, understand the larger cycles in which we are operating, and relate these factors and forces in meaningful ways to the practical work at hand—in our careers, our relationships, our service, and our self-improvement.

There are times in anyone's life when it is necessary to reevaluate convictions, goals, and talents. The forces of Sagittarius work in subtle ways to promote precisely this kind of review, so that we can move forward into the future. They do this by highlighting our ambition, our will to serve, our aspirations, and our sense of obligation. They also stir up our intuitive faculties, so that we can penetrate the confusion and deception we have built up around us, or others have carefully built up for us.

Unless we are consciously working to cooperate with the forces of Sagittarius, much of this drama is likely to be played out at hidden, unseen levels. The curious aspect of Sagittarius is that it forces our attention on treading the path before us and absorbs us in the practical issues of life, yet our sense of direction, as we tread the path, originates in inner, hidden levels. These inner, hidden levels may be benevolent—the soul, the Hierarchy, or the plan of God. But for many, they are less than noble—the repressed desires, ambitions, and irritations of the subconscious.

Indeed, our response to the forces of Sagittarius may sabotage the process of rediscovery, not heighten it. In some, Sagittarius will be a time of increased confusion, irritation, and even egotism. The highly emotional will tend to lose control of their ambitions and desires. The narrowminded and rigid of thought will become more shallow and stubborn than ever. But if we are dedicated to following the inner light of the soul, Sagittarius will be a time when we tap extra illumination about the changes we need to make in our direction and approach to living. We will rediscover the love, wisdom, joy, and strength of the higher self; realize that they have never waned in their power or influence, even during our time of trial; and align ourself with these forces, thereby enriching our sense of direction.

Sagittarius is therefore a time to strive to act multidimensionally—to realize that the focus of these forces is to implement plans, duties, and activities in the physical world, but always in alignment with our emotional, mental, and spiritual direction. Many people create chaotic conditions because they go in different directions physically, emotionally, mentally, and spiritually. Instead of acting multidimensionally, they act without a unifying purpose or plan. Their spoken words contradict their noblest intentions. Their emotions sabotage their attempts to be successful. If we are interested in using the time of Sagittarius constructively, we must understand that the sense of direction which guides us should be used to integrate the many dimensions of our self-expression.

In this context, it is appropriate to observe that the different levels of quality will be more pronounced during Sagittarius than at other times. We will be struck by the differences between the gross, the subtle, and the sublime levels of expression—our own, the expression of others, and the expression of society. The spiritual aspirant should strive to sense the sublime elements and work with them to guide and direct the more dense and gross elements. This idea is expressed nicely in the symbolism of Sagittarius, the centaur-archer. The animal nature of the centaur represents the gross aspects of life, the human nature of the centaur symbolizes the subtle qualities, and the arrow flying through the air portrays the sublime. It should be the arrow which guides us, and the lower nature which follows.

Still, it must be emphasized that the primary focus of Sagittarius is in attending to the pragmatic aspects of life. If we are consumed in esoteric studies, Sagittarius will tend to stir up a mild level of dissatisfaction which forces us out of our ivory tower into practical application of esoteric principles in daily life. If we are confronted with difficult problems to solve, we will find that practical solutions will work the best. If we experience conflict in dealing with others, the best course to take will be to improve our capacity to get along with these people in practical ways.

Sagittarius is a time for new understanding and increased generosity in our self-expression—a time for recognizing the tremendous resources of our personality and circumstances in life and taking action to use these resources in enlightened ways. There is an enormous potential at this time to take charge of our life and stay in charge. This heightened sense of self-determination, if properly used, can in turn become the source of much inner poise. But to tap this potential to take charge of our life, we must harness two forces:

• We must orient ourself to the true source of direction within us. An excellent way of doing this is to ask ourself: "What do I serve? Do I serve my own selfish interests—or the divine ideals of life?" If we serve our own selfish interests, our capacity to take charge of life will be limited to its lowest octave.

But if we serve divine ideals there is a basis for real progress.

• We must be willing to change and learn, so we can better serve the divine ideals. In a strange way, this need to be willing to learn is usually the most critical for those who have already demonstrated great competence and skill—even mastery.

THE SYMBOLISM OF SAGITTARIUS

The symbol of Sagittarius is the centaur—a mythological figure that is half man, half horse. He is shooting an arrow from a bow. In modern times, the image of the centaur has often been transformed into an archer—and sometimes the archer is left out as well, and only the arrow in flight remains.

All of these elements of the symbolism focus on aspects of the energy of Sagittarius and how it influences us. Personal ambition and desire are accentuated, represented by the animal nature of the centaur. The question that confronts us is: will our ambition be selfish—or dedicated to the idealism of the soul?

The archer—no longer half beast—indicates that the mind is able to control the emotions and refine its self-expression. Transformation and growth are possible; spirit and spiritual purpose are to be grasped and brought to earth—hunted down in the heavens and carried back to earth.

The arrow in flight implies that the archer has spotted his target and has released his arrow of self-expression. It is the nature of Sagittarius to concentrate energy and release it in forceful blasts. The archer's arrow is aimed high, leading him along his chosen path. Once it has been shot, the archer must then pursue it, to claim his quarry. The forces of Sagittarius, in other words, impel us to focus our aspirations and desires, then follow them into the realm of our imagination and dreams. If the impulse is strong enough, the force of our dreams and expectations will drive us to fulfill them, until we reach our objective.

The spiritual aspirant tries to shoot an arrow that will rise from earth to heaven, creating a link between the conscious levels of our being and the divine aspects of the inner being. The path of the arrow becomes what is known in Norse mythology as Bifrost, the rainbow bridge, and what is known esoterically as the antahkarana. The flow along this path can then be reversed, and the soul can use it as a channel for expressing love, wisdom, and power through the personality.

When this occurs, the symbolism of Sagittarius will change; the centaur will be outmoded. The true spirit of Sagittarius will be better expressed by the symbol of the knight (the symbolic opposite of the centaur), who brings the ideals of heaven to earth through his two-edged sword. Above all, the knight symbolizes *service*—in medieval times, service to his lord, the king. Esoterically, the knight serves his lord, the soul.

Thus, Sagittarius is a time when it is especially appropriate to make a greater dedication to the life of service—not a time to let ourself get bogged down in the conventional traits of the sign—gullibility, zeal, impracticality, cheerfulness, and excess. It is a time to orient ourself toward new and higher objectives.

Let us think, therefore, of the archer as a huntsman—a hunter of new spiritual ideals and purposes. If we do not hunt these elements of the life of spirit on our own initiative, the forces of Sagittarius will become the hunter—and we the hunted. We will be hunted down and forced to recognize the will of spirit. So let us not forget the meaning of Sagittarius—we are to be the archer!

HOW THE FORCES OF SAGITTARIUS AFFECT US

The cosmic influences of Sagittarius are very much like arrows of light shot into our consciousness. These arrows of light tend to awaken most of us to new possibilities, lifting up the quality of our thoughts and aspirations while giving our thinking and activity a greater sense of focus and direction. The arrows of light will be distressful only to those who resist guidance from the higher self and scorn self-discipline—or those who stubbornly cling to the status quo and refuse to grow.

As the light of these arrows penetrates our awareness, new directions are etched in the patterns of our subconscious feelings and thoughts. These new directions have been taking shape at unconscious levels since the influx of new divine energy in Aries, but only now are they becoming a conscious part of our personal equipment. Only now are they becoming "set" as a permanent feature of our self-expression.

The effect of these arrows of light on the average person will be to stimulate a stronger sense of ambition, desire, and self-centeredness—but with a catch, for the futility of the shallow life will be exposed. Those who have built their lives on "looking out for number one" will suddenly find their intense selfishness rejected by others. Those who have insisted on preferential treatment will be in for a rude awakening. Those who have grabbed for power and recognition without earning it will find they are unable to continue holding it. The force of reality will rub off the rough edges of their ambitiousness.

The effect on spiritual aspirants will be different. The forces of Sagittarius will energize the spiritual nature with a stronger impulse to manifest it in their lives. This will lead either to the enrichment of their character or the quality of their work—or to major friction and resistance, if their human nature is still stronger than their spiritual nature. Those who are sincerely interested in healing the flaws of their character, for example, are likely to gain new insights into the nature of these flaws—and the power to mend them. Those who have lacked skill in some area of life, yet have sought to overcome this lack, are likely to get unexpected help in making the desired change.

The effect of the forces of Sagittarius on the advanced person will be a heightened capacity to work at abstract levels of thought and energy—to tap the essence of spiritual forces and use them in his or her creative work. There will also be a stronger sense of identification with the network of spiritual people working together to serve humanity.

The forces of Sagittarius will affect our **motivation** by emphasizing the principle of accountability. As every spiritual aspirant knows, we are accountable to the will of spirit and the order of the universe. We are meant to have personal desires and ambitions, but we are responsible for focusing them in such a way that they add to and enrich life, not take from or impoverish it. In Sagittarius, our motivations become colored by a stronger sense of accountability—of making sure that our actions are in harmony with the principles of life, so that they lead to productive results.

The effect of these forces on our **awareness** will be to focus our attention in two important ways:

1. On a deeper understanding of authority. We may discover new meaning in the authority of the higher self, and decide to initiate new lines of activity or reform old lines of behavior to conform with this authority. Or we may simply be annoyed by the expression of authority in others.

2. On a more enlightened sense of direction. Those who are already goal-oriented and have taken the time to revise their goals in keeping with changing conditions will become more aware of how much they control their direction in life, as well as the problems and opportunities that come to them. But those who are passive and prefer to "go with the flow" will become more aware of the need for achieving greater skill in guiding the direction of their life.

The effect of the forces of Sagittarius on the **mind** will be to stimulate new insights and clarity of thought. It will be an excellent time to refine and refocus convictions, values, and ideals; after some confusion in the early stages of the sign, there will likely be a rapid burst of new realizations which clear away the clutter of undigested ideas and experiences and help us put our thoughts in order.

The effect of these forces on the **emotions** is considerably different, however. Sagittarius stimulates emotional reactiveness, leading to stronger desires, heightened conflicts, and possibly a measure of sorrow. It also has the effect of pumping up the emotions so that they believe that they understand more about life than the mind, and ought to rule the mind and make important decisions. As a result, we are likely to hear a lot of nonsense about how "feeling" is superior to "thinking." But nothing could be further from the truth.

The effect of Sagittarius on our **self-expression** is a most remarkable one, encouraging us to expand it and appreciate its fuller potential. In undisciplined people, this could easily lead just to greater self-centeredness, but ideally, we will respond by dedicating ourself to using the personality as an *enlightened vehicle* for the intent of the soul—developing such a close rapport with the soul that it is able to act through our talents, qualities, opportunities, and achievements. In this way, we can begin to express our own potential for greatness in all that we do.

THE CHALLENGES OF SAGITTARIUS

The challenge of this sign can be summed up in the need for each of us to manage and build with spiritual forces. It will not be possible to coast through Sagittarius maintaining a selfish or materialistic perspective; to make the most of the opportunities of this time, it will be necessary to recognize and work with the inner levels of life.

This does not mean that we have to be consciously "spiritual" to make the most of Sagittarius, but we will need to think and act in ways which honor and express the essence of our wisdom, goodwill, compassion, and creative skills. A scientist would do this by seeking out the full implications of his investigations; an educator would do it by finding ways to harness the eagerness to learn of his students; a statesman might do it by responding more intelligently to the spirit of his nation. The key lies in rising above our own personal perspectives and capacities and learning that there are rich, inner levels of meaning and spirit which ought to guide our life and efforts.

Fortunately, there are a number of steps we can take to prepare ourself to act in these ways. The most important are:

1. Cultivating right silence. The power of silence and quiet confidence will never be more evident—or more beneficial. Keeping silent does not in any way mean being passive. Rather, it means learning to work without noise, gaudy display, vanity, or the kind of pointless confrontation that draws unwarranted attention. The power of silence is that it gives us a better chance to listen and hear the subtle dimensions of life. We quiet down our *reactions* to outer life so we can restore our connections with the inner life, be inspired by its direction, and then set forth with even more vigor than before toward our common goals—the goals we share with the soul. If we work in this way with the poise and quiet confidence of silence, Sagittarius can become one of the most productive periods of the zodiac, as it lets us see more clearly the action we must take toward our goals.

2. Making life better. There is a tremendous opportunity in Sagittarius to make improvements, both in the material circumstances of life and our character. This is true for the individual and for society as a whole. Some of the things we ought to strive to make better during this time include: our skills, relationships, habits, material circumstances, business efficiency, self-confidence, ethics, knowledge, and self-control. In fact, there is the potential for very rapid gains, *if* we actively seek to make improvements which serve the intent of the inner being.

3. Right focus of attention. The way in which we focus our

attention is one of the prime factors determining the outcome of Sagittarius in our life. Our challenge is to discipline ourself to focus our attention on those priorities which genuinely have meaning to us, and not be distracted by other forces and conditions. In improving a relationship, for example, we need to focus our attention on the good qualities and potential of the other person, not dwell on those characteristics which annoy and irritate us.

The challenge of Sagittarius to parents is to help their children become more responsive to new directions of self-discipline, maturity, self-initiative, and more enlightened habits. There are few gifts parents can give their children which are more valuable than a strong sense of self-initiative and self-determination. This is cultivated throughout the whole time of childhood, of course, but Sagittarius is an especially good time to focus on these themes.

The challenge of Sagittarius in our relationships in general is to update our appreciation for where our friends, family members, and colleagues are headed in their personal growth and development. All too often, we cling to an image of a person we formed when we first met, and stubbornly refuse to reevaluate it as the years pass. This is unfair to the other person—and to the relationship. Our friends, colleagues, and family members change and grow just as we do. Instead of dealing with them as they were five, ten, or more years ago, we should try to understand them in terms of what they are becoming—in terms of how they are responding, or struggling to respond, to the force of new direction in their lives.

The challenge of Sagittarius in business is to refocus on the fundamental principles of business, eliminating worn-out policies which no longer serve a purpose, cleansing the management structure, and setting new directions. Sagittarius is an outstanding time for implementing policy changes which have been taking shape over the last half year or so.

The challenge of Sagittarius in government is to simplify bureaucratic procedures, eliminate waste, and streamline the delivery of services. It is also a good time for developing new strategies and approaches to the chronic problems of society.

In terms of our personal growth, the challenge of Sagittarius is to discover the creative potential of *self-control*. Many people equate self-control with repression and self-denial, but Sagittarius encourages us to see that self-control is actually very much different. The choices we make during Sagittarius set the course for our involvement in life and growth during the next year. If we drift unintelligently through the month, we will be swept along by forces we do not control. As a result, a pattern is set for the coming year that we do not control. But this is neither an intelligent nor a very productive way to live our life. If we make intelligent choices during Sagittarius, and exercise a mature level of self-control, the matrix we create for the coming year will be one we can cooperate with, benefit from, and use productively. Sagittarius is meant to be a time when we work intelligently to set the right forces in motion for our individual self-expression.

If we refuse to exercise reasonable self-control, Sagittarius will call us to task for it. It will call us to observe the consequences of our acts and failures to act; it will call us to review our mistakes, false assumptions, and self-serving deceptions. If we have approached life by trying to outsmart the universe and play on the goodwill of others, we will be called to account for this as well.

At the same time, however, Sagittarius can just as easily call us to enter into a greater partnership with the universe and the inner dimensions of spirit. We can become more aware of the direction spirit is leading us. We can become more aware of the perspective of the soul toward our problems, opportunities, and desires. We can become more aware of our own potential to enrich our work, friendships, family life, and community.

335

At the highest level, in fact, Sagittarius calls us to become a guardian of the light within us, and to recognize it as our most precious treasure. How can we best preserve and honor the light within us? If we answer this question wisely in Sagittarius, it can carry us successfully through the coming year of experience and opportunity.

THE PROBLEMS OF SAGITTARIUS

The problems of Sagittarius are most frequently related to the misuse of personal ambition and the refusal to learn from the lessons of life. Often, our desires and ambitions are blind and unintelligent as well as selfish and basically destructive. As a result, they become forces which inexorably draw to us problem situations—often quite subtle and easily misunderstood, until we gain the experience and wisdom to see through them and resolve them. Therefore, the more we can look at our problems from the perspective of spirit, the more quickly we can see them in their true light.

The most common problems of Sagittarius include:

1. Pettiness. In relationships, there will be a tendency to focus on petty differences and personal needs, overlooking the true richness of the relationship. Misunderstanding may be exaggerated; in some cases, the "rules of the game" may suddenly change without one party knowing it. Even minor inconsistencies may become highly irritating. In life in general, our attention will be easily absorbed by irrelevancies or inconsequential details. There will be a constant danger of being sidetracked, unless we keep ourself well focused in our most important themes and work.

2. Strong reactions to injustice. The forces of Sagittarius promote a heightened awareness of justice. This may well work in our favor, if we have been wronged, but it can also generate a

large measure of resentment and frustration if we are overly zealous in demanding justice. We need to be an agent of justice ourself, treating others with thoughtfulness and fairness, and not carelessly use the ideal of justice to criticize, attack, or gain personal advantage. The aggressive demand for justice will be apparent both personally and nationally.

3. Impatience. The tendency to rush ahead with projects and ideas that have not been thought through may lead to foolish and precipitate action which later cannot be reversed. As always, prudence and patience are two of the most important elements in focusing new directions of self-expression.

4. A guilty conscience. The forces of Sagittarius can be almost surgical in cutting through our self-deceptions and pointing out the deficiencies of our behavior—especially our record of how we have treated others. If we have any conscience at all, these discoveries are likely to lead to a greater measure of guilt—and quite possibly defensiveness and irritability as well. To grow most effectively, we need to be able to confront our errors without being defensive or irritated—and without wallowing in excessive guilt.

5. Competitiveness. The idea that someone else may be pulling out in front of us or gaining some kind of advantage over us will tend to blind many of us and fuel our competitive nature. We need to place the emphasis instead on learning the value of genuine cooperation with others—and the inner life.

6. Escapism. When pressed with the need to reexamine their life and principles, some people will simply ignore the problem, by changing the subject, retreating into ivory tower speculations, or escaping into a fantasy world of their own creation. This does not solve the problem, however; it just traps these people in recurring cycles of frustration.

7. Inexperience. If we allow ourself to be ruled by overconfidence, we may find ourself taking on duties and commitments we are not sufficiently prepared to handle. If this is so,

our lack of experience will be exposed, leading to embarrassment. This is a potential threat not just to the average person, but to the spiritual aspirant as well, who may be tempted to take on duties and assignments pertaining to spiritual service that he is not yet qualified to handle. We must remember that incompetent service is far worse than no service at all. If we do find ourself in situations we do not know how to handle, we should not try to cover up. Instead, we should seek out and be guided by someone more experienced than ourself—be that our own soul, a competent teacher, a senior colleague at work, or a good advisor. Above all, we must beware the temptation to feign competence we do not have!

8. Separativeness. There will be a tendency to want to withdraw and work apart from others. While this is appropriate in some cases, it may also separate us from those we need in order to achieve success in life. The temptation to assume that we have an exclusive franchise on some kind of talent, knowledge, or ability is especially dangerous at this time.

9. Resentment. Our temper may be triggered easily as a result of being unusually sensitive to our obligations or the pressures placed on us by others. Resistance to change and reform, cynicism, and sarcasm may be a few of the forms this resentment takes.

10. A false sense of security. Certain trends and circumstances in our life may become deceptively silent and quiet, especially in comparison to all the noise of Scorpio. This must not lull us into a false sense of security, however. The problem may well remain at inner dimensions, even though the outer conditions are more quiet. We should therefore continue to work to resolve the basic problem.

11. False generosity. Insincere people will be even more prone than usual to act in an apparently helpful way with their words and gestures, but not follow through with their hearts and minds. Many will deceive themselves by thinking that they are

338

acting in magnanimous ways, when in actual fact they are only being patronizing.

12. Forcefulness. Sagittarius has a way of bringing out the boldness and aggressiveness of people. This may cause them to be more forceful in their self-expression and dealings with others than is necessary or appropriate, leading to misunderstandings, hurt feelings, and insults.

13. Instability. As the energies of Sagittarius stimulate our character, unseen or repressed patterns of behavior may be magnified as well, "rocking the boat" for no apparent reason. As a result, unless we have been in the regular habit of examining our "inner territory," and know what is there and what is not, we may experience headaches, uneasy feelings, or a general malaise without having any idea why. The tides of mass consciousness may also be more influential than normal.

14. Extremism. Sagittarius is meant to be a time when we strive for balance, but not everyone does. Some people overdose on aspiration and become self-righteous and fanatical on certain issues. Singlemindedness is a virtue, especially in the spiritual aspirant, but it must be balanced by sensible emotions and reason, so that our self-expression is aligned with the noblest elements within us—not extremist positions.

15. Disillusionment. Glamours and illusions of all kinds will be heightened at this time, and there is an enormous temptation to pursue the shallow life. But the forces of Sagittarius will tend to puncture these glamours and illusions and force us to look at reality. This is commonly known as "disillusionment"— a healthy process, actually, but one that the personality tends to melodramatize. If we are to grasp the new directions emerging at this time, we must take care to discern reality as it is—not as we would like it to be.

16. Self-pity. Sagittarius brings insights about our potential as a spiritual being, and this means there is a definite possibility of glimpsing what might have been, if we had played our cards

with greater wisdom. This may lead some to wallow in destructive self-pity, or indulge in an orgy of blaming others for their own mistakes. The spiritual aspirant should recognize the harmfulness of this and work instead to free up the personality for more enlightened action and thought in the future.

17. Ignorance. One of the worst mistakes which can be made during Sagittarius is to turn our back on the larger implications of any situation and pretend they do not matter. These larger implications represent the doorway to our growth and expansion during Sagittarius.

18. Fear. Our sensitivity is heightened, and if we have made no effort to discipline and focus it, it may well fall prey to excessive fear and anxiety. If this becomes a problem, the only real solution is to work on a daily basis to cultivate faith and hope in such large measures that they overwhelm and eliminate our fears and anxieties.

19. Erratic behavior. The tendency of this time is to move forward in spurts rather than with smooth consistency. This can easily have an unsettling effect, which can be magnified by overreacting to it, either in ourself or in others. If our own behavior is erratic, it may be because our intentions and motives are not properly coordinated, and we are approaching our activities with ambivalence, doubt, and hesitation. In such cases, it is our own lack of strong values and commitments which is generating our erratic behavior. By working to redefine our purpose and values, we can achieve greater consistency in our actions.

THE OPPORTUNITIES OF SAGITTARIUS

The opportunities of this time generally lie in our ability to mobilize spiritual force and project it from the realm of theory into our daily self-expression. To whatever degree we can focus our skills and efforts on meaningful accomplishment, in harmony with the plan of the soul, we create a new momentum of opportunity and success. Sagittarius is a time for giving pragmatic focus to our highest aspirations and ideals. But this means considering each major area of our self-expression, contemplating the ways we can blend in more of the new directions of spirit and then formulating specific goals which will serve this purpose. In this way, we launch our "arrow."

Specific opportunities of Sagittarius include:

1. Cleansing and purification. As we tap new levels of meaning, we begin to see that most of the problems we have faced have resulted from our own selfish orientation, incomplete understanding, or misdirected attitudes. To harness the new levels of meaning, therefore, we must cleanse and purify our consciousness. But this is not just an exercise in self-restraint or inhibition. Correctly done, the cleansing of consciousness revitalizes and refreshes us, just as taking a shower helps wake us up physically.

At the spiritual level, we can cleanse ourself by renewing our dedication to serving spirit.

At the mental level, we can cleanse ourself by refining our priorities, values, and patterns of behavior.

Emotionally, we can cleanse ourself by exercising our ability to forgive others, heal emotional wounds, and reduce irritability.

Physically, we can cleanse ourself by building new and better forms of self-expression.

In these ways, we can revitalize our desire to make a worthwhile contribution through the work we do, our relationships, and our personal interests. We can also cleanse away any lingering patterns of defeat, purposelessness, or martyrdom.

2. A new revelation of our fate. To most people, fate is something the ambitious person must conquer and tame, but this is a serious misunderstanding. To the spiritual person, our fate is the fabric of our opportunity for achievement and contri-

bution. As we work to define who we are and what we are doing, we learn important new insights into just what our fate is, and how best we can work with it in seizing the opportunities of the coming year.

3. Compassion. As we understand more about our own destiny and what the soul requires of us, it becomes possible to see the real potential of others and what they must do to tap it. Through this kind of realization, we can develop a true measure of compassion toward others—a deeper respect for the noble elements within them, as well as a stronger measure of benevolent concern for their well-being.

4. Brotherhood. Sagittarius focuses our attention on our individuality and selfhood, but always with the goal of helping us see ourself from a higher perspective. This higher perspective includes not just ourself as an individual but also the role we play in the universe. We are part of a larger body of consciousness, and this larger body is linked together through the bond of brotherhood. It is therefore useful to take time to contemplate what the force of brotherhood actually is—and how it enriches and adds many new dimensions to our life.

5. Self-healing. Those who have been tormented by doubts will find Sagittarius a good time to rediscover the patterns of intelligence and meaning which will restore their faith and trust. This will not happen automatically, of course; we must initiate the work of self-healing by searching for these insights and focusing their power in our ideas and convictions.

6. A greater sense of mission. Sagittarius stimulates our capacity to set goals and follow the direction of experience and growth set by our own destiny. When this is combined with an expanded awareness of our potential for greatness, the result is a better grasp of our spiritual mission in life.

7. Clarity of thinking. For those who have developed the mental faculties, Sagittarius will stimulate and enhance both rational and intuitive thinking. Time spent in reflection on the

342

meaning of events and opportunities will very likely produce important new insights. Even for people who have not pursued the development of the intuition, common sense and empathy with others will be stronger.

8. Friendship. Sagittarius promotes a deeper level of sharing in friendships and other relationships, including work and professional relationships. It reveals common points of humanity we share with others, and how we can build on them.

9. Optimism. Because Sagittarius helps us appreciate more fully the talents and strengths of character we already have, it will be possible to build a stronger sense of optimism for the future. It will also be possible to remove the various inhibitions which have obscured our psychological vision in the past, letting us see more clearly the hope and potential for the future as well as the potential greatness within us.

10. The right use of material resources. There is a marvelous opportunity at this time to review our use of money and the values and principles that guide the way in which we express ourself materially. Most people spend money to indulge their ego, and so it enslaves them. The spiritual aspirant needs to learn to be guided by the principles of productivity, generosity, and growth in his or her use of money and material resources.

11. Harmony. There are many ways to focus harmony in Sagittarius—in relationships, at work, and in the way we interact with our environment. But the most important is to establish and sustain a harmonious response to the ideals and principles we serve. This is the heart of all opportunity at this time.

In a curious way, there is also a provocative opportunity to become more aware of the workings of the "harmony of the spheres." This will not apply to everyone, but does contain a hint which may be of value to some.

12. Transcendence. If our aspiration is strong enough, Sagittarius can become a time of genuine transcendence, as we begin working with the transcendent elements of life. This will

343

most typically print out as a stronger appreciation for the larger perspective on specific situations—the "soul's point of view." But it may also involve a new ability to work directly with divine qualities such as harmony, goodwill, joy, and wisdom.

13. Dignity. Our sense of personal honor is heightened, and we begin to see it is a privilege to serve the higher principles and ideals of life. This, in turn, can give us a renewed sense of self-esteem and a deeper awareness of our connections with spirit.

14. A fresh measure of hope. Hope can be thought of as the higher correspondence of faith and optimism, which are primarily emotional attitudes. Hope springs from the awakening of our higher faculties and new insight into our plan and future. It is perhaps the greatest gift of Sagittarius. But to achieve this new measure of hope, we must be willing to stretch ourself beyond our current limitations. This is no time for smallmindedness or pettiness, for these attitudes shrink the mind. We must act with a nobler purpose than ever before, a greater capacity for goodwill and tolerance than ever before, a stronger measure of peace and patience than ever before, and a higher level of comprehension than ever before. The old and comfortable ways will no longer suffice. We are headed toward a peak experience or rebirth that will change many of the rules and formats in which we work—and it would be shortsighted indeed to think that the old style of handling problems and the wealth of our accumulated experience will be sufficient for the challenges ahead. We must expand to new dimensions. As we do, we generate a fresh measure of hope. We must invest this hope wisely in our future.

TUNING INTO THE FORCES OF SAGITTARIUS

The forces of Sagittarius are practical in focus. Tuning into them requires much the same kind of focus. To work effectively with these energies, we must be able to balance our *aspiration* with our *self-expression.* Our awareness of the inner life is heightened, but we should not become so absorbed in it that we withdraw from responsibilities or "space out." We are meant to aspire to a more enlightened capacity to act in the world and bring heaven to earth. In this way, we achieve balance.

One of the best ways to tune into the forces of this time, therefore, is to examine our goals and where they are leading us. Is this where we want to go? Is this where the soul wants us to go? Are we pursuing our goals haphazardly—or intelligently?

As we proceed with this review, we may be able to use our intuition to gain glimpses of the future. By taking a plan and considering alternative ways of reaching our goals, we may receive impressions that some approaches will be more successful than others. There is also the likelihood that certain events will be omens portending the future. The challenge, of course, is to interpret such omens correctly.

The best way to teach in Sagittarius is by radiating light—by illumining the mind with the light of wisdom, insight, and knowledge—and inspiring others to respect the truth.

The best way to heal is by shattering glamours and illusions, replacing them with a strong devotion to reality.

The best way to lead is by revealing a new direction which unites the group with a stronger sense of common purpose.

The work done in Sagittarius lays the groundwork for Capricorn and Pisces. The arrow launched toward the heavens in Sagittarius draws a response like lightning in Capricorn—and guides us to a more profound sense of service in Pisces.

A SONG FOR SAGITTARIUS

Two pillars stand as gateway between the desert and the fertile ground. The breach between the pillars is many leagues in breadth. To the inhabitants of the desert, the pillars are a gateway to a great void, for they can see nothing through the breach.

Long eons pass, until the time is ready. Then, an arrow, streaming fire behind, shoots through the pillars, piercing the heart of the desert. The inhabitants gather to inspect it, and for the first time know that something lies beyond the pillars—something which shot this arrow. The arrow seems full of power and promise, and stirs great interest. But further eons pass before it is proposed: why not send the arrow back?

A great debate ensues. Some say it would destroy the pillars forever, and thus the cosmos. Others are enchanted by the arrow, and would not give it up. Eventually, the arrowshooters win. Together, the inhabitants of the desert work to shape a giant bow, strong enough to launch the arrow. They shoot it forth, bisecting the pillars once again.

As the arrow flies, it heals the breach—and reveals the fertile ground, to the wonder of the dwellers of the desert. Passing through the pillars, they follow the arrow to where it has landed, pointing to yet another set of pillars in the misty distance.

A PARABLE FOR SAGITTARIUS

A foolish man had the habit of riding his donkey from town to town in a most peculiar manner: he never followed the straight roads, but always wandered erratically through the countryside, often covering two or three times the necessary distance. Many people laughed at him for this odd way of traveling—but then, what would one expect from a fool?

One day, a well-meaning friend offered the fool a compass. "This will help you find your direction, so you can travel in straight lines." To the friend's surprise, however, the foolish man refused the gift. The friend asked why.

"If I ever start traveling in straight lines," the fool replied simply, "people would stop thinking I was foolish."

15

Capricorn

CAPRICORN

Keynote: New initiative.

Mantra: "I build upon a solid foundation of light."

New moon focus: The vision of the work unfinished.

Full moon focus: The vision of service unbegun.

Rays 1, 3, 5, and 7 dominate.

Primary archetypal forces:

Unification, patience, order, reverence, majesty

A Prayer For Capricorn:

O heavenly Mother-Father God, help us seize the opportunities of this time to act as agents of Your plan.

Fill us with the strength we need to take new initiatives in serving the life of spirit.

Fill us with the dedication we need to honor and manifest our inner wisdom and purpose, and to use these forces to transform our life and character.

Fill us with the vision we need in order to penetrate the blind spots still within us, so we may recognize the light of spirit and see how it can be focused here on earth.

May we walk in the presence of Your benevolence, so that we, too, can learn to act benevolently.

All this we ask so that we may better serve Your plan of light and love.

Like a bolt of lightning from the heavens, the forces of Capricorn will stir up our life, challenging us to face the real issues of life and set in motion new initiatives. These lightning bolts will bring disruption to some, but a new focus for work and self-improvement to others. In some cases, they will force old issues to a conclusion, but only so the next phase can begin with a clean slate. In other cases, they will recharge our psychological batteries with a greater measure of spiritual strength than ever before. So even though these lightning bolts may be shattering, they will not be destructive; if we respond intelligently to the changes of this time, we will find that Capricorn brings us many new revelations and opens up many new possibilities.

The average person, of course, does not like to have his or her comfortable world disrupted and shattered, and will tend to view the sudden changes of Capricorn as unsettling, perhaps even threatening. But the spiritual aspirant will find that his or her capacity for perseverance is greatly increased—that with the disruptions of this time also comes a much greater capacity to triumph over adversity. Capricorn is, in fact, an excellent time to test our personal strength and discover just what inner resources we can call on and rely on.

If we meet the lightning bolts of Capricorn with patience and intelligence, therefore, we will be able to glean the full benefit of this time. For as they shake up the limiting conditions of our life, they simultaneously expose the light of new purpose, insight, and direction in our work, relationships, and growth.

Capricorn will call on us to make certain sacrifices in order to take advantage of its full potential for progress. We may have to give up cherished beliefs, comfortable habits, wornout philosophies, or relationships which have exhausted their purpose. Change often means exchange—not just the simplistic adding on of something pleasant. If we see the time of Capricorn as an opportunity to exchange old elements of our life for something new and better, we will be able to handle the challenges of this time with calmness and detachment. Even more importantly, if we can greet the emerging directions of our life with enthusiasm, we can sail through the appearance of adversity with dignity.

In this regard, it is helpful to understand that the forces of Capricorn encourage us to launch new initiatives. A lot of dead wood has been cleared away during Virgo, Libra, Scorpio, and Sagittarius, and Capricorn will bring this effort to completion. Even though we may not yet be able to recognize it, this has simplified our focus at work and in life in general, so that we can concentrate more effectively on the important issues before us. But this does not guarantee that we will respond in this way. It is still left to us to focus the initiative and momentum we need to carry us into the next phase of our creativity and development.

From an esoteric point of view, the work of Capricorn is to bring to our attention unfinished business and unresolved conflicts, so that we can carry them to a proper conclusion. If we do not cooperate intelligently with this aspect of Capricorn, it may mean that some of our ongoing problems will have to get so bad that they erupt into crisis. It is the story of Humpty-Dumpty brought to life in our own experience. Humpty-Dumpty would be those conditions of life we have refused to change. Capricorn knocks them off the wall and they are shattered into thousands of fragments, so that not even all the king's horses and all the king's men can put them back together. We have no choice but to leave them behind and get on with the rest of our life.

The force that knocks Humpty-Dumpty off the wall is really nothing more than a sudden movement from inertia to a burst of energy—from yin to yang, as the Chinese would express it—and consequently nothing to fear. In fact, those people who are already oriented to taking new initiatives will be in full control of these forces. But those who just passively drift with the flow of events may find Capricorn rather destabilizing.

Capricorn can be thought of like a divine weaver, who takes the strands of destiny and weaves them into a cloak of self-expression. The patterns of our life, the structure of our ideas, the framework of society, and even the fabric of cosmic life all take shape on the loom of Capricorn. If we are attentive to these patterns and strive to understand their structure—and how it is changing—there is much we can learn at this time.

For this reason, *experience* is of major significance. The forces of Capricorn draw us into new experiences which broaden the scope of our understanding and involvement in life. If we are alert, we can see how these new experiences fit into the ongoing fabric of our life, and learn from them a great deal about the larger patterns of who we are and what we are doing.

Each experience has a lesson of its own, of course, and we should be alert to this as well during Capricorn. The business person may be drawn into a series of experiences which provide new insights into the way the public views his or her policies. The "tough negotiator" may be drawn into experiences where he or she learns the value of compassion. The cynic may be drawn into experiences where he or she is forced to rely on and appreciate the goodwill of others. The spiritual aspirant may be drawn into experiences where he or she learns that good works and practical intelligence must be added to faith and aspiration.

But the experiences of Capricorn have a deeper meaning as well—it is time to act. An analogy from the world of business is appropriate in this regard. Having planned a new product and worked out all the preliminary details, it is now time to go into production. The last nine months have introduced us to a number of new themes and possibilities for each of us. We are more or less aware of these possibilities, depending on how diligently we have worked to contact and understand the forces which gave rise to them. But now, in Capricorn, it is time to move out of the realm of theory and speculation. It is time to bring these new directions into manifestation. It is time to *ground* our values, ideals, and plans.

The concept of grounding is a subject of universal importance, for we all need to learn to extract from the seemingly vague and nebulous realms of the inner dimensions whatever is useful and practical and give it focus as a dynamic force in our life. We need to translate our good ideas into achievements and concretize our philosophy and values into definite paths of action.

For this reason, the best preparation for Capricorn is to work carefully at the level of the mind to recognize, as they arise, practical opportunities which will advance our major goals in living. This will only be possible, however, if we have identified our short and long range goals and have prepared ourself to take advantage of the opportunities which arise for meeting them.

In a very real sense, the universe has done its job; the forces of the zodiac have created precisely the conditions we need in order to ground our inner values and ideals and expand the sphere of our effective responsibility. Now *we* must act. No one or no thing can thwart us, if we are determined to involve ourself more intelligently in the work at hand. Only our failure to act can obstruct the forward progress which can be ours at this time.

Let us therefore nurture the opportunities and responsibilities which constitute the work at hand, and help them flourish. This is not a time for sitting idly by, waiting for someone else to take the initiative. It is a time for taking action.

THE SYMBOLISM OF CAPRICORN

The most common symbol for Capricorn is the goat. In some traditions, it is depicted as a sea-goat or crocodile. The esoteric symbol, according to Alice Bailey, is the unicorn, in which the two horns of the goat have been fused into one.

The goat symbolizes the forces of Capricorn which emphasize the materialistic and desire side of mankind—selfishness, earthiness, and degradation. Indeed, Capricorn is a time when the vulgar often becomes more vulgar. Conversely, it is also a time when the very best can be expressed in its full glory. The goat does not just give into vulgarity; he transforms it. This is symbolized by its habit of eating all manner of garbage and transforming it into his sustenance.

Like the goat, the crocodile of ancient Egypt lived on refuse thrown in the Nile. But it acts out the theme of transformation in another way as well, through its ability to rise out of the water and walk on land. In this way, the crocodile represents the personality's capacity to evolve into a spiritual being of light.

The unicorn symbolizes the crowning glory of transformation—the one who will sacrifice himself so others may grow.

While not usually tied to Capricorn, the star of Christmas is also a good symbol for this sign. The Christ came to earth to demonstrate the light within us all, and what it means to embody heavenly light in a human form. Taking something as abstract as light and giving it form through our work, relationships, and daily activities is a transformation of the highest degree. The star also reminds us that the enlightenment of the personality occurs through the cultivation and use of the mind. In this way, it picks up one of the symbolic themes of the unicorn, which concentrates the light of the mind in its horn—symbolizing illumination and integration of the personality. And indeed, one of the results of Capricorn is to stimulate the mind, thereby opening up the higher levels of human expression.

HOW THE FORCES OF CAPRICORN AFFECT US

The impact of the lightning bolts of Capricorn on our consciousness can also be compared to the force of an ax striking a log, splitting it in two. From the perspective of the man wielding the ax, this represents the power to achieve productive results, as symbolized by the splitting of the wood, which can be used as fuel for a fire. From a less enlightened perspective, however— say, from the point of view of the log—the impact of the forces of Capricorn may *seem* divisive or even destructive.

In the average person, immaturity will become more flagrant, ambitiousness will be heightened, bad habits will be strengthened and become more addictive, the emotions will be irritable, impulsive, and stubborn, and dullness will become the ruling force. It will be perfectly obvious what *needs* to be transformed—but little if anything will be done about it.

In the spiritual aspirant, the active mind will be greatly stimulated, leading to new capacities for analysis, discrimination, problem solving, and creativity. If the aspirant allows the mind to rule, and seeks to cooperate fully with its greater capacity to make sense of life, he can establish a rhythm with the swinging ax which will lead to heightened productivity.

In the advanced person, a new appreciation of selfhood is stimulated, allowing him to discover more fully the inner meanings of his birthright as a noble child of God. As the advanced person integrates this new appreciation into his self-respect, values, and dedication to serve, he discovers that he is the one that wields the ax—and he does so with purpose, authority, and self-assurance. His force is properly directed toward an enlightened goal—building the fire.

The effect of the forces of Capricorn on our **motivation** will be to give us a stronger interest in the work of transformation. The primary transformation humans must make is to move away from a selfish, materialistic motivation toward a more loving, spiritual expression. This is a constant theme of Capricorn and has many practical applications.

We can transform the physical body from a tool for sensory indulgence, motivated by greed, desire, and lust, into a vehicle for creative activity and productivity.

We can transform the emotions from a selfish barometer of

feelings and moods into a warm, loving expression of goodwill, charity, hope, and companionship.

We can transform the mind from a collector of knowledge into an active, living source of light and wisdom.

We can transform our relationships from issues of convenience into opportunities for genuine caring and sharing.

We can transform our work from a drudgery into an opportunity for self-expression, responsibility, and competence.

The effect of Capricorn on our **awareness** is to make us much more aware of gaps and differences. The energies of Capricorn tend to drive wedges and divisions into the heart of our affairs. This will be apparent at all levels—in groups, our own self-esteem, ideas, personal labors, and relationships. But these wedges will not necessarily weaken the overall purpose being served. In fact, they are meant to strengthen it, just as splitting a log is meant to serve the purpose of building a fire.

The splits of Capricorn will not produce schisms so much as the animation of certain pairs of opposites which have been dormant. The result will be the arousing of new opportunities and creative potential, but also new challenges and problems. An example of the splitting action of Capricorn would be the case of two people drawing different conclusions from the same evidence. If they respond immaturely to this division, they will become opponents, each believing himself right and the other wrong. The more mature response, by contrast, may be to see that both interpretations contribute in part to a complete understanding of the underlying truth of the evidence.

In terms of awareness, the stimulation of the mind which will occur in Capricorn will produce many new insights and lead to a new level of determination to be productive, but may also lead to resistance and rebellion from the emotions. This split could become quite serious, unless we work to reconcile the division by discovering the reason for the rebellion, removing it, and strengthening our ideals and values.

The effect of the forces of Capricorn on the **mind** will be to promote precision and accuracy. If the shoe does not fit, Capricorn is not the time to hobble about and get blisters. It is a time to buy a proper shoe. Many people will get blisters by retaining old habits of carelessness and thoughtlessness in thought, word, and deed—but if we seek to use the mind according to its design, we will find a much greater capacity than usual for precision, accuracy, and carefulness in our thinking.

The effect of the forces of Capricorn on the **emotions** will be to stimulate any area of emotional immaturity, which will then conflict stridently with the areas of our maturity, threatening to spoil the good that we would do. Yet it is important to sense the real drama of these conflicts. If we can give up our immaturity and forge new skills of talent and strength, we will in effect bring the old cycle of immaturity to an end and inaugurate a new cycle of opportunity, interest, responsiveness, and activity.

The effect of the forces of Capricorn on our **self-expression** is to stir up our interest in acting and doing something useful with our skills and talents. The focus of Capricorn is on working productively and creatively with what we have. In fact, physical activities will be so energized that we must take care that they are linked with adequate plans; there would be danger in engaging in an enthusiastic burst of work which served no purpose. We must also take care not to approach our work in an excessively mechanical and unthinking manner.

THE CHALLENGES OF CAPRICORN

Capricorn will ask us a fundamental question: what are we doing to manifest our ideals and values in daily life? What practical steps are we taking to involve ourself more fully in the work of mankind and to initiate new projects or activities which increase our expression of the inner life?

This is therefore a time for attending to "the work at hand," seeking always to approach it with the maximum measure of inspiration and love, even while pursuing pragmatic achievements. Capricorn is an earth sign, and it encourages practical and pragmatic approaches to the work before us, putting the emphasis on organizing resources, coordinating efforts, and increasing productivity.

In this regard, it will be useful to evaluate just what "the work at hand" is, for not only will it define the challenge in contacting and establishing a better rapport with the higher self, but actually all of the challenges of this time.

For parents, the work at hand involves helping their children become more mature, aware of their talents, motivated to achieve, and responsive to spirit. The challenge to parents, therefore, is to teach their children to take initiative in these areas of life.

In our relationships with others, the work at hand is to heal wounded relationships and establish healthier bonds—to place the emphasis on what we have in common with other people and build upon this solid foundation. The challenge of relationships, therefore, is to work together toward common goals.

In the business world, the work at hand is to find ways to improve the conditions of the workplace, to set in motion plans for the coming year, to develop new commercial ventures, to refine business ethics, and to achieve greater efficiency. The challenge to business, therefore, is to discover the inner forces and principles motivating the economy in general and an industry or company in specific, and work to honor these inner forces more fully in pragmatic ways.

In society as a whole, the work at hand is to build upon the foundation of tradition and custom which is the fabric of civilization, and push humanity forward into its next phase of experience and growth. The challenge to society, therefore, is to realize that it has a destiny which it is meant to fulfill, and to move more consciously toward the goals which unite us all.

In terms of our personal growth, the work at hand is to honor the best within us and around us, and to initiate changes which will enable these elements of our life to become more dominant. In this regard, the work at hand consists of:

• Improving that which is already a strong part of our character. We should look for character traits which already are self-renewing and enduring. Habits of integrity, goodwill, steadfastness, courage, self-respect, tolerance, and patience are examples of traits that have proven their value again and again. As we seek out these enduring qualities and apply them consciously in our daily thought and action, we center ourself in a stable core of health and intelligence.

• Developing new avenues of creative expression. Even though we are usually threatened by changing conditions, the odds are much greater that change and new cycles will bring us fresh opportunity, not disaster.

• Honoring the cherished traditions of society and the primary groups we belong to. Important traditions which are the basis for social interaction can help bring order, unity, and security in changing times, especially if we view these traditions as the *foundation* for moving toward a well-ordered life.

As we respond to the challenge to focus on this work and complete it, we will discover more fully what the Christ meant by His statement that "the kingdom of heaven is at hand."

THE PROBLEMS OF CAPRICORN

The problems of this time will tend to arise from the inertia of our life—areas in which we have allowed the momentum of life to slow down, in which we have permitted our conscience to become deadened, or in which we have lost interest and failed to fulfill our responsibilities. In order to stir up new initiative and progress, Capricorn must shake up these deadened areas. But in so doing, it will also awaken the force of our inertia and resistance, thereby setting the stage for a number of problems:

1. Embarrassment. We may suddenly realize that we have been acting improperly in some aspect of life, and become deeply embarrassed—because we were the last one to see it. The potential for embarrassment and humiliation is also especially high in terms of the assumptions we have made about what others expect and enjoy. It is important not to compound embarrassment, if it occurs, with defensiveness or the effort to cover up. A straightforward apology for the error is enough—and then we should get on with new business.

2. Grimness. Perseverance in the face of adversity is a virtue in Capricorn, but grim determination and humorless endurance are not. Yet when confronted with the need to persevere, most people respond with grimness rather than the strength of their spiritual self. This, however, plunges them into materialism. We should make sure that the substance of our strength and power to persevere is derived from the treasures of spirit, not the forces of the earth.

3. Intransigence. Some people sidestep the need for perseverance simply by withdrawing into stubbornness—they become as immovable as a rock. But rocks are notably not human, being neither loving nor intelligent. We should understand that intransigence is almost never a healthy approach to any problem; in fact, it magnifies the underlying conflict and drives those who might help us further away.

4. Confusion. There may well be times in Capricorn when we are uncertain about what stand to take or what to do next. The experiences of Capricorn often unfold in hard-to-predict ways, and we may have to take the next step without knowing for sure where it will lead us. In addition, we may find that old methods will not work as effectively as they once did. The only way to overcome this problem is to make sure that we take each

step with a dedication to doing the right thing. If we act on instinct, or just respond blindly, we could end up in a lot of trouble. The person who acts from a clear set of values, however, has little trouble piercing the confusion of this time.

5. Misanthropy. There is a tremendous potential for isolation and the cynical rejection of the trust and goodwill of others at this time. Even if we are affected only a little bit by this kind of attitude, it is still a poison which eats away at our basic humanity. It is therefore very important to nurture compassion, goodwill, and generosity in our dealings with others.

6. Selfishness. The "every man for himself" syndrome is heightened at this time, and this can produce an intensification of selfish desire. Even intelligent people will have a tendency to respond more to instinct and the lowest common denominator than to spiritual qualities and the nobility within themselves. It is therefore a good idea to spend extra time cultivating altruistic values and a generous heart.

7. Bigotry. Stereotyped and narrow modes of thinking will be common. We must not let preconceived prejudices blind us to the real dynamics of any situation, relationship, or issue, however, lest we miss opportunities for our own development.

8. A sense of loss or waste. Those who identify with their possessions and personal habits may be paralyzed by a crushing sense of loss or waste. But we will actually not lose anything of value during Capricorn, even though it may seem that we do. There is a strong need at this time for cultivating the "impersonal life"—the capacity to view the ups and downs of life with detachment and an awareness of the larger plan which is unfolding and carrying us forward into the future.

9. Apathy. If we become exhausted from working too hard, or simply assume that the work ahead is too much to bear, we may be tempted to relax our focus so much that we become apathetic. If this occurs, it is important not to dwell just on the specific tasks ahead and our own role in completing them. In-

stead, we should take a practical look at what must be done and balance this against our inner values and creative resources. It may in fact be necessary to gather new creative strength before apathy can be overcome.

10. Manipulation. The urge to manipulate and boss other people around will be strong. Nagging, meanness, and cruelty will likewise increase, as we view life through our own perspective and demand that others conform to it. But this kind of behavior irritates others and makes us unhappy with ourself. We need to accept others as they are and act with tolerance.

11. Naivete. The simpleminded tendency to propose simplistic solutions to complex problems will be heightened, as the lure of superficiality eclipses, at least temporarily, the deeper issues involved. We must not be blinded by cliches and platitudes, but study the implications of problems at every level.

12. Entrapment. We can fall prey to a powerful sense of being trapped in Capricorn, as we overestimate the strength of the limitations imposed on us by the nature of our work and our standing in the community. This may produce a great deal of frustration and doubt, undermining our reservoir of optimism. However, this sense of entrapment is largely a form of blindness imposed on us by our own superficiality. We can break out of the trap by renewing our vision of the future, our talents, and our initiative—and by acting appropriately.

13. Instability. Problems which have been left unattended may suddenly become critical, absorbing far more of our time and attention than we had expected. There is a strong likelihood that outer events may upset our inner equilibrium, unless it is well-established and *maintained* at this time.

14. Alienation. There is a strong potential for feeling isolated or even ostracized—rejected by others or at least "marching to the sounds of a different drummer." In particular, those who are striving to rise out of materialistic priorities may at times feel out of step—and there may also be some who feel that

only their efforts count and that no one can, or will, help them. But there is danger in these attitudes; if we become too isolated in our focus, we may fail to appreciate the role we are meant to play as a member of society. In fact, we may even become rebellious, taking the attitude that "if they aren't with me, they must be against me." This rebelliousness is best neutralized by maintaining a steady faith in the value of our life and work, and by appreciating that what we stand for and do has value not only to ourself, but to others and God as well.

15. Depression. Feelings of depression often increase in Capricorn, as we fall short in our efforts to maintain our vision of the beauty and strength of the inner life. There is therefore a need to cultivate our own sense of individuality and to focus the strength of our self-determination in such a way that we are able to begin enjoying life again.

16. Vanity. A great deal of emphasis will be put on outer appearances and the image of success, in lieu of cultivating inner maturity and wisdom. As a result, a lot of silliness will be generated during Capricorn, as shallow people try to impress one another with the appearance of substance and character.

17. Sentimentality. Certain people will put far too much emphasis on their feelings, thirsting for "warm fuzzies" and wanting other people to "stroke" them, especially in group situations. The "all for one and one for all" syndrome will be heightened, especially in corporate settings and society. But this is more commonly a distraction from the work at hand than a benefit, since it is almost always limited to the emotional level. The enlightened person will look beyond mere gratification of the emotions and will keep focused on productive achievement.

18. Acts of sabotage. There may be acts of sabotage, including not only chaotic acts of vandalism but also psychological sabotage as well. This could be something as simple as a series of obscene phone calls—or something as subtle as one person trying to tear down and undermine the accomplishments of others.

There may also be an increase of vandalism and terrorism at the international level. Any tendency toward sabotage or chaos should be stoutly resisted, with a sense of fairness and justice.

THE OPPORTUNITIES OF CAPRICORN

The opportunities of this sign come to us as we penetrate beyond the outer conditions of life and tap new revelations and spiritual power. If we drag our feet, we may be pushed forcefully into these opportunities, and only realize after the fact that they were indeed opportunities and not restrictions. But if we take the initiative to meet the challenges of Capricorn, we will see from the outset the rich possibilities of these opportunities.

Some opportunities of this period will also emerge from within, as insights and mystical experiences lift the veil of our awareness of the inner life. This could be a shock, of course, if we discovered something about ourself which disturbed us. But even if the discovery is unpleasant, it is an opportunity—an opportunity to grow in awareness and maturity.

Indeed, the most important opportunity of Capricorn is often our chance to establish a new and closer relationship with the inner side of our life, as well as the inner life of others. In order to take advantage of this opportunity, however, we must be properly aligned with the inner life, looking for ways to cooperate with the changes and new cycles which are unfolding, seeking to translate the power and purpose of the inner life into our own self-expression and creative projects.

The purpose of Capricorn is to help us refine our ability to work with the pure essence of divine energies even while immersed in imperfect or stagnant conditions. The creative applications of Capricorn are therefore great. And if we work correctly with the energies of this time, we will not be the same person at the end of the month as we were at the beginning.

The most significant opportunities of Capricorn are:

1. Increased strength. Capricorn provides us with an unusually great opportunity to invoke new measures of strength and support from the higher self—for our work, relationships, and personal growth. In a very real sense, this increased strength will have the power to refresh our consciousness and renew our initiative.

2. Greater efficiency. The forces of this time likewise cause us to draw together our resources and find a better, more efficient focus in using them. Through new plans and a better coordination of our goals, we will find that we are able to streamline our efforts and become more productive. The key to this effort is *simplicity*. The more we avoid complicating issues and keep to the barest essentials, the more effectively we can operate. This opportunity can also lead to a higher level of coordination between our thoughts and feelings, as we discard ambivalent attitudes and ambiguous beliefs and focus on what is really important and meaningful to us.

3. Self-approval. There is an excellent opportunity for self-approval and greater self-esteem, as we review the pattern of our experiences and see what we have actually accomplished in life—in our work, relationships, spiritual growth, and service. This is usually far more than we give ourself credit for, especially if we are the type of person who broods excessively on our problems and weaknesses while disregarding our successes. If we reverse this tendency, however, and set aside some time in Capricorn for intelligent self-approval, we will find that we gain many new insights into the meaning of what we have done.

In this respect, it is also a good time for parents to help their children build up their self-approval mechanism, and to realize that this is one of the most important ways we generate the strength for self-initiative and personal accomplishment.

4. A nurturing attitude. There is great value in taking a maternal, nurturing attitude toward our work and career, lov-

ing the goals we have set and the purposes we serve through our profession or major life focus. We should view the work we do as an offspring of our creative or productive talent, and realize that we have a responsibility for caring for it, preserving it, and helping it grow and develop, so it can reach full maturity.

5. Self-control. Because outer events are prone to cause turmoil and disruption, Capricorn is an excellent time to learn the value of self-control and an impersonal response to life. We will have to choose many times between *acting* and *reacting*, and will also be given many object lessons in self-control by witnessing the hysterical reactions of others. There is great virtue in preserving our self-control at this time and acting like a mature adult, not an immature child.

6. Planning. Capricorn is an excellent time for revising our plans and reshaping our goals, and for coordinating both of them with a renewed sense of purpose. The so-called "New Year's resolutions" that many people make are usually just an expression of wishful thinking; they do not embody sincerity or dedication. But we can use this time profitably to intelligently forge new and more effective plans for self-expression.

7. An intuitive sense of correct principles. The tendency of the forces of Capricorn to foster pragmatism will also stimulate a deeper understanding of the principles of successful living. Even though it arises from the intuition, the awareness of these principles will seem to develop just as a matter of common sense—something which becomes obvious as the result of thoughtful reflection on our immediate concerns. If we take time to search within ourself for these principles of success, we will be richly rewarded.

8. Practical intelligence. While Capricorn is not a time for flights of fancy or wild bursts of imagination, it is a time when the mind is stimulated and able to make sense of the practical challenges of our work and responsibilities. During Capricorn, the mind has the opportunity to fulfill its potential for bring-

ing the light of the inner levels into expression on earth.

9. Productivity. The urge to be productive and make a meaningful contribution will be exceptionally strong, but we must take care that this does not merely become the demand to produce results. We must make sure that our building efforts are truly constructive, not just the superficial appearance of success.

10. Testing our limits. Sometimes we need to explore how much we can do and what we cannot do, in order to determine the most effective focus for our work and the most efficient pace at which to do it. This testing then permits us to allocate our time and energy more wisely, as well as helping us recognize our most valuable and reliable talents.

11. Refinement of work habits. In the same way, Capricorn is a good time to review our daily work routines and evaluate how well these routines serve our true objectives and efficiency. Many habits outlive their usefulness once conditions change; others become a hindrance as we grow in competence. This is a good time to clean out patterns no longer serving our needs.

12. Security. Capricorn provides a good opportunity to review realistically what we need to do in order to make our life, career, and most important relationships more secure. The search for security can easily become a trap for the chronically anxious and fearful, however, so care must be taken to look for our real needs for security—not at what we fear.

13. Right remembrance. Memory plays an important role in Capricorn. Esoterically, memory is the key to the structure of thought and habit. We build up habits by repeating a certain kind of expression until a pattern is formed that we automatically "remember." To change the habit, we must rebuild the structure. Capricorn is an excellent time to use memory as a key to evaluating the structure of how we think and act. The average person, of course, will simply relive the memories which arise, basking in the pleasant ones, suffering through the unpleasant ones. But the enlightened person will see the patterns of

memory which arise at this time as valuable clues to what must be dealt with—clues to talents, areas of growth, problems, and opportunities which need attention. The purpose of this evaluation is not so much to journey into the past as it is to restructure the foundation of our thinking and behavior so that it leads us wisely into the future.

At its highest level, of course, right remembrance is the state of automatically remembering that our source of all good things and opportunities is the higher self, the wellspring of love, wisdom, and power within us.

14. Recognizing the symbolic within the real. Due to the role of memory in Capricorn, it is easier to review our experiences and see the larger patterns of meaning they represent. Even though the increased materialism of Capricorn may blind some people, many others can look forward to breaking through the blind spots and gaining insight into how spirit has led them, indirectly, to where they are now. Our life exists within the context of universal force, and this fact may become much clearer to us during Capricorn, if we look for the symbolic meaning within outer circumstances.

15. Greater patience. Patience is not just the ability to wait, but more importantly the capacity to build the readiness to act when the time is right. The person who is prepared to act is not caught off guard by unexpected reactions from others, new opportunities, or twists of fate. It is an invaluable asset during Capricorn—and something which is more easily developed at this time.

16. Common sense. Most of the problems we encounter during Capricorn can be managed successfully if we but apply common sense. Wild ideas and long shots are ripe for failure, but common sense will prove effective. We should therefore emphasize the conservative side of our nature in making decisions.

17. Majesty. The full scope of divine purpose and beauty, as it manifests in physical life, is *majesty*—and Capricorn is an

excellent time to become aware of majesty and integrate it more fully into our life. We need to appreciate that we are part of the divine pattern of majesty, and that as we bring our life and work into order, we add to and enrich the divine tapestry of majesty.

18. Reverence. As our awareness of the majesty, order, and beauty of divine life increases, it is natural to respond with a heightened sense of awe and reverence. It is the quality, in fact, which gives us the power to stretch ourself beyond our present limitations and become more aware of the grand drama of universal life and how we fit into it. The expression of reverence can even become a *celebration* of life.

19. The enrichment of life. In Capricorn, we can also realize that we are the channel through which divine life is focused into our projects and activities. We are not a robot plodding stupidly through life, nor a worm who is unworthy of the One who created him. We are *a giver of life*—a giver of life to our work, our relationships, our duties, and our interests. Through the labors of an active mind, a loving heart, and generous and building hands, the lightning bolts of Capricorn do not just light the sky—but are brought to earth where they give life to all we do.

TUNING INTO THE FORCES OF CAPRICORN

One of the best exercises for tuning into the quality of the forces of Capricorn is to periodically review and express gratitude for the good things in our life: our strengths, talents, friends, successes, opportunities, and material resources, as well as the support we have received, from others and the higher self.

As much as possible, however, this should not just be a rote exercise, but deep, heartfelt gratefulness and appreciation for the inner forces which are continually at work, just below the surface, guiding and inspiring us as we act in the physical plane. If we can achieve this, then our gratitude will be a constant link keeping us in touch with the inner dimensions of life. Some of the best themes for gratefulness during Capricorn would be:

Gratefulness for the beauty of our life and the inner life.

Gratefulness for the maturity we have acquired and the lessons we have learned through the experiences of our life.

Gratefulness for enlightened elements of our cultural traditions, which enrich the fabric of our life.

The best way to teach in Capricorn is by demonstrating our own deep enthusiasm for learning and growing.

The best way to heal in Capricorn is through the transformation of the barriers to the life of spirit.

The best way to lead in Capricorn is by taking initiative and setting new forces in motion that will impel the group forward.

The work done in Capricorn sets in motion new projects that will bear fruit in Leo. If we fail to strive for practical results now, however, the forces of the zodiac will continue to prod us during the coming year until we do respond as we are meant to.

A SONG FOR CAPRICORN

The light draws, and ambition stirs.

We move toward the light many times, only to find it is the false light of our reflected desires.

The light draws, and aspiration stirs.

We see a higher light which traces a mysterious course. This higher light eludes us, yet impels us to leave behind the false and cast the light of our desires in shadow.

The light draws, and aspiration deepens.

Higher and higher we climb, until we reach a new summit and glimpse the rising sun for the first time. We comprehend what has eluded us, for now we see with a single eye, and our whole body is filled with light.

The light draws, and ambition and aspiration are fulfilled.

A PARABLE FOR CAPRICORN

No animal in the kingdom had a greater reputation for care-fulness and mastery of his environment than a certain goat who lived high on a mountain. The reputation was well-deserved, too; his daily treks took him over the most treacherous terrain. One false step and he could fall thousands of feet. But he was sure of foot and famous for it.

Indeed, his fame became so great that many animals sought him out for advice on coping with the adverse aspects of envir-onment. In time, he began conducting regular survival expedi-tions, wrote books on the subject, and became very popular among the young.

One day, as he was teaching a class in mountaineering, a fierce storm suddenly came up. The students were buffeted and battered by the wind and rain, but the goat resolutely led every-one to safety. Once back, one of his students was overcome with awe at the calm and self-assured way the goat had met the crisis.

"Oh, it's really not very difficult to make your way about the mountain in a storm such as this," the goat remarked. "The conditions are so unfavorable you have no choice but to keep yourself focused on the outer environment. The most danger-ous time to be on the mountain is when the weather is fair. That's when the inner storms of the emotions and mind tend to mount; memories, worries, and daydreams rise within you. If you aren't careful then, you can easily be distracted—and forget what your feet are doing. Years ago, two of my friends fell to their deaths this very way."

"And what has spared you from the same fate?" the student asked.

"I have always saved my worries and daydreams for when I am not climbing mountains."

16

Aquarius

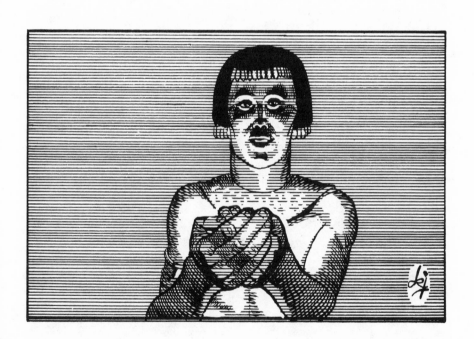

AQUARIUS

(January 20 through February 18)

Keynote: Generosity in attitude and act.

Mantra: "I embrace the light, the light pours through me,
and thus I serve."

New moon focus: Understanding the forces
which impel us to serve.

Full moon focus: Harnessing the forces which enable us to serve.

Rays 2, 4, 5, and 7 dominate.

Primary archetypal forces:
Generosity, prosperity, goodwill, brotherhood, strength

A Prayer For Aquarius:

May the one light which brings life to all draw us together in bonds of goodwill and brotherhood, and reveal to us our true relationship to light.

May the power of divine love cast out all hate and sense of separation, and fill us with perfect compassion.

May the presence of divine wisdom dispel all ignorance, and fill us with perfect understanding.

May the divine life in which we dwell, as individual members of a single body of light, inspire us to treat one another as God would treat us.

And may we respond to the call of this time with goodwill, tolerance, a sense of unity, and the willingness to act as an agent of light.

In a number of profound ways, we are now entering into situations and circumstances which are largely *unformed.* New cycles are taking shape within the context of our individuality and environment. It is as though we were a painter standing before a blank canvas. Our inspiration has taken shape at inner dimensions; we have responded to it; and perhaps even made some preliminary sketches and studies. Nevertheless, we have not yet taken action to translate the inspiration into art.

For some, the experience of standing before the blank canvas of the art of living is a frightening one. They identify with the emptiness on the canvas and believe it to be their own emptiness. They may even go so far as to believe their life to be purposeless. But nothing could be farther from the spirit of Aquarius. Having seen the empty canvas, we are meant to harness the purpose and meaning of our inner self and get on with the work of creating a noble masterpiece in our life.

As a result, the forces of Aquarius stimulate us to become more fully responsive to the needs of others, to conditions in our physical and spiritual environment, to the intent of the inner self, and to our impulse for self-expression. Metaphorically, we are motivated in Aquarius to pick up the paintbrush of our creativity and begin to work on new projects. It is important that this new effort to act be controlled by the wisdom and love of the higher self, however, and not be allowed to degenerate into randomness and "blind stabs in the dark."

Throughout Aquarius, the energies of brotherhood and love will be heightened. It is therefore an ideal time to strive to develop practical applications of these forces, by making an effort to help others in meaningful ways and by embracing greater responsibilities. All efforts to nurture a greater ability to care will be handsomely rewarded. But to take advantage of this opportunity, we must move beyond self-centeredness and self-concern, which will also be stimulated.

The best way to do this is to increase our sensitivity to

forces and factors beyond our personal sphere—to become more sensitive to the groups we belong to (even those we disclaim), to group problems, and to the higher self. The forces of Aquarius will automatically stimulate this kind of sensitivity, but we can only expect to benefit from it if we are willing to work intelligently with it. After all, sensitivity to national problems and international pain could become somewhat disabling if we did not simultaneously recognize our capacity to act in mature and responsible ways to diminish, at least to a small degree, the burden of these problems.

In other words, it is important to understand the ideals of brotherhood and caring, so that our increasing sensitivity will be properly harnessed, and not precipitate us into depression or irritation.

Whatever we truly serve will rise to the surface and be revealed. If we serve our own vanity, this will become obvious. If we serve the shrine of greed and materialism, this, too, will be uncovered. On the other hand, if we genuinely serve the plan of God, the intent of the higher self, and the ideals of love, wisdom, and peace, the next step to follow in these noble endeavors will become clear to us. Both the vision within and without will be more completely focused.

Partial commitments, however, will be exposed for what they lack. For those who waver in their commitment as they struggle between their aspirations and their resistance, Aquarius may be something of a Valley Forge experience. For them, the words of Thomas Paine will once more ring true:

"These are the times that try men's souls. The summer soldier and the sunshine patriot will, in this crisis, shrink from service of their country, but he that stands it *now* deserves the love and thanks of man and woman. Tyranny, like hell, is not easily conquered; yet we have this consolation with us that, the harder the conflict, the more glorious the triumph."

For those who do have a genuine commitment to serve the

374

plan and purpose of the higher self, there will be no danger of shrinking from the task. Instead of crisis, Aquarius will present a marvelous opportunity to enrich life with new meaning and a higher level of understanding. It will lead to a deeper appreciation of the presence and power of the inner ruler or higher self, not in the mode of aspiration but in the mode of service.

Indeed, it could be said that the time of *seeking* is largely past, both in terms of this stage of the zodiacal cycle and of the growth of humanity. In a very important sense, seeking must now give way to *striving*. Having found the ideals we ought to serve and learned something of them, it is now time to *strive:*

• To master the talents needed in order to express these ideals wisely in daily life.

• To integrate the life and quality of these ideals into our own attitudes and feeling, so that we are better able to cooperate with them, moment to moment.

• To serve the spirit and purpose of these divine ideals through all that we do, at work, in our relationships, and through the groups we belong to.

It is very important in Aquarius to cooperate with the inner ruler—the inner teacher. If we do, we will be successful in translating a greater measure of the inner life into outer expression. But if we do not, the sense of emptiness which can occur in Aquarius may well be justified.

This, then, is the archetypal challenge of Aquarius—to touch the real presence of life in all that we do, and convert this inner presence into meaningful, constructive action. The inner presence can be discovered in our own higher self, in the spirit of groups, and in the meaning of the work we pursue. But it is our challenge to convert it into service and help.

Expressed poetically, the time of Aquarius might be called the month of the "flowering of consciousness," as though the service we can perform now is like a rose blooming in midwinter, when no one expects it. This is always the true miracle of life: to look for and find areas of emptiness, coldness, aridity, or boredom in our life and activities, and ask, "How can I enrich this emptiness, so that my talents and love and joy will flower, even here? How can I serve?"

THE SYMBOLISM OF AQUARIUS

The symbol of this sign is the water bearer, who carries water in a vase or pot and pours it forth to nurture the growth of life. Conventionally, this symbol is interpreted as representing the loosening of bonds at the end of a cycle, followed by death and then renewal. This does describe an aspect of the energies of Aquarius, but the esoteric meanings are far more powerful. The most important is the theme of service and brotherhood. The water bearer is motivated by a deep kinship with all life, and carries water to help this life grow, whether it is human or otherwise. But implied in the symbol of the water bearer is also the idea that he must be *ready* to carry the water. This is a point often disregarded in connection with Aquarius.

Many of us are confused about service, believing that to serve is to impose our beliefs fanatically and militantly on others. We mistake righteousness for love, dogma for light. This is *not* the true spirit of service. As long as we act in these ways, we may be ready to serve, but those we would serve are not ready for us!

During Aquarius, the soul approaches the personality for the purpose of activating it to greater service. But the soul will be unable to make contact, unless we have built something of a pathway to heaven—to the inner dimensions of our life. This is the purpose of prayer, meditation, aspiration, a dedication to the life of spirit, and the cultivation of good habits and noble ideals.

Only when this pathway exists can the soul approach us,

and fill our chalice or vase with the spiritual waters we are meant to carry forth to others. The water, of course, is love and light—our capacity to love the work we do, nurture the growth of others, act wisely, and support and assist where we are needed.

HOW THE FORCES OF AQUARIUS AFFECT US

The light which nurtures wisdom and goodwill also has a way of stirring up conflict with *anything* which opposes these forces on earth. We should therefore expect to meet with subconscious resistance and opposition from within ourself, groups, and nations during Aquarius. This will be most noticeable in those who have invested a great deal of time and energy in sustaining illusions and false goals.

At the same time, however, Aquarius will be a time when those who are confused begin to see, when those who are lost find their way, when those who waver tap new resolve, and when those who are selfish learn the value of altruism. There may be a lot of people who do not learn these lessons, but some will. Aquarius has the power to be a turning point in our life.

The forces of Aquarius will affect the average person by heightening the "herd consciousness"—the impulse to conform. Instead of seizing his inner potential for greatness and nobility, he will scorn those who dare to lead and set an example. The average person will also tend to descend further into pettiness and selfishness.

The effect on the spiritual aspirant will be to heighten sensitivity and underscore the need to rise out of the astral plane, with its heavy focus on feelings, sentiments, flashy visions, and glamours, and learn to work and act from a mental and spiritual focus. This will not be easy, because most aspirants are still addicted to the warm and rich sensations of the astral plane. They much prefer to play the games of spirituality than confront the issues of responsibility, goodwill, and humanitarian service. But rising out of an emotional focus and learning to act with intelligent mastery of our character is indispensable to spiritual aspiration in Aquarius.

The effect on the advanced person will be to deepen his humanitarian concern and his commitment to helping others. The advanced person will also experience heightened sensitivity, but will carefully attune it to Hierarchical plans, thereby giving himself a renewed and stronger focus for service. He will be drawn further into the heart of the groups to which he belongs.

The effect of the forces of Aquarius on our **motivation** will be to foster a strong urge to heal and to give.

The urge to heal can be considered an intelligent response to the force of brotherhood. As our sense of unity with others increases, we become more oriented toward playing an active role in correcting imbalances in our relationships, helping those in need, and adopting a more wholesome attitude toward life. To some degree, we all become healers during Aquarius—physically, psychologically, politically, or spiritually. The healing we render is often simple and quiet—a kind word to a friend or support for someone who is suffering. For some people, the help that is offered will mostly be just a projection of what they want in return; for others, it will be more a form of self-serving publicity for themselves than genuine healing of a problem. But in many people the urge to heal will be correctly focused. These people will sense what is genuinely needed—knowing that what is wanted and what is needed are often two entirely different things—and seek to help as best they can, in practical and effective ways.

The urge to give develops as we discover that life itself has been generous with us—and seeks to support our noble and inspired efforts even more, if we will but cooperate with it. People who are still mired in selfishness will not understand the real

nature of generosity; they will continue "giving to get" and looking for ways to procure money and attention while appearing to
serve. But those who are escaping the traps of selfishness will
find their own generosity, kindness, and helpfulness strengthened at this time, along lines of service they are already performing. And in those who are sincerely committed to a life of service, Aquarius will be a time when new opportunities to help
will open up, or new insights into the work already being done
will be gained.

The impact of the forces of Aquarius on our **awareness** will
be to promote a new understanding and appreciation of communion. Communion is not just a religious sacrament; the sacrament is itself a symbol for a deeper reality—the interaction of
brotherhood and kinship that we can experience through our
own involvement with other people, groups, and humanity as a
whole. Communion is not just an awareness that we are part of
this group and share its problems and opportunities, however; it
is a direct perception of the inner bonds which magnetically
draw the group together and nourish its growth and usefulness.
To honor the spirit of communion during Aquarius, therefore,
we need to act in ways that effectively translate the reality of
these inner ties into our established group relationships.

The forces of Aquarius affect the **mind** by flooding it with
light; there is therefore a great potential to educate and train the
mind to work more efficiently and brilliantly. Indeed, it is quite
possible that first-class brilliance will be expressed, both mentally and creatively. This potential should be seized and put to
work; we must not let the mind lie fallow.

There will be a number of opportunities for increasing our
powers of mental observation during Aquarius. Instead of just
believing in certain principles or facts, for example, we should
endeavor to observe and understand what is relevant and what
is workable. The workings, laws, and patterns of life can be
more readily discerned at this time, especially as they influence

our life and activity. Our connections with universal law, the soul, and the groups we work with will also be more highly visible. We can potentially learn much about the opportunities available to us for enriching our life—through the work of civilization, our professional involvement, and our responsibilities.

The forces of Aquarius affect the **emotions** by stimulating our capacity to express harmony. But if our emotions are not oriented toward expressing harmony, the likely impact at this time will be increased conflict. This may be conflict with others, inner storms of conscience, or clashes between the old order and the new. For some, there will be unpleasant reactions to the realities of present conditions, but any attempt to return to the old order will be a mistake. The resolution of conflict comes as we examine what controls us and what we serve. If we truly serve God and our noblest ideals, we will resolve the conflict wisely. If we serve only our personal wishes, however, the conflict may prove stronger than us. As much as possible, we should strive not to be overly irritated by the conflict, but seek to handle it compassionately and in harmony with the ideal. Above all, we should not aggravate the differences we encounter.

The forces of Aquarius affect our **self-expression** by encouraging our productive involvement in life—and by shifting our attention away from what we can do for ourself alone, focusing it instead on what we can contribute to the welfare of humanity. There will be more emphasis placed on the needs of society than on those of the individual. It will be important to learn to serve these larger needs, in order to seize the full force of Aquarius.

THE CHALLENGES OF AQUARIUS

The time of Aquarius challenges us to begin thinking of ourself as an agent of light who expresses universal forces through everything that we do—our work, our duties, the way we treat others, and our contributions to life—knowing that we are the only way light can shine into our personal world.

There is a great measure of goodwill in the universe, but it can only enter our world if we become its agent.

There is a great measure of compassion in the universe, but it can only enter our world if we treat others compassionately.

There is a wonderful treasure of joy in the universe, but it can only become our treasure as we learn to express joy in the face of difficulties and share it with others.

There is enormous genius in life, but it can only enrich our life if we take stock of our talent and seek to expand it to a point of true genius—and then do something worthwhile with it.

In fact, Aquarius is a time when real genius can break forth and make its mark—if we respond to the challenge. Anything we can do to cultivate our genius and use it productively will be worthwhile. This need not be grandiose—Aquarius will stimulate any real genius, whether it is a genius for parenting, a genius for hospitality, or a genius for creative and innovative work.

The challenge of Aquarius to parents is to honor their obligations and responsibilities. All too many people become parents without any real commitment to taking on the responsibility of cultivating spiritual, mental, emotional, and physical maturity in their children. Aquarius is an excellent time to review our commitment to serve the needs of our children over our needs as parents. In this regard, we might ask ourself: "What am I called to do as a parent that I have not yet recognized?"

The challenge of Aquarius in our dealings with others is to cultivate the inner levels of friendship and learn to *commune* with the inner essence of our friends, colleagues, and family members. The fact that barriers of rigidness and standoffishness will be lessened will help make this easier. In addition, the desire to be involved in sharing life with others will increase.

The challenge of Aquarius in business is to enrich and improve relationships between management and employees, or the unions that represent them. It is also an excellent time to understand that we make a contribution to human life through our business or professional activities, and that this contribution is more important than profit alone.

The challenge of Aquarius in society is to control and properly focus the perception of world need. Some individuals may be more susceptible than usual to depression, especially the kind of depression which results from a heightened awareness of *Weltschmerz* or world pain. And international relations and world opinion are also subtly affected by these conditions during Aquarius. This can make it easier to see world need—but if it is uncontrolled, it can also lead to unwarranted ultimatums, foolish propositions, and the blurring of the real issues of world service.

The challenge of Aquarius to our personal growth is to learn to take crises in stride. Various lines of force tend to come together during Aquarius to produce the tension which often results in crisis. Yet there is great opportunity in any crisis—if we have the skill and self-control to tap it. Aquarius is a time for mature, sensible action—quick, fearless, and decisive, but in no way rash or impulsive. To seize the opportunity of crisis, we must know what we stand for and what we are trying to build in our life. If we can honor our values and our responsibilities and continue to build toward our goals, we can turn most crises into productive opportunities.

Whether or not there is a crisis in Aquarius, we should always look for the focal point of tension which is the key to growth. This focal point can be described as follows:

• At the level of the will, it is the tension between our urge to be helpful and our immersion in self-centeredness.

• At the level of the mind, it is the tension between our understanding of our spiritual self and our perception of chaos, pain, and confusion in the personality.

• At the level of the emotions, it is the tension between

our goodwill and our fear of having our goodwill abused.

• At the physical level, it is the tension between our intention to be a constructive influence and our insecurity.

Out of these differing kinds of tension, we can learn to identify with both our spiritual nature and the genuine needs of growth for humanity—including ourself. When we have mastered enough self-control that we can hold these twin identifications in steady balance, then we have learned to take crisis in stride and use it purposefully. Our own growth will accelerate rapidly, and we will be able to offer genuine help to those who still struggle to grow.

THE PROBLEMS OF AQUARIUS

The major problems of this time are those which arise in opposition and selfish reaction to the spiritual forces of Aquarius—and the sense of responsibility which guides all enlightened people. But the forces of Aquarius also have a way of subtly influencing our attitudes and awareness, making us vulnerable to a variety of unfortunate tendencies.

The most critical problems of Aquarius are:

1. Gullibility. The greater sensitivity of Aquarius may cause us to become too open and trusting of others, and willing to believe in their flattery. Friendliness and trust must be tempered by intelligence, lest we expose ourself to exploitation.

2. Self-indulgence. The easy complacency and gentleness which come with a lack of discipline and a retreat into immaturity may be overwhelming at this time. This may be especially true if we substitute intelligent philosophizing for intelligent behavior. As a result, our susceptibility to temptation will be higher than usual.

3. Severity. On the other hand, some people will be excessively rigid and demanding in the way they make others—and

themselves—"toe the line" at this time. This is not a proper anti-dote to self-indulgence—it is a problem in its own right. It is necessary to moderate both extremes and focus our attention on responding intelligently to the inner plan or authority which governs the situation.

4. Idle speculation. Instead of intelligent reflection on our life and its problems and opportunities, we may end up only ruminating and speculating on what might have been. If we focus on our honorable values and motives, however, and seek intelligent insights and answers instead of self-serving ration-alizations, we can avoid this trap.

5. Malicious speculation. It is also likely that all forms of gossip and pettiness will increase, and be more damaging than usual. The reputation, dignity, and nobility of some people may be unjustly infringed. We need to refrain from participating in such immature behavior—and if we are the target of it, retain our dignity and not compromise it by fighting back with petti-ness of our own.

6. Glamours. Emotional fascinations and obsessions, especially those associated with the themes of service, goodwill, and unity, are likely to be stronger. This could result in a serious distortion of any effort to help others or encourage a sense of brotherhood. The need for service may only be met with sympathy. The need for brotherhood may only be met with racism or nationalism—the "us against them" syndrome. It is important to examine these issues with the mind, not the emotions.

7. Intrigue. In personal relationships, business dealings, and at the national level, alliances will be repositioned. In some cases, this will result in rather strange ties. It may also plant the seeds for eventual betrayal. But in most all cases, this realignment of alliance will represent a distraction from pur-pose, not a step forward.

8. Staleness. Apathy will be a big problem in Aquarius,

fueled by a tendency to continue working as usual with worn-out ideas, run-of-the-mill solutions, and hackneyed responses. There is a need for new vigor and vitality in the way we think about life and the way we act in fulfilling our duties and responsibilities.

9. Mimicry. In some, the impulse to be sensitive toward others may be expressed as nothing more than mere mimicry. While the emulation of heroes can uplift our thought and behavior, it is important to understand that the mimic usually imitates more than just the noble elements of the people around him. We are called in Aquarius to cultivate our own understanding of life and values, not mimic others.

10. Hypocrisy. Especially among spiritual aspirants, there will be a strong temptation for old, selfish ways to suddenly be reborn as "noble service to humanity." We must discriminate between genuine service on the one hand and the ego trip which has been coated with benevolence and recycled as a "noble and selfless gesture" on the other.

11. Superficiality. The tendency to rely on outer appearances and ignore the inner substance will be heightened. This can lead to bad judgments about others and situations, as well as indifference to the deeper levels of meaning. Aquarius is meant to be a time when the relationship between the inner and the outer worlds stands revealed. But superficial people will miss the revelation entirely.

12. False assumptions. There will be a tendency to jump to conclusions on insufficient evidence. First impressions should be evaluated before acting on them. Some may be misleading or only partially true. Beware of misconstruing fragments of evidence for the whole truth. One method of teaching in Aquarius is to give the student a few pieces of the puzzle, then challenge him to speculate on and reconstruct the rest.

13. Self-doubt. As we become more aware of the needs of people around us, our usual concepts of ourself and our work

may become slightly blurred, so that we are not sure about our values and our interests. This, in turn, may cause us to look back over recent events and discover that we may have been more selfish than we had realized. Or, we may be tempted to second guess ourself in other ways. Insecurities in general will increase, and we may turn to others for reassurance. But this self-doubt and insecurity must not be allowed to become excessive.

14. Abuse of responsibility. Whenever a sense of duty or responsibility is heightened, as it is in Aquarius, resistance to it also increases, leading to abuses and abandonment of responsibility. Ingratitude toward those who are helping also increases.

15. Burnout. Those who do serve and try to be helpful, yet without a fully defined set of values concerning service, may find their dedication severely tested as they encounter opposition, ingratitude, and a failure to respond in those they seek to help. This can lead to conditions of burnout and disappointment. When this is the case, we need to reexamine exactly what our motives for serving are. Are we serving in order to fill a need of our own—or to help those who need what we have to offer?

16. Unexpected surprises. There is a potential for being caught off-guard during Aquarius. We need to be as prepared for the unexpected as possible, but if it happens anyway, respond with as much dignity and poise as we can. If necessary, we should choose silence rather than respond in a way that would be damaging to ourself. But we should not be mute when it comes to honoring the principles and values that we cherish.

17. Artifice. There will be a strong tendency for people to hide behind masks. In their action and speech, they will try to assume different disguises and artifices. The form of their activity will veil the truth of their motives. We should be alert to this possibility, and pierce beyond the shell of artifice. In addition, we should be sure not to hide behind pretenses ourself.

THE OPPORTUNITIES OF AQUARIUS

A tremendous quality of compassion permeates Aquarius, and is one of the strongest motivating forces of this time. If we can attune ourself to this quality of compassion, and not let it descend into mere sentimentality or political opportunism, it can open many doors for us. It can help us become aware of the true needs of those around us and humanity in general, thereby preparing us for a higher level of responsibility. It can open the door to becoming sensitive to people we have never met, both physically and nonphysically. If we limit ourself by being concerned only about our own needs, these opportunities will be closed to us. But if we are sincerely concerned about the well-being of others and humanity in general, the compassion which is the heart of Aquarius will draw us into a transcendent realm of spirit where we can tap the forces we need.

We should use this compassion to develop the following opportunities of Aquarius:

1. A greater awareness of the inner life. Aquarius stimulates introspection and sensitivity. We will therefore find that the time we spend in meditation and reflection will be exceptionally fruitful. Our rapport, alignment, and accord with the inner life will be easier to achieve and sustain.

2. A stronger sense of relationship with other people and society. The sense of belonging to a group—a family, church, community, race, business, or nation—will be enriched. We may therefore come to recognize more clearly how we benefit from—and have an opportunity to assist—these groups.

3. Reconciliation. Aquarius is a time for healing personal relationships, reconciling with old enemies, and resolving old conflicts. Aquarius promotes a greater awareness and understanding of others and their problems. As it also fosters our capacity for goodwill, there will be rich opportunities to mend fences and promote tolerance, fairness, and forgiveness.

4. Consolidation. To some degree, the forces of Aquarius merge complementary or parallel efforts and elements to produce a more efficient synthesis of the whole. There may therefore be a singular opportunity at this time to join forces with others in such a way that the common purpose is better served. This can happen in working with ideas, personal relationships, business enterprises, or at a national level.

5. Reassessing priorities. The forces of Aquarius help us discern higher levels of purpose and motivation, thereby making it an excellent time to review our priorities—to take a fresh look at what we are doing, what we are trying to accomplish, and why. Are we actually devoting an appropriate measure of time and skill to our highest priorities—or are we wasting them on non-productive activities? As much as possible, this review of priorities should be conducted at the level of the mind, not emotionally.

6. Charitableness. The forces of Aquarius foster a recognition of how and where we can be helpful in the world and how we can render this service most effectively. It enriches our capacity to *care* for the growth and enlightenment of others.

7. The enlightened use of influence and power. The forces of this time stimulate insight into a higher and more spiritual orientation to life. As a result, we are able to better understand how to relate to others effectively and efficiently while preserving our principles and values. We are able to blend noble purpose with our practical skills of living, especially as we interact with and influence others.

8. Building on the past. One of the great opportunities of this time is to add our contribution to the rich legacy we inherit from the past—to find ways to enrich and expand the meaning or influence of traditions, ideas, and achievements we have long admired. We must take care, however, not just to retreat into the past without building on it, as this would be a regression.

9. Generosity. The charitableness of Aquarius likewise

stimulates a deep sense of generosity, which is the willingness to reinvest in life that which we have in abundance. Generosity is not just the simplistic act of giving money or kindness away; it implies a dedication to making intelligent decisions to use the resources we have been blessed with so that the blessing is spread to a larger number of people, and humanity's evolution is helped. In a very real sense, it is the investment of the best within us—our abundance—in the best within others—their potential to grow.

10. Endurance. There is a marvelous opportunity to discover the real meaning and power of endurance at this time—not endurance in the sense of grimly and stoically hanging on in the face of great obstacles (which is antithetical to the Aquarian spirit), but endurance in the sense of the ability of the life of spirit to endure and prosper. During Aquarius, it will be possible to tap and learn to express:

• The joy which endures in spite of hardship, elevating consciousness.

• The nobility which endures in spite of personal embarrassment or disgrace, elevating self-esteem.

• The goodwill which endures in spite of rejection or opposition, elevating our emotional responses.

• The wisdom which endures in spite of error and confusion, elevating our intelligence.

• The sense of beauty which endures in spite of coarseness, elevating refinement.

• The harmony which endures in spite of conflict, elevating our capacity for cooperation.

11. Group work. Our ability to work in groups is strengthened, as well as our capacity to become more fully aware of the role we play in groups, the impact groups have on us, and so on. In ordinary groups, team spirit and greater cooperation will be stressed. In advanced groups, the ability to focus energies and ideas for the good of mankind—to serve as a collective agent—

will become more obvious. Those who are able to work at this level may gain new insights into the importance of groups and of inclusive solutions to the Aquarian spirit. Aquarius is an exceptional time to link our goals and efforts to projects which will benefit vast numbers of people.

12. Overcoming limitations. The forces of Aquarius have a powerful capacity for awakening us to the ways in which we have been limiting and restricting our efforts and self-awareness—and then supporting us in the effort to break down our limitations and transcend them.

13. The enrichment of consciousness. The soul itself is enriched during Aquarius, by its contact with the forces of love and brotherhood. This is true both individually and collectively. As a result, we can look for increased awareness of:

- The meaning of world affairs.
- The group minds that influence us.
- Our capacity to refine our self-expression.
- Our niche in the world—the role we are designed to fill in bringing new aspects of heaven into expression on earth.
- Our ability to be helpful.
- The larger purpose of the work we do.

14. Building abundance. For those who meditate, Aquarius is a good time to build up a reservoir of joy, harmony, and goodwill for our creative self-expression—a time to contact the penetrating influences of the soul and focus them into our acts and thoughts. By doing this regularly, we can build an abundance of these qualities which will serve us in good stead whenever we need them. The best way to build this abundance is to work at expressing them in ways which stretch our normal expression. Many of us, for example, are quite capable of expressing goodwill and joy in the presence of friends, but still balk at expressing these qualities toward enemies. We cannot acquire an *abundance* of these forces until we overcome these limitations.

15. Prosperity. By striving to build an abundance of these

qualities of the life of spirit in our character and self-expression, we set in motion the forces of self-determination which will cause these forces to prosper in our life. In general, we become more interested in helping the projects and activities we participate in to prosper and do well.

16. Magic. Aquarius is an excellent time for esoteric studies and practices. In many regards, it is almost a magical sign; what we hold in our mind and imagination has a way of becoming manifest. It is for this reason that it is so important to hold our mind steady in the light of our ideals and values, lest the magic we work turns out to be self-destructive. Obsessive concern at this time about fears, worries, and pettiness can magically reinforce these negative elements. Instead, it is much healthier to concentrate on *making the most of what we have*, in terms of skills, blessings, and natural capacities. That is the real magic.

17. Charm. Perhaps the greatest form of magic to use in Aquarius is the charm of personal graciousness and goodwill—not the superficial charm which is used to enchant and manipulate people, but the mature, spiritually-motivated charm of liking other people and responding always to the best within them. The person who delights in the company of friends and is able to express the joy and companionship of the soul in their presence is one who has touched the magic of the art of living, and is acting in harmony with the essence of Aquarius.

TUNING INTO THE FORCES OF AQUARIUS

The spirit of Aquarius can be summed up in the idea of becoming a spiritual adult. Immaturity will be consistently and relentlessly exposed as it occurs during this time. It will not be accepted. Instead, we will be called upon to act as an adult—an adult who is responsible, disciplined, true to our values, able to deal with conflict effectively, stable, reliable, and strong. What may have been appropriate behavior for adolescence must be abandoned as damaging to an adult. It is time to grow up—in every facet of life.

For this reason, a good exercise for tuning into the forces of Aquarius is to contemplate what it means to be an adult, especially in the spiritual context. Far too many people are content to be a child of God. There is virtue to that state, to be sure, but it is even more significant to be a responsible adult cooperating wisely and creatively with God. As Paul wrote, "When I was a child, I spoke like a child, I thought like a child, I reasoned like a child; when I became a man, I gave up childish ways."

We can therefore ask ourself:

What does it mean to be a spiritual adult?

In what ways do we still think, speak, and act as a child—both in ordinary living and in our pursuit of the life of spirit?

How does a spiritual adult approach his work?

How does a spiritual adult treat other people?

How does a spiritual adult respond to tests of personal integrity and honor?

How does a spiritual adult approach the use of money?

How does a spiritual adult interact with family?

How does a spiritual adult approach the duties of citizenship?

How does a spiritual adult respond to the call of service?

By asking and answering these questions as an ongoing exercise in Aquarius, we can do much to stretch ourself beyond our present limitations, and enter into a new sphere of maturity.

The way to teach in Aquarius is by setting a humanitarian example and laying the groundwork for a true acceptance of humanitarian ideals.

The way to heal in Aquarius is by bringing the inner design into physical reality.

The way to lead in Aquarius is by expanding one's own duties and responsibilities for the work to be done, thereby demonstrating that service is a central principle of human life.

The work done during Aquarius makes possible the inflow of new energies in Aries, at the beginning of the next cycle.

A SONG FOR AQUARIUS

The opening notes are sounded, but are not heard. Again and again they are sent forth, penetrating the stillness, until they are faintly recognized. But the listeners are not ready to accept what they hear, and the call is ignored. Still, it does not cease. The notes continue to be sounded.

At last, the listeners leave their isolated caves in order to hear more clearly. They sense it is a summons, calling them, but they do not grasp its message. Yet in leaving their caves, they find one another, and join together in their common quest.

Collectively, they learn to respond to the notes, and help one another journey toward the mountain from which the summons seems to come. The call becomes clearer and stronger, until they reach the mountaintop. There, it is clearest of all, and the listeners hear what they have never heard before. It is not a summons, but a song—a mighty psalm which fills the heavens and charges everyone with a single chord, until the very ground on which they stand vibrates in harmony with the opening note.

A PARABLE FOR AQUARIUS

A city installed a water fountain in its town hall. When the first person tried to use it, however, the fountain was dry. The company which installed the fountain was called in to repair it, yet no defect could be found. It was in perfect working condition. But no matter who tried it, no water came.

Word of the fountain which gave no water spread quickly,

and jokes abounded about "typical government services." Eventually, the city stopped trying to get the fountain to work, and just let it be. But everyone who visited the town hall made a point of stopping by the fountain to get a drink—knowing they would not. The town became famous for it.

One day, a man who was pure of heart and wise in mind came to the city for a visit. Hearing of the fountain, he went to investigate this strange phenomenon for himself. But when he stepped up to it and pressed the lever, the fountain worked! He drank deeply and stepped back.

Naturally, the others in the building were amazed at this event, and immediately rushed to the fountain to be among the first to drink from it. But when they tried, the fountain stopped working again. None of them could get a drink. Finally, they called the man back. "Try it again," they cried.

He did—and once more the fountain flowed freely.

"Are you some kind of magician," a man in the crowd asked, "that you can make this fountain work?"

"No, it is life itself which is magical," the wise man replied. "This is just an ordinary fountain, as I am an ordinary man, but the water you seek is water that no city can supply for its people. It can only be found by each person on his or her own, by developing an unselfish heart and a noble mind. So stop looking for the city to quench your thirst."

And having explained the magic of the fountain, he cupped his hands to catch the water, and let everyone drink from what he had collected.

17

Pisces

PISCES

Keynote: The healing power of God's love.

Mantra: "I am a light in the world, illuminating the path we all must follow."

New moon focus: The work of redemption.

Full moon focus: Fulfilling the plan of God.

Rays 1, 2, and 6 dominate.

Primary archetypal forces:
Benevolence, wisdom, will, devotion, compassion

A Prayer For Pisces:

O heavenly Mother-Father God, help us to meet the challenges of daily living with a fuller awareness of Your universal qualities and timeless ideals.

Help us attune our thoughts to the inner light, so that we may act with intelligent guidance and insight.

Help us center our desires and aspirations in the inner love, so that we may enrich our lives with goodwill and serenity.

Help us affix our intention to act on the inner will, so that the purpose of all we do is revealed.

Help us focus our awareness on the inner life, so that we may "lose" our sense of personality in Your life and be reborn.

Let wisdom guide, goodwill prevail, the inner emerge, and the old disappear, fulfilling divine purpose and releasing Your light so that all may see.

And be guided on the path before them.

Pisces is a time when the inner person has an excellent opportunity to overshadow and even dominate the outer person and its activities; a time when the purpose of an enterprise or group can become clear and compelling; a time when the spirit of a nation has increased opportunity to call forth a mature response from its citizens. The forces of Pisces encourage us to distinguish between the real and the unreal and invoke the power of the real to master and transform the unreal. Yet none of this happens automatically. If we respond to the forces of Pisces by aligning ourself with spirit and our activities with purpose, both individually and collectively, the promise of Pisces can be fulfilled. But if we react rebelliously to these forces, Pisces will be little more than a time of greater confusion, frustration, and irritation.

In a very real sense, Pisces is a time for distilling the meaning of our experiences, thereby manufacturing wisdom and refocusing our will to be involved productively in life. Yet wisdom is a precious metal, not easily forged. Simply undergoing a series of tests or experiences in life does not in any way guarantee that we comprehend their meaning or learn anything from them.

The power of Pisces lies in being able to step back from the immediate triumphs and hardships of our daily experiences and discern their underlying meaning and purpose. Once we have tapped this meaning and purpose, we then draw from it a new measure of strength and spiritual vitality, which prepares us for the challenges ahead.

Yet we must take care not to let sloppy habits distort the power of Pisces. It would be all too easy, for example, to step back from daily experiences so far that we lose track of what we are supposed to be doing. There are several ways this can happen:

• By becoming passive and indifferent to life. We detach, but without tapping the new understanding and wisdom which is the reason for detaching.

• By devoting a lot of time to "finding our own space." Looking for "our own space" is a good way to get locked into a highly personal view toward life. Most of us need to find the inner qualities and ideals which enrich the meaning of life, not private space.

• By feeding the tired old illusion of "creating our own reality." This is a very attractive idea for many people, but it is a distraction from the real business of Pisces. It tends to isolate the person who believes it from others, and makes it impossible to abstract any real wisdom or strength from our experiences and lessons.

Stepping back from our close identification with daily problems does not in any way mean that we are stepping away from them. Instead, we are meant to draw closer to the inner power and ideals which will renew our capacity to act wisely and maturely in solving these problems. The forces of Pisces work together to promote this kind of renewal:

• They increase our sensitivity to the inner life, so that we can see more clearly what these inner powers and ideals are.

• They increase our awareness of subconscious patterns and the significance of outer events, so that we can see where and how we ought to be using these inner powers and ideals. Of course, this increased awareness may also lead to irritation and frustration, if we are not truly interested in tapping new understanding of our life.

• They reveal any lack of experience we may have in successfully pursuing or managing the key roles of our life, so that we can seek out a new perspective or develop a more effective way of acting.

This will be a poignant experience for some people, especially those who have been battered by the crises which were the challenge of Aquarius. But it must be remembered that the purpose of crisis and tension is to set the stage for transformation and more rapid growth. If we get bogged down in our personal reactions of pain and distress, we may well miss the opportunity for this new growth.

Nevertheless, it is equally true that any crisis has a way of leaving us disenchanted with the course of our life, sapped of strength, unsure of ourself. If we let such reactions go unchecked, they may lead quickly to a serious loss of personal momentum. The great healing power of Pisces, if we choose to tap it, is its capacity to help us convert confusion into understanding, understanding into wisdom, and wisdom into a new strength to act.

This new strength to act is generated out of our ability to love. The magnetic attraction of love is a strong force in Pisces. We will be drawn toward whatever we love the most. If we love intelligently and wisely, focusing our love on the noble qualities and ideals of the soul, we will draw to ourself rich opportunities for growth and success. But if we love foolishly and selfishly, or cannot love at all, we will draw to ourself chaotic, destructive forces and conditions.

The intelligent use of love, discerned and tapped in Pisces, can help us refocus in the inner strength of our own potential. It can refresh our sense of purpose and vitality in living, so that we can be more fully aligned than ever to the joy and intent of the soul, and thereby strive gladly to fulfill its will. Our relationship to the inner life becomes one of cooperation, not resistance.

Pisces completes the twelve-month cycle of the zodiac, bringing to fulfillment the new trends released in Aries. Each Aries, a new divine impulse is set in motion. During Aries, Taurus, and Gemini, we are largely unaware of this new impulse, as it saturates the unconscious levels of life. During Cancer, Leo, and Virgo, the new directions begin to interact with us; we still may not understand them, but we begin to react and respond to them. This stage is followed by Libra, Scorpio, and Sagittarius, in which we begin to understand more fully whither these new energies are moving us, and incorporate them into our plans. In the final three months, Capricorn, Aquarius, and Pisces, we become aware of the real creative power of these forces, their potential to be integrated into our active service, and the ways in which they affect humanity as a whole. We become much more aware of the *group* implications of these new directions.

In this great drama, Pisces is almost as pivotal as Aries; during Pisces, we have the opportunity to fulfill the promise of Aries and to bring this yearly cycle to successful completion. This does not mean that the new projects which have been set in motion must be completely manifest by Pisces; in most cases, they will continue for years and years. It just means that we need to strive to understand, integrate, and apply the new forces and directions by Pisces—and draw from them the full significance of their meaning to us—so that we can then be ready for the next challenge of living, when it arises in Aries.

For this reason, one of the great characteristics of Pisces is that it is a time of synthesis—a time for finding the common themes of the rich diversity of our experience and drawing them into a single realization of who we are and what we are doing. In this way, we extract the full force of our journey through the zodiac, and prepare ourself for the next one.

THE SYMBOLISM OF PISCES

The symbol of this sign is a pair of fish, facing opposite directions and bound together. In this way, the basic duality of life is once again emphasized, only this time the implication is quite clear that the duality has been harnessed.

Still, we may not perceive it that way; the forces of Pisces tend to present us with many more paradoxes than solutions. The duality of Pisces widens the gap between the mundane and the sublime elements of life, and we will be affected by this, until we discover what it is that harnesses both poles. We may feel caught in the middle, or isolated at one extreme or the other, or even tossed back and forth between the extremes. If we tend to be defensive by nature, or prone to "dig in" and protect the status quo, the time of Pisces may be quite irritating, and not at a symbolic level! But if we are able to see that resolving these paradoxes will lead to greater maturity, it will be a productive period.

The major paradoxes or dualities of Pisces will include:

1. The personal versus the universal. The problems of Pisces are the problems of humanity as a whole; the opportunities of Pisces are the opportunities of humanity as a whole. As a rule, the forces we deal with at this time are not personal, but universal. And yet our sense of personality and individuality will be heightened. At the very moment when we can achieve success by embracing a larger, more universal perspective, we will be tempted to retreat into a very personal perspective. Yet if we do become bogged down in personal woes and reactions to the events of Pisces, we may well come to grief. Indeed, the greatest source of conflict in Pisces lies in the interaction of the personal and the universal, the individual and the group.

The two fish symbolize our personal desires and our personal reactions to universal impulse, plus the power of temptation to keep us focused personally; the ocean in which they swim represents the universal forces of life.

2. The inner versus the outer. We will tend to become more aware of the *differences* which exist between spirit and form, soul and personality, intention and behavior, observation and interpretation, and the invisible and the visible. These differences will be quite real to us, but we must understand that they are real only because we do not fully comprehend the true relationship between the inner and the outer. As long as we are primarily submerged in the outer facts of life, the differences do not trouble us too much. But when the inner life is stirred up, as

it is in Pisces, the differences become more noticeable, and we wriggle uncomfortably as we try to make sense of them. We begin to wonder if life is rational. It is, of course; our perplexity is merely a sign that we are not as rational as life is!

3. Practicality versus idealism. There is a renewed sense at this time of wanting to get on with the business of bringing good ideas and plans into manifestation in daily life. Yet there may well seem to be a conflict between what is effective and practical on the one hand and what best honors the ideal on the other hand. In extreme cases, this duality may plunge those who are practical by nature into a frenzy of earthbound activity, while sending those who habitually eat lotus petals farther into "outer space." The best way to resolve this paradox is to focus our efforts on fulfilling the responsibilities we have set for ourself. In this way, we unite the practical with the ideal; we learn to be active on earth without becoming earthbound. We also learn to be active in heaven without becoming a space cadet.

4. Meekness versus self-esteem. The self-image is one of the primary focal points of Pisces, and many of us will struggle with achieving a proper posture for the spiritual life. Both the tendency to grovel and the tendency to be vain and pompous will be accentuated. To avoid problems of this kind, we must understand that neither of these extremes is healthy. The true posture of the spiritual life combines a deep reverence for the glory of God with a willingness to use our talents and strengths to serve as an agent of the plan of God.

5. Attachment versus detachment. Attachments and relationships are strengthened and highlighted by the forces of Pisces—especially our attachments to family and groups—yet so is the need for detachment. While this will seem to be a major paradox, it need not be, if we realize that the purpose of attachments is not to enslave us but to provide channels for self-expression. The cultivation of detachment therefore does not cut us off from our attachments; it merely liberates us from being con-

trolled by them—or by the people on the other end of the attachment who may be trying to manipulate us.

The ribbon tying the two fish together represents both our attachments *and* our capacity for detachment.

HOW THE FORCES OF PISCES AFFECT US

Throughout Pisces, many false teachers will arise which could lead us astray, if we listen to their lessons. Most of these teachers will be in our own consciousness—the voice of authority in our attitudes, feelings, and thoughts. Our challenge is to learn to recognize these false teachers within us, reject them, and pay heed to the genuine lessons of the month.

As always, the rule for separating the true teaching from the false is the classic statement by the Christ, "By their works you shall know them." In other words, we will learn the most in Pisces through the good works we do—through our efforts to be helpful and constructive, mentally, emotionally, and physically. The time for building up a reservoir of wisdom and goodwill has passed. Pisces is a time to *express* these qualities and talents, for the good of mankind.

The average person, of course, will be a willing victim of his own false teachers. He may come face to face with higher qualities and ideas at this time, but will not recognize them, or know what to do with them. As a result, he will tend to sink further into his personal needs and vanities.

The spiritual aspirant will be the one who most feels the tugs and divisiveness of the duality of Pisces. If he is relatively new to the spiritual path, and still captivated by its superficial aspects, he will be even more impressed than usual by the "wow wonderful" aspects of the spiritual life and spend his time pursuing pretty visions and dreams that have no real value. Given the opportunity to be a constructive force in humanity, he will tend to spurn it in favor of the never-ending pursuit of personal bliss. But this renders him vulnerable to being seduced by the real wolves in sheep's clothing, not just the ones inside his own character. The more mature aspirant, however, will be able to sidestep these distractions and use the power of transcendence to contact new insights into the subtle dimensions of life.

The advanced person will be presented with a series of lessons on using the force of spiritual will to empower the expression of love through healing and teaching.

The effect of the forces of Pisces on our **motivation** will be to increase our dedication to redeem life. The forces of goodwill and wisdom which pour into our awareness at this time help us see more clearly the elements of imperfection, both in our own character and in society. If we just sit by and do nothing, the goodwill and wisdom will pass through us and leave us behind, unenriched. But if we seize these energies and use them to redeem imperfection wherever we find it, the goodwill and wisdom will stay with us and be a part of our life.

The effect of the forces of Pisces on our **awareness** is to encourage us to reverse our thinking in a number of key areas, so that we begin to think in universal instead of personal terms. Instead of aspiring to better conditions, we begin working to establish them. Instead of longing for the inner light to illumine the dark areas of our life, we become the light itself, seeking to redeem and enlighten conditions of darkness wherever we find them.

Pisces is not a time when fate works reversals on us, yet it is a time when we have the chance to work major reversals in our attitudes, lifestyles, priorities, and acts. It is a time when we can truly "reverse the dualities" which have entrapped us for so long and begin to use them creatively. For this reason, the forces of Pisces tend to highlight the gap between the best and the worst within us, stimulating not just the impulse to help and redeem life, but also the emotional reactiveness, negative psychic sensitivity, and conflict. It makes plain the dualities which are of great importance to us, so we can reverse our way of approaching them.

The effect of the forces of Pisces on the **mind** will be to enslave it to the emotions, unless we have already established the mind as the ruling force within the personality. In that case, the mind will be enriched by the strong measure of benevolence and compassion which characterizes this time, helping us understand the true needs of others more precisely.

The effect of the forces of Pisces on the **emotions** will be to stir up their reactiveness. It will be easy to get carried away with emotional outbursts and excesses, unless we exercise reasonable caution and allow common sense to rule. In fact, it is possible to become drowned in emotionalism at this time and not even realize it, because the subtle elements of the emotions will be controlling factors in many people. Glamours will increase. Temptations will reappear in new and more subtle disguises. Our thinking will often be distorted by what we want, what we believe, or what we fear.

The effect of the forces of Pisces on our **self-expression** is to encourage us to serve and be useful. We will be more naturally inclined to look for ways to improve the conditions of life. This could be something as simple as a worker making recommendations for improving a company's product or instituting new safety procedures; or, it could be something as complex as finding new ways to serve the plan of God.

THE CHALLENGES OF PISCES

The major challenge of Pisces is to be helpful and participate in the work of redeeming life. The variables or ingredients we need to be helpful have all been given to us, in one way or another, throughout the course of our life in general and throughout the course of the last twelve months in specific. They exist in our life, both in inner and outer dimensions.

Do we know what these ingredients of helpfulness are? This is the question Pisces asks us.

What can we make of them?

What hinders us from being helpful in life?

What are our opportunities to become a force of help and redemption in our life?

Many people do not know the answer to these questions, even though they do have the ability to serve. Having the ability to serve does not guarantee that we have the *will to serve*. Many spiritual aspirants get caught in a state of limbo where they know the value of serving and how they might help, yet do not have a strong will to serve.

The help we offer, of course, must be given with benevolence and generosity, not arrogance. It is not meant to be a case of a strong person condescending to help a weaker one. We all are meant to help, we all are meant to receive help, each in our own way. In this manner, we all grow in our ability to participate in the life of spirit.

The challenge of Pisces to parents is to help their children learn the value of maturity and competence. Excellent role models of maturity can be found during Pisces if we are alert for them, but children need to have these role models pointed out to them so the value of maturity becomes a living, obtainable goal. All too many of the role models set before children in our culture are just the opposite; they encourage children to remain childish and adolescent.

The challenge of Pisces in improving our human relationships is very similar: to strive for a genuine level of maturity in our friendships, family relations, and professional associations. The human proclivity in Pisces will be just the opposite, however; the immaturity of this time will heighten contentiousness and argumentativeness. This kind of petty bickering, of course, tends to spoil the rich promise of opportunity in Pisces.

Other problems likely to arise in relationships include difficulty in sharing authority and extending trust. Possessiveness and manipulation will be more apparent. We should be careful not to respond in kind if treated in these ways—or stage a showdown. Instead, we should find strength in responsibility and duty.

The challenge of Pisces in business is to build a greater group awareness of goals and purposes. Combativeness and competition within groups will be heightened; different departments or divisions within a single business will treat one another like enemies, instead of partners. Corporate policy will often clash with individual enterprise. But these trends do not have to prevail. It is an excellent time to stress teamwork and cooperation, and to make the members of a corporate group more aware of the common themes and goals which do unite it.

The challenge of Pisces in society is really the struggle for the control of the thoughts and opinions of the masses. Nationalism, dogmatism, demagoguery, and fanaticism will increase at this time, as various special interest groups and political leaders vie for the support of large blocs of citizens. It is therefore important for those who have the mind to think to understand exactly how these forces are seeking to influence public awareness, and do what they can to decrease the ill effect.

The challenge of growth to each of us individually is to tap more of the potential of our noble human mind. We have a tremendous resource of wisdom within our innermost self, but it means nothing to us until we develop the mind and teach it the skills of thinking required to tap into this reservoir of wisdom. The word "potential" comes from "potent," meaning powerful. The mind is indeed potent, when properly trained:

• It is our direct link to the higher levels of will. As the mind develops, it can be trained to interpret the will and focus its power into our character and self-expression, so that we are able to maintain a steady measure of motivation, courage, and the power to act.

• It is our mechanism for understanding life. The emotions can tell us what we like and dislike, what we fear or covet, but they cannot understand what is happening and why. Only the mind can bring us the gift of understanding.

• It is the key to operating multidimensionally. There are many levels to our humanity—physical, emotional, mental, and spiritual. Most people are focused almost exclusively at the emotional level, but we are meant to act at all four levels simultaneously, guided by spirit. This cannot occur, however, until the mind is developed, for it is the mind which is capable of consciously embracing the multidimensional scope of our being.

• It is our key to creative activity. Many people link creativity with the "feeling" side of our nature, but they are actually confusing "feeling" for "intuition." The highest level of creative activity is that which brings the actual life of archetypal patterns into expression on the physical plane. Only the mind has the strength and capacity to focus this kind of power.

• It is the key to effective service. All too much of the help and service offered in the world is motivated by good intentions but executed with sloppy feelings. As a result, we often end up serving our personal needs far more than the needs of those we profess to help. Before we offer help, we must understand our own capacity to help and what will constitute genuine help.

• It is the key to harnessing the basic duality of life. The emotions get very frustrated in trying to deal with dualities. But the mind can be trained to see not only the twin poles of a duality but also the higher reality which harmonizes the two and enables us to reconcile the division. And when the mind is trained to work in this fashion, it truly does tap its full potential, for it is out of duality that the creative impulse emerges.

Let us therefore take the challenge of Pisces, and work to refine and expand our use of the noble human mind.

THE PROBLEMS OF PISCES

The forces of Pisces tend to stir up our awareness of and sensitivity to the influences and conditioning factors of our environment, subconscious, and mass consciousness. Others will be more sensitized to these impressions as well, leading to situations where misunderstanding can easily arise, reactiveness may be overstimulated, and feelings may be easily hurt or insulted. This could lead to conflict or stress which might not arise at other times. The major problems to be alert for include:

1. Arrogance. Excessive confidence in our own views and beliefs may blind us to the perspectives and opinions of others. Moreover, we may feel so confident and correct in our own views that we may feel justified in rejecting the ideas of others. Such arrogance and righteousness, however, are antithetical to the effort to cultivate a wise and mature expression of love.

2. Self-serving rationalizations. There is an enormous temptation in Pisces to use noble causes and ideals to justify what are basically self-serving propositions. Selfishness and self-indulgence are likely to increase, and the mind may well be employed to find ways to justify these excesses, rather than see their emptiness and put them to an end.

3. Vanity. The need for ego strength is an important theme in Pisces, but many people will try to attain it by cultivating vanity and the illusion of self-importance, rather than tapping the impersonal strength of the soul. We need to see beyond vanity and understand the real basis of our identity.

4. Impulsiveness. We may launch new plans and activities without understanding their potential for success—or their impact on others. Pisces is no time to act out of desperation or rashness. The plans and new directions we launch at this time should be the natural outgrowths of what we have learned from past experience, and should be directed at meeting genuine needs. Projects launched in defiance of the lessons of the past—

or in defiance of legitimate need—are almost certain to fail.

5. Introversion. There can be a pronounced tendency at this time to become excessively absorbed in the petty elements of one's "inner life"—our feelings, reactions, and hurts. Finding life difficult, we may be tempted to become the turtle withdrawing into his shell or the ostrich burying his head in the sand. Such withdrawal into reactiveness will only tend to magnify frustration, worry, and fear, not heal them.

6. Deviousness. The temptation to manipulate others secretly and deviously will increase, but so will the likelihood that such underhandedness will be exposed. If we have tended to be devious in these ways in the past, it is also likely that we will be treated in like manner by others (or mistakenly believe others are treating us deviously)—and not tolerate it very well. If this happens, it is important to look first at our own tendencies to be devious and manipulative and eliminate them, before we complain about the treatment we receive from others.

7. Jealousy. There can be an intense longing or yearning for what we have not yet achieved. If this yearning is focused on growing in maturity and responsiveness to our inner potential, it will be beneficial. But in the majority of cases, it will be focused instead on resentment of what others have, envy of their accomplishments, and jealous lusts. These are all destructive and can poison our state of mind during Pisces.

8. Confusion. Events and relationships may seem to be more complex than they actually are, as glamours and illusions are heightened, and we begin to question our own attitudes and priorities. This can lead to ambivalence and ambiguity. In addition, our previous confidence in our capacities and skills may be shaken by events which force us to reexamine our assumptions. The key to working through such problems of confusion is to rise out of our emotional turmoil and rationally evaluate what is real and what is unreal in our beliefs, values, and priorities.

9. Fear. The fear of growth, the fear of the unknown, and

even fear of the authority of the higher self will be stronger than usual. This results from not being sufficiently attuned to the source of love and wisdom within us.

10. Imposition. Others may try to encroach on our privilege, rank, freedom, or goodwill for their personal advantage. We may even invite this encroachment by ignoring our duties and responsibilities, or by failing to exercise our freedoms or goodwill maturely. The key to preventing such imposition lies not in defensiveness but in working actively and intelligently to express our values and fulfill our obligations.

11. Collapse. Where old conditions have been weakened or undermined, they may fall into ruin or disuse. There could be a collapse of enterprises which have served their useful purpose and no longer have their original vitality. But such collapse should not be viewed with excessive alarm. The rubble should be swept up and new progress initiated.

12. Grimness. It is easy at this time to fall into a rut of grimly plodding forward, devoid of all enjoyment of life. This problem could range all the way from feeling awkward and out of step to real grimness and pessimism. Yet grimness blocks out the light of the soul. As we discover areas in which we have slipped into grimness, we should relax our intensity a little and discover the soul's capacity for delightenment, even in the midst of struggle.

13. Excessive zeal. A mature response to the divine ideals of life is always valuable, and Pisces does encourage this. But in immature people, the impulse of idealism can easily become excessive, leading to unrealistic thinking, blind ambition, and unbridled zeal. If the idealism of Pisces is not harnessed correctly, it will produce a great deal of frustration—and can actually sabotage the projects it is directed toward.

14. Short cuts. The temptation to take short cuts will be great, but also quite costly. The forces of Pisces encourage us to grow, but our progress must be won honestly, by acquiring the

knowledge we need and the competence we must have to be successful. The person who habitually seeks short cuts may painfully learn it is not possible to get something for nothing.

15. Silliness. Capriciousness and naivete are likely to increase. There are some who embrace "spontaneity" as a spiritual virtue, but these are usually people who have no guiding principles or specific plans for service. Immaturity is immaturity, no matter how it is disguised or rationalized. This is no time to indulge in foolishness, but rather a time to strengthen our efforts to be self-disciplined, lest we do and say things which dishonor our best interests and opportunities to help.

16. Criticism. It will be easy to be judgmental and critical—of others, ourself, and life in general. When this occurs, it indicates that the impulse to help is being shortcircuited and directed into destructive channels, instead of constructive ones. When confronted with imperfection, we are meant to get busy and help correct it—not pass judgment on the imperfection. The tendency to judge and condemn will also result in increased irritability, both in the giving and the receiving of criticism. As a consequence, there may be many rough moments in interpersonal communications. It is important not to take umbrage at what others say to us, but rather discern the subtle meanings of their communications.

17. Martyrdom. Self-pity and a sense of being a martyred victim will be greatly aggravated at this time, as well as a guilty or troubled conscience. Yet all of these reactions to the problems of life are destructive. They hold us trapped in what is wrong and the mistakes we and others have made. The true spirit of Pisces is just the opposite—to strive always for a greater expression of what is good.

18. Astral vandalism. The heightened emotional reactiveness of this time will not only affect us individually, but will also poison and pollute mass consciousness and the astral plane. The time is ripe for astral vandalism—the attempt to sabotage the

412

good works or happiness of others psychically and psychologically. We must take care to focus our emotions and feelings only in healthy ways—never destructively.

THE OPPORTUNITIES OF PISCES

The basic relationship or connection between the soul and personality is strengthened during Pisces, making the work of spiritual integration easier. In general, this creates opportunities for any activity that brings the treasures of heaven to earth in order to enrich the life on earth and redeem that which is imperfect. Nonetheless, this process usually requires the alteration of the personality in some ways; old ways and ideas must die off, so they can be replaced by something new and more spiritual. This *can* be painful, unless we proceed with an understanding of the purpose and meaning behind it.

Pisces, in other words, is a time when change does occur. The only real question is: will this change come crashing down upon us, or be intelligently initiated by conscious effort?

The greatest opportunity for change in Pisces lies in expanding our capacity for nurturing and caring for our responsibilities, ideas, personal growth, inspired work, and creative projects. The universal forces are quite active and powerful during Pisces in supporting and nurturing activities that bear light, even if we do not happen to see the evidence of it. To work effectively as an agent of these universal forces, therefore, we must seek to work as they work, and make a diligent effort to nurture, support, and care for the worthwhile projects of our life and humanity as a whole. We should strive to be a loving, compassionate parent, not just toward our children, but toward all worthwhile projects we are involved in.

In this regard, it is also important to consider how effectively we are attuned to these universal forces of nourishment and support. Are we in the habit of invoking and focusing them to support and enrich our efforts? Or are we burdened with selfish and defiant attitudes that obscure them?

One of the great roles of the emotions is to enrich the quality of our self-expression, but for the emotions to fulfill this role, they must be oriented toward *adding* to the quality of life. Our primary effort in Pisces should therefore be to infuse our self-expression with the treasures of spirit, and teach the emotions to embrace and express them.

The specific opportunities of Pisces are:

1. Right receptivity. The ability to be more consciously aware of the subtle side of life is greatly enhanced. Dreams and psychic sensitivity are stimulated. While glamours and illusions are also stirred up, our ability to see them for what they are will also be stronger, giving us the opportunity to break through them and work at a higher level. In particular, we should take care not to substitute fantasies for genuine psychic perceptions.

2. Refinement. The civilizing force of the well-trained mind can be a major influence during Pisces, leading us to a deeper appreciation for the quality of life, a more profound comprehension of meaning, and the refinement of attitudes, tastes, concepts, and cooperation with others. This capacity to refine the quality of life is a major force to use in neutralizing egoistic and self-serving impulses.

3. Innovation. As we discover new dimensions to our life and new meaning in our experiences, we will probably be inspired to become more creative in our approach to work, relationships, and activities. In fact, some situations will demand that we work out new and better ways of approaching them.

4. Courtesy. There will be unusual value in tact and diplomacy as we strive to manage—or prevent—problems. An investment in courtesy now may well pave the way for enduring harmony in our relationships.

5. A greater sense of spiritual purpose. Purpose is the

force which spirit uses to impel us toward its goal. If we ignore it, we begin to be troubled by an ever-deepening sense that what we do lacks meaning. This can be a real problem, especially for the aspirant. But Pisces provides us with a marvelous opportunity to grasp the spiritual purposes of our life more fully—*if* we are willing to look beyond our personal needs and indulgences and consider the broader purposes which motivate and impel humanity.

6. New strength. The challenges of Pisces may call forth every bit of strength we have, but therein lies a marvelous opportunity for discovering just what we consider strength to be. Is it the strength to beat down opposition, to always get our way? Is it the power of money, position, anger, or vengeance? Or is it the strength to unite that which has been divided, to forgive those who have injured us, to heal that which is imperfect, and build that which is yet unbuilt? Our true strength lies in the wisdom we have acquired, the goodwill we have learned to express, our capacity to help, and our ability to cooperate with the soul.

7. A deeper sense of unity—an awareness of the common strength of humanity. Nothing weakens us more than the personal views and prejudices which cut us off from the rest of humanity; nothing adds more strength to our self-expression than the intuitive recognition of the oneness of humanity. The challenge of Pisces is to enrich our individual self-expression with an active love for the unity of life.

8. Excellent meditative contact. Pisces stimulates mysticism and a deeper interest in the life and plan of God. As a result, we are better able to perceive the "still waters that run deep"—the inner levels of life. By tapping into these "still waters" in moments of reflection and meditation, we can greatly stimulate our intuitive capacities.

9. A strong sense of triumph and celebration. Pisces is an excellent time to recognize the genuine achievements we have

won, the duties we have fulfilled, and the growth we have attained. It is also important to rejoice in our common ties with others—the ideas, values, and ideals that tie us together.

10. Self-renewal. Pisces is a good time for cleansing and renewing the tools of consciousness, reflecting on what we have done and how we could have done it better, and for reviewing how we interpret observations and intuitive perceptions.

11. Appreciation of the poetry and beauty of life. A sense of music or poetry is stirred up in Pisces, thereby putting us more in tune with the symbolic and creative facets of our nature.

12. The recognition of those who have always loved and supported us, even when our trust and loyalty have wavered. There will be an opportunity in Pisces to perceive the deep undercurrent of goodwill that has never been broken—in family relationships, inner groups, and our own relationship with spirit. In this way, it becomes possible for the unconscious ties and connections which unite us, one with the other, to become fully conscious and active in our life—not to bind and constrain, but to enable us to serve as a liberated agent of light.

TUNING INTO THE FORCES OF PISCES

The primary archetypal force of Pisces is love—the spiritual love which impels us to become a force of helpfulness and redemption in life. The many expressions of love—kindness, compassion, goodwill, reverence, devotion, affection, and benevolence—are the greatest sources of enrichment known to mankind. Yet all too many of us have little experience with this level of love, either in expressing it or recognizing it in others.

Where we have become disaffected, we do not love; where we have become alienated, we do not love. If we are dissatisfied with our work, for instance, we have lost the capacity to love it. If we are disenchanted with a relationship, we have lost the ability to love its potential. Many people, in fact, live in a bankrupt state of being unable to love themselves. This is especially true of many aspirants, who see their shortcomings and difficulties and conclude that they are not worthy of love—even their own.

Such attitudes poison our state of mind, ability to grow, and capacity to achieve. Love is the wavelength on which all healing, growth, and service occur. One of the best ways of tuning into the forces of Pisces, therefore, is to ask ourself:

How intelligently do I use the power of love?

Do I love excellence and honor it in all that I do?

Do I love the work I do?

Do I love my own potential and nurture my growth wisely?

Do I love the potential within those close to me?

Do I love the ideals and purposes of the inner life?

Do I love myself?

If we are unable to love in any of these ways, we should use the time of Pisces to magnify our ability to love in mature ways. We should try to discover the love of the soul for our potential and duplicate this love in our attitudes and perspectives.

The best way to teach is to give students the tools of discipline they need to develop the mind and higher skills of thinking.

The best way to heal is by attunement to the ideal and the transforming power of compassion.

The best way to lead is by striving to fulfill divine purpose.

The completion of work in Pisces enables new energies to be released in Aries, so that new fulfillment and synthesis can be attained the following year in Pisces.

A SONG FOR PISCES

The light shines forth, descending into darkness.

In the depths, the darkness stirs to engulf the light. The light is captured, encased in a shell of darkness.

417

The shell seems solid, strong enough to trap the light forever. But the imprisoned light burns quietly, seeping through the shell. The shell begins to glow faintly, even in the dark.

Slowly, the darkness is drawn into the imprisoned light, which flickers and grows. Layer after layer of darkness is dissolved, and the shell begins to move toward the source of light, above the depths, drawing the darkness with it. It is now the depths of darkness which are captive.

The light consumes the dark, and all is light.

A PARABLE FOR PISCES

Experience is not always a reliable teacher.

A fish was caught by a fisherman one day, only to be thrown back into the water because he was too small. Alarmed at first by his near encounter with death, the fish soon became ecstatic, believing himself the beneficiary of a "divine deliverance." Not understanding the reason why he had been spared, he concluded that the entire episode had been a test of his spirituality—a test he had passed triumphantly. Moreover, he decided that only a fish who had endured such a test could truly be considered a "fish of God."

He therefore sought out his friends and related his experience. "I have been blessed by divine providence," he proclaimed, "lifted into the heavens and then sent back into the waters. You, too, should undergo the test I have passed; you should subject yourself to the trial of the hook. To be a complete fish, you must prove the purity of your piscience."

The other fish accepted his story without question and swam off eagerly, in search of a heavenly fishing line to bite. Unfortunately, they were all larger than their friend the prophet, and never returned. The fish who had been thrown back lived into dignified old age—but he lived alone.

18

The Challenge
To Astrology

THE GLAMOUR OF THE STARS

To put it bluntly, modern astrology is not fulfilling its potential for helping humanity grow and become more creative—it is not meeting its challenge. Far too often, in fact, it is used only for the most petty types of fortune telling—or to judge people by the most trivial of standards. And it has become mired in the mind set of suspending all activity unless the heavens have been consulted for the opportune time to act.

Each of these uses of astrology could have some merit, of course, if it served a noble purpose instead of a selfish one. Astrology can help us understand the psychological trends which are leading us into the future—but this is not the same as flatly stating that the stars predict this success or that failure, as so many astrologers do—especially those who claim most loudly that "the stars do not control." Astrology can likewise help us understand a great deal about the personality and human nature, our own or that of others. But if we are sincere about learning these lessons, we should strive to understand them in the context of the soul, not our potential for romantic fulfillment or the manipulation of others, as so many astrologers are content to do. Our total character and spiritual potential is *not* something which is tapped by the usual analysis of a natal horoscope. And astrology can also help us cultivate an enlightened sense of right timing, so that we can act in harmony with the rhythms and cycles of divine life. But this is not the same as evaluating when we should act to gain an advantage over other people—or life itself—as so many astrologers love to do.

To be fair, the problems of modern astrology are really nothing more than the problems of human nature; the majority of people are only interested in the mundane applications of astrology. They could care less about the spiritual aspects of this science. Being petty and living at a soap opera level, they are only interested in astrology because it seems to add a cosmic dimension to their pettiness and lust for romance—and may help them get ahead of others. At times, this pettiness is dressed up in fancy labels such as "the spiritual quest for fulfillment" or "the realization of self," but once it is stripped of its embellishments, it is still smallminded and selfish.

Actually, for many centuries astrology could probably do no better than serve these mundane needs. But today there are large numbers of people who are ready to understand and use astrology to aid them in their quest for spiritual insights, the purification of thought and emotions, and the illumination of their self-expression. These people deserve something better than what astrology has traditionally offered. They deserve a system which will help them interpret the real power of astrological forces.

As long as modern astrology continues to serve the mundane interests of the masses, however, it will remain trapped there, burdened by the praise of the unenlightened and suffering the success of feeding our emotional reactiveness. And intelligent people will for the most part ignore it and look elsewhere for the help and guidance they need.

This does not mean that the whole of modern astrology has failed to acknowledge the growing interest in a more esoteric approach to this subject. There has been a response—but unfortunately, it has not been all that enlightened, except in a very few cases. It does little good to put on esoteric clothes and pretend to esoteric knowledge, if in fact there is a general lack of understanding of the nature of spirit and its plan for the evolution of consciousness! Just recognizing the role spirit might play in astrology is not enough; the astrologer must undergo a transformation, so that his motives and purposes truly serve the soul—and not the tired traditions of mundane astrology. After all, what does it matter if we know the exact nature of our karmic obligations, if our orientation to life is still one of *avoiding* all distress instead of *confronting* and resolving it? What does it matter if we know the nature of our spiritual plan for service, if we still are primarily concerned with satisfying all our desires, not serving the soul?

Without a unifying core of understanding about the life of spirit, new interpretations of planetary and zodiacal forces, aspects, the houses, and transits are useless. Yet getting astrologers to understand this problem and take action to correct it is like trying to dislodge an immovable object. From the inside looking out, it is hard to see the limitations and blind spots the traditions of astrology have imposed on it.

To put this in esoteric terms, modern astrology has fallen victim to a wide variety of *glamours*. A glamour is an emotional distortion or illusion which results from allowing certain sentimental fascinations to distort our perception, judgment, and behavior. The way teenagers idolize singers, movie stars, and sports figures is a common example of glamour—the fascination with popular heroes.

Many glamours are not as blatant as the example of hero worship, however. They are often very subtle and hard to detect—and insidious in the way they deceive us. The most difficult of all glamours to detect would be those that find their way into the traditions and popular ideas about a subject, thereby distorting our ability to comprehend it and leading to serious disruptions in our values and behavior.

Because astrology is viewed by many people as a mysterious and arcane subject, it is filled with glamours—glamours which affect not only the thinking of the average person but also those who are professionally involved in studying and using astrology. Until these glamours are seen for what they are, and dispelled, it will not be possible to tap the esoteric potential of astrology. And astrology will not be able to meet its challenge as a spiritual tool for the new age.

The principal glamours enchanting the practice and use of astrology today are:

The glamour of intuition. Many astrologers inflate their egos out of proportion by offering an intuitive analysis of the horoscope. While some astrologers do use the intuition most productively in interpreting horoscopes, much of what is claimed to be intuitive analysis is not intuitive at all. Instead, it is just the operation of the associative mechanism of the subconscious, which remembers all the material read, all the speculations made, and all the cases worked on in the past. As new charts are worked on, similar memories are triggered in the associative mechanism and well up in the mind of the astrologer. But it is just a rehashing of old ideas and interpretations, not a fresh revelation or penetration beyond traditional interpretations—which intuition would produce.

A healthy associative mechanism is indispensable to all analytical work, including astrology—but it should never be mistaken for intuition! If it is, it will produce a powerful glamour of intuition which leads the astrologer to reconfirm his misconceptions and traditional assumptions time after time after time. Instead of producing bold new breakthroughs, this glamour of intuition will produce nothing more than the same old thing with a few new frills—and astrology ends up back where it started in the first place.

The competent astrologer does not have to be intuitive to be effective, any more than a person driving a car needs to be. Both have their "roadmaps" to guide them to where they are going, both can check their location if they think they are lost, and both can predict where they will end up if they keep heading in the same direction. It is just a matter of doing the homework and then making sense of all the instruction. And if the average astrologer would leave the intuitive interpretation of the horoscope to those who have genuine, demonstrable intuitive skills, the art of astrology would be greatly benefited.

The glamour of spirituality. A particularly deadly glamour which holds back the evolution of astrology is the strange notion that the study of astrology makes us spiritual—or that we are "called" to study astrology because it is such a spiritual body of knowledge. This idea probably arises because astrology is the study of cosmic forces and universal order. But electricity and gravity are also universal forces which reveal something about the very fabric of universal order—and yet the study of electricity and gravity does little to make the average person spiritual. Neither does the study of astrology.

It is true that the forces of the zodiac are divine, but like the rain, they affect the just and unjust, the spiritual and the unspiritual alike. If we are already spiritual, the study of astrology will help us make our study of spirit and esoteric principles more practical and useful. But if we are not already spiritual, the study of astrology will do little if anything to transform us. In fact, it may well make us more materialistic!

And yet, it will be protested, astrology reveals the inner life. But the "inner life" that conventional astrology explores is not the life of spirit—it is just the life of the subconscious and the astral plane. And to describe the force and nature of our wishes, wants, and reactiveness as "spiritual" is absurd; it distorts our thinking not only about spirit but also about the proper role of astrology in our lives.

The glamour of being an expert counselor. The opportunity to influence (or control) others and be viewed as a great counselor who knows all secrets seduces many astrologers. This type of glamour is an occupational hazard for all kinds of counselors, not just astrologers, but it is perhaps more of a problem in astrology, because it leads to a state of intoxication in the astrologer and an unhealthy exaggeration of the role astrology plays in life.

The glamour of complexity. One of the hallmarks of the false teacher is to offer such complex explanations and theories about life that they *seem* profound, even though they are without meaning. And indeed, it is very easy to mistake a complex system of ideas for knowledge itself. Some people love mazes and all the intellectual stimulation they provide. But that does not make them relevant to our life—or helpful to us in any practical way. An ant farm, after all, is exceedingly complex—but irrelevant to our daily problems.

There is no doubt that astrology deals with a complex range of forces, and many of the more refined theories of astrology will, as a result, be complex. But some people use complexity to cover up the fact that they are not actually doing anything worthwhile, and all too often, this is the case in astrology.

The glamour of complexity can bury us in a maze of fascinating details which distract us from a sensible focus on the central issues of life. We therefore need to approach the study and use of astrology with a healthy pragmatism and an equally healthy respect for our own responsibility to act. We should make sure that astrology enriches our understanding of who we are and what we can do to become a better person—not hide it under an avalanche of meaningless trivia.

The glamour of fatalism. Perhaps the greatest indictment which can be made of modern astrology is its emphasis on fatalism—that certain configurations of the stars and planets, when appearing in a chart, will lead to conditions and circumstances we cannot control. The stars and planets never control—they merely influence. The power which is meant to take charge of our life is our own individuality and spiritual self—not astrological forces. Astrological forces play a major role in shaping the time and atmosphere in which our problems and opportunities arise, but we alone determine what those problems and opportunities will be!

Obviously, when astrologers leave the impression that our problems and opportunities are caused by the stars, rather than our own initiative or indiscretions, they undermine a very important part of our self-determination. They also set the stage for rampant superstition. Because mass consciousness is highly pessimistic and negative, many people are all too willing to believe in predictions of calamity and disaster. In fact, some people lust for them. And it is easy to look ahead at the transits or future positions of Saturn and Mars in a chart and conjure up all kinds of frightening prospects. The fact that most of these possibilities will never manifest is immaterial, however; the damage has already been done.

Some people may be able to override such fatalism with their innate cheerfulness and optimism, but in the average person it shatters whatever self-confidence and self-determination there might be. Astrology has produced a great deal of mischief in exactly this way, and will not be able to break free from this glamour of fatalism and live up to its true potential until it sets the record straight and teaches the general public that the stars only influence—they do not control.

The glamour of mystery. Almost everyone loves a mystery, and because astrology deals with occult forces, it can have a strong appeal to many people *because of its mystery alone*—especially those who are seeking to escape from the dullness of their lives. Unfortunately, the thrill of the unknown is not a good motive for investigating astrology, as it tends to make us discard reasonable interpretations in favor of more exotic explanations. In fact, the truly powerful and meaningful influences of the zodiac are apt to be overlooked while excessive attention is given to minor but exotic esoteric points.

The great tragedy of this glamour is that it leads many people to abandon their common sense and maturity as principal ways of solving their problems, and look instead for magical explanations and deliverances from the heavens. An unhappy spouse, for instance, might find it far more appealing to search the heavens for the reason he or she is having difficulty in the marriage, when five minutes of common sense reflection would reveal the unpleasant truth of the matter—that he or she is demanding, clinging, or parasitic.

427

The glamour of manipulation. Many people love to be "the spider in the web," able to control events and the lives of people around them. Because astrology can detect the innate rhythms of life and analyze the reactiveness of people, it would seem to provide the basis for predicting behavior. This ability to know in advance the moves of others has enormous appeal to those who are obsessed with having an edge on others. It also gives us the false belief that we are in control of events—or have some special connection with universal order so that it works for us!

There is no doubt that we have both the right and the duty to investigate order and understand how it works in our life—so that we can bring our personality into greater alignment with our divine nature. But when this opportunity is abused, and the knowledge we gain is used only to satisfy our egotistical wishes and wants, we become trapped in our own web. The glamour of manipulating others and the universe itself reinforces the innate desires of the personality and our materialistic focus on life, at the expense of genuine spiritual growth. And yet it is an immensely appealing glamour, because it does often lead to materialistic success and emotional satisfaction—until the emptiness of these achievements is exposed by the light of reality.

As any spiritual student knows, the only way to eliminate glamours is to shatter them. This is one of the great challenges to astrology today: to recognize the glamours which beset its thinking and destroy them with the light of understanding. This will not be easily done, however, because the group mind of conventional astrology is very strong, inbred, and attracts the very individuals who refuse to change. It is held together, like a religion, by an elaborate tradition of beliefs, techniques, and narrowminded prejudices—the intense commitment, for example, to the horoscope as the only means of discerning astrological influences. This group mind is also characterized by an insidious tendency to discount new ideas and reinforce the old— to claim to incorporate esoteric principles into the practice of

428

astrology, for example, but then continue to rely on the same old mundane methods and orientation.

The basic tool for shattering glamours is the *mind*, and there are two primary ways in which the mind can be used to do this. The first is to develop enough intuition to be able to penetrate beyond the glamour and discover the truth *as it actually is*. The second is to cultivate a refined capacity for keen observation of life and people, always comparing the conclusions we draw with the actual events of life. This is what the conventional astrologer notoriously fails to do—he has a keen sense of observation, but frequently fails to compare his assumptions with what is actually happening in life. And so, traditions go unchanged—and unexamined.

A TOOL FOR CHANGE

Astrology is meant to be the premier occult science. As a science, it can and should be approached with a respect for truth, with a pragmatic intention to test the validity of its assumptions, with an experimental attitude about searching for new ideas, and with the eventual expectation that we will derive some practical benefit from this research. Unfortunately, few professional astrologers currently use the scientific method in their studies or their practice. Some would say that this is only natural—that the study of astrology is largely subjective and cannot be approached scientifically. But this is nonsense. Subjective speculations do not have to be endured when life itself, and all its phenomena, serve as a great laboratory for verifying or disproving our theories and hypotheses.

A second great challenge to modern astrology, therefore, is to embrace scientific methods and raise the quality of its research and practice. If those who practice astrology will begin viewing it as a legitimate science, not a pseudo-science, with a body of verified facts and principles, theories, and practical applications, astrology would take a giant leap forward. For one thing, it would tend to eliminate much of the mystique which cloaks the real potential of this body of knowledge. It would also weed out those who are involved in astrology only because there are so few standards to judge their competence by.

This would also help us begin to recognize the true value of astrology as an aid to enlightened living and spiritual realization. It is a fact that astrology holds many of the secrets of both human and divine psychology. This body of knowledge is not yet fully developed, but its potential is real. The mapping of the human subconscious can be done quite expertly through a skillful interpretation of a natal horoscope. Eventually, it will also be possible to map the life of the soul as it works in and out of incarnation—not with a natal horoscope, but its higher correspondence. And even though this cannot be done fully today, we do already have some clues as to what a horoscope of the soul would consist of, as we work to map the basic temperament, rays, patterns of karma, focus of life purpose, degree of initiation, and the esoteric value of the ascendant of an individual.

The great promise of astrology lies in its ability to show us how to align ourself with spiritual and universal forces. The universal force most easy to find with astrology is the force of divine intelligence, especially as it is reflected in divine order and the cycles of expression and involution which mark the phenomena of life. But *all* divine forces, including divine will, wisdom, and love, can be tapped and investigated by the skillful use of esoteric knowledge about astrology.

The third great challenge to astrology, therefore, is to recognize the role it is meant to play in helping us understand human psychology, divine life, and our capacity to grow. But as long as astrology is in the hands of fortune tellers and those who toil so that we can get more money, sex, and power, this challenge means very little. How can a psychologist be expected to respect the contribution astrology could make to his practice, as long as the ordinary uses of astrology are so banal and selfish? Yet the failure to respect this potential of astrology impoverishes psychology as much as it does astrology.

It is not the purpose of this book to comment extensively on every possible way astrology could reform itself. Instead, we have concentrated on presenting, as thoroughly as possible, a bold new way of using astrological information which is meant to complement, not replace, the traditional use of the horoscope. Yet many of the ideas which inspired our new approach can also be adapted to upgrade and refine the current practices of traditional astrology.

The most important of these would be to begin seeing the natal horoscope in a more enlightened context. Instead of looking at it as a device for mapping the personal subconscious, with all its character weaknesses and strengths, we should begin to see it as a *personal message from the universe*—a personal message from God. What this personal message—the horoscope—tells each person is not what is going to happen to us, but rather what the nature of our design for growth and achievement is, and how we can best contact the divine forces of life.

As an example, a natal horoscope might indicate that there are favorable prospects for partnerships, communications, and public activities. An esoteric interpretation of this horoscope would not stop there, however, but go on to indicate how this individual can tap into cosmic power to build these partnerships, improve his skills of communication, and make a meaningful and enlightened contribution through public involvement. It would teach him to be something more than just a passive beneficiary or victim of astrological forces—to become, in fact, a person who can skillfully wield archetypal forces and integrate them into his character and self-expression.

The natal chart should also be interpreted in such a way that it indicates how the inner life—not just the subconscious—

431

is being strengthened and used by spirit so that it can find expression in the physical plane through the personality. This would give us clues as to the nature of our spiritual will and direction, even though the feelings and prejudices of the personality may be dragging us elsewhere.

Many astrologers, of course, would claim to be doing this already. It would be wonderful if they were, but most of them are not. Most of these so-called esoteric or humanistic astrologers are interpreting only the influence of *mass consciousness* on the individual—not the influence of the soul or the spiritual forces of life! This traps them in a very limited world of human experience.

Astrologers need to train themselves to relate to the cosmos as a whole—not as a sterile mathematical model, but as a living, dynamic system of divine qualities and forces. If they will look for this living system, sooner or later they will find something they can tap as a resource of power and help, and this will let them begin interacting with the zodiac as it really is—not as they subjectively think it to be. But as long as they remain plugged into traditions and unsupported theories, they will miss the real power and challenge of the zodiac.

Whether or not we have any deep interest in conventional astrology, as we work with the ideas presented in this book, we will be training ourself to approach the investigation of cosmic forces correctly. We will understand from the outset that astrology is meant to be a *tool for change,* not just a means of understanding the personality or manipulating our environment. Astrology is meant to help us understand the nature of divine forces and how we can harness them for growth in awareness, creativity, and self-expression. As a tool for change, in fact, astrology carries with it a *responsibility* to use these divine forces wisely and constructively. The old notion that we are a passive beneficiary or victim of the astrological forces which spin about us, conditioning our environment while we remain the same, is a primitive belief which reflects materialistic misconceptions about the nature of life and astrological forces. It needs to be discarded, both from our own thinking and from the traditions of astrology.

The scope and power of astrology is virtually unlimited. This book does not pretend to be an exhaustive study of the subject—or even a comprehensive one. It is meant to be an introduction to how each of us can intelligently interact with divine purpose, plan, and energy. There is a lot of room for experimentation with and expansion upon the ideas presented in this text. Each one of us will have our own unique focus for applying these ideas—and it is important to determine what this focus is and cultivate it.

Ultimately, it is neither this book nor the traditions of conventional astrology which reveal to us the forces of the zodiac and their relationship to us. Only the forces themselves can do this, as they respond to our intelligent inquiry and investigation.

19

Companions
of the Soul

In the final analysis, whenever our imagination reaches out to the stars, it should lead us back to the light within us—our own individual capacity to respond in meaningful and enlightened ways to the direction and power of the forces of the zodiac. It is a mistake to think of the zodiac as something "out there" and ourself as something "in here." The forces of the zodiac are companions of the soul—and are meant to be our companions as well, as we become acquainted with them and learn to work and think and act in harmony with them. In a very powerful way, we live and move and have our being within the scope of the zodiac—and this means that the zodiac can and does have a powerful impact on our consciousness.

And *consciousness* is the proper stage upon which to study and research the forces of the zodiac—not the twists and turns of fate as it shapes outer circumstances and conditions. The real triumphs of humanity, after all, begin first as an achievement in consciousness, not circumstance. Genuine growth likewise begins first in consciousness; only later is it expressed through the events of our life.

As we grow in awareness, we recognize more of the potential for greatness within ourself, and the constructive possibilities of the circumstances we face.

As we grow in knowledge, we organize our life to make it more efficient, solve our problems, and seize opportunities.

As we grow in ability, we become more productive and are able to serve spirit more effectively.

Consciousness does not unfold all at once, of course. As a child, we draw our direction from those around us—our parents, siblings, and friends. We learn by imitating them and following their instruction. Through this, we acquire the basic abilities and knowledge we need to become self-sufficient.

Later, we learn to make choices, assigning a high value to the opinions of certain people and a lower value to the ideas of others. We learn to study the phenomena of life directly—and

437

to determine what is important to us. Eventually, we learn that the lessons of previous generations are embodied in the traditions of culture, literature, science, and religion, and we begin studying them. In this way, we refine the quality of our consciousness and begin to nurture our individuality.

Finally, as an adult, we learn to take initiative in developing our consciousness. We begin exploring the roots of human behavior and the nature of conscious awareness which gives rise to it. We may do this because we know we can be a better person than we are, and we want to tap this greater potential—or we may be forced into it, by being given problems we have to solve. But whether we recognize it or not, we are guided by an inner impulse to grow which shapes much of our life.

Each of these stages of learning contributes to who we are— and holds a key to our consciousness.

Because the roots of our consciousness lie in part in the period of childhood, we can come to understand these roots by examining the meaning and subtleties of childhood memories. Modern psychology has already established the significance of these memories; by studying them, we are able to comprehend the patterns of habit and reaction in our *personality*.

Because the roots of our consciousness lie in part in the collective beliefs and traditions of our culture and mass consciousness, we can come to understand these roots by exploring the rich treasures of human religion, sociology, history, literature, and the arts. In this way, we can become more aware of the forces which have influenced and shaped the values and convictions of our *character*.

But the roots of our consciousness also lie in part in our inner life and the cosmos. These are the transcendent elements of our consciousness; they have been a determining influence on our life since before our birth, and are largely responsible for the development of our temperament and dominant personality patterns. Mysticism and the esoteric aspects of religion and psychology can help us discover some of these roots, but we can only come to know them in full as we explore them in our own awareness. The study of these transcendent elements of consciousness can help us comprehend our *spiritual individuality.*

The effort to interact with the forces of the zodiac as companions of the soul is one of the best ways we can discover and map the roots of our consciousness in both our inner life and the cosmos. It helps us learn to work simultaneously in two worlds or spheres—the personal world of our daily activities and the cosmic world of divine influence. Through the companionship that we cultivate, we steadily integrate the heavenly influences of the zodiac into the mundane affairs of our personality. We link divine force with human activity, *through consciousness.*

Much of this, of course, can be accomplished through conventional astrology. Since astrology is concerned with the relationships of heavenly influences at the time of birth, it can provide a great deal of insight into the nature of our subconscious. Basic personality patterns, interests, reactiveness, problems, and best outlets for self-expression are all codified in conventional interpretations of the natal horoscope. Astrology is also good at mapping the tides and currents of mass consciousness.

Yet even though this has value to the average person, it is of little use to those who are trying to explore the spiritual roots of consciousness. In fact, one of the tests to determine the degree to which the soul controls the personality is to examine the accuracy of the transits in an individual's horoscope—the relationship between the current position of the planets and their position at the time of birth. If the standard interpretations of the transits describe what is happening in the person's life and development fairly accurately, then this is a sign that the personality, not the soul, is still in control! But if the usual interpretations of the transits are consistently off the mark, then this is a good indication that the soul controls and directs the personality.

It is easy to become trapped in the life of the personality, allowing only slight remodeling of our convictions and attitudes. Habits and blind spots have a way of recycling themselves in ever more sophisticated forms. Rationalizations can always rescue us from genuine change, and prejudices usually find their own justification. We therefore need any help we can get, whether of the earth or of the heavens, to free us from this trap.

But we must choose with care. One of the most sophisticated ways to stay trapped in the life of the personality, after all, is to pay too much attention to conventional astrological advice! In principle, the study of the natal horoscope is as useful as the study of the forces of the zodiac, as outlined in this book, in helping us explore the inner dimensions of consciousness. But conventional astrology all too often leads the spiritual aspirant back into mass consciousness, rather than into the realms of spirit. The "cosmic forces" with which it deals are mainly the energies of human emotions. The "great insights" the typical astrologer taps are mostly the byproducts of the wish life of humanity. And the rhythms conventional astrology charts are primarily the tides of collective emotional reactiveness. If we follow conventional astrology indiscriminately, we are likely to get stuck in our emotions—and getting stuck in the emotions is the most common way that the life of spirit is blocked.

We must understand that it is possible to contact astrological forces at many different levels: at the level of their archetypal purity, at the level of our personal reactiveness to them, and at the level of collective human emotions—the subconscious of the human race. Most astrologers are able to see beyond the level of personal reactiveness, yet very few are able to work directly at the level of archetypal purity. By default, therefore, they contact the forces of the zodiac at the level of the collective human emotions. And because there is great power there, the forces contacted in this way are generally mistaken for their spiritual counterparts. The result is an alignment to forces and rhythms the spiritual aspirant should be learning to master—not *submit-*

ting to! Although this fact is rarely grasped, the consequences of it can be devastating to effective work and progress on the spiritual path.

In no way does this imply that the study of astrology is any more dangerous than the study of any other aspect of consciousness. It is simply a strong and compelling statement that our primary attention and interest in this study should be to discover and relate to our spiritual self, the soul. The soul transcends the personality, mass consciousness, and most of the forces described by conventional astrology. It is the center and heart of our life, and in this spiritual center, new forces, qualities, and rhythms can be tapped to direct our life in more enlightened ways, to heal our problems, and to enrich our self-expression with new talent. If we dedicate ourself to the life of our soul and seek to express its qualities and energies, self-mastery and spiritual self-expression will automatically ensue.

The soul, in other words, is designed to be a *clearing house* for all cosmic energies, including astrological forces. When the personality is viewed as the clearing house for these forces, then the personality is strengthened at the expense of the soul—a fact that all conventional astrologers should ponder on at great length. If, however, the soul is given primary authority in our life, then we will be able to use the forces of the zodiac most beneficially in our life. We will be able to tap them not through the collective emotions of the human race, but as companions of the soul. And contacted at this level, these forces can have a tremendous impact on our life, giving birth to many spiritual qualities, talents, and powers in our consciousness, as they move through our life. If we learn to use these forces intelligently and constructively, we can greatly accelerate our development of soul consciousness.

In this book, we have described how the forces of the zodiac can be used in this way—to liberate the life of spirit. We have tried to portray these forces as they are at the level of spirit. As a result, our descriptions are frequently at odds with "traditional wisdom" about these same forces. We hope the serious spiritual aspirant will understand the reason for these differences, and make a concerted effort to interact with these forces at the dimensions of spirit—not at the level of conventional astrology.

Throughout, we have stressed the usefulness of these forces as a resource for transformation. As a result, we have done a great deal more than just list the good and bad features of each sign—we have shown how to use the good features to transform and spiritualize the bad features. This also represents a radical departure from conventional astrology, which largely ignores the serious work of transformation in favor of helping people achieve personal power, success, and happiness. While it may seem that "getting what we want" is all anyone should worry about, it is nonetheless a point of view which totally neglects the life of spirit and its rich potential to enrich our awareness.

The work of transformation needs to be focused on reforming our identity and selfhood—not just what we do or how we do it! For this reason, the commentaries have been written to inspire us to transform:

• Our habits of thought and feeling. The habit patterns of our mind and emotions form the structure of our awareness. As we work to transform them, we elevate our ability to deal with the issues of life, which helps us resolve our problems more effectively as well as seize the opportunities which come to us.

• Our relationships with others and our work. These relationships extend the scope of our consciousness, through our involvement in life. By transforming them, we enable the soul to express itself not only through our values and convictions, but also through the major investments we have made in life.

• Our identity. Our identity is what we identify with. All too many people identify with the things of the physical plane, rather than the life of spirit. As we transform our identity, we leave behind patterns left over from more immature years. This liberates our orientation so we can perceive more of our rich potential and act with greater enlightenment in all that we do.

• Our self-expression. Our self-expression is what we do, think, say, and feel, day in and day out. As we transform it, we are able to become more productive and tap more of our creative potential. More importantly, we will be better able to serve the life of spirit in our daily activities.

• Our relationship with spirit. By transforming the quality of our values and aspirations, we also transform our relationship with our spiritual self, enabling us to draw on more of its treasures and integrate them into our daily life.

If this theme of transformation is recognized and accepted as the central feature of working with the forces of the zodiac, it will be possible to use this book as a handbook for spiritual growth—a text which will become a central tool for learning to recognize the many ways in which the soul speaks to us and leads us to new levels of maturity. *Forces of the Zodiac* is not a book to be read once and then set aside—or even to be used for one yearly cycle of the zodiac and then forgotten, as though we had absorbed all the wisdom of the soul in twelve months' time!

Our life is not neatly tucked into the package of a single year, and neither is our growth. Genuine spiritual growth is built on cycle after cycle of evolution; the intelligent person begins to recognize these cycles and tries to cooperate with them. It is for this type of person that this book has been written—the person who is beginning to realize that the forces of the zodiac *are* companions of the soul, and can become our companions as well, if we have the patience, intelligence, and dedication to learn to recognize their presence in our life.

There are many rhythms of growth we can become familiar with, as we use the forces of the zodiac year after year. We will be able to see, for example, the order and intelligence with which the soul orchestrates major new developments in our life—and better understand what it means to cooperate with them. We will also learn, if we continue working with this book, the steps in successfully conceiving, developing, launching, and sustaining new projects—or new habits, values, or responsibilities.

The stars are a powerful resource—if we learn to work skillfully with them as *energies*, not just as *intellectual concepts*. After all, the idea of love or the intent to be forgiving must be impelled by the energy of love just as much as our automobile must be propelled by actual fuel. It will not run on the idea of fuel! It is the *forces* of the zodiac that we must learn to harness, therefore, not the idea of astrology.

If we fail to work actively, we will be a passive victim of mass consciousness and its immature interaction with the forces of the zodiac. This is why it is so important to learn to interact actively and with enlightenment with these forces.

Spiritual aspirants are sometimes impatient, unwilling to work step by step to achieve their goals. They want enlightenment, and they want it now! But the soul does not operate in this fashion—and neither do the forces of the zodiac. To learn to harness the forces of the zodiac as an aid to the work of spiritual transformation, we must come to respect them as powerful cosmic forces which are greater than ourself. We must learn to cooperate with them, not expect them to respond to our wishes, demands, and impatience.

The hidden secret of the forces as "companions of the soul" is to learn to use them as the soul uses them—as forces for building new and better patterns of consciousness, which in turn will give rise to new and better forms of self-expression. The average use of astrology will never reveal this secret, no matter how many horoscopes are cast; while aspiring for the heavens, its methodology keeps it earthbound, trapped in illusions. But if we rise out of these limitations, we can penetrate the secret, and learn to use it.

We, too, can become the companions of these forces, and learn to walk in the light they cast.

444

Appendices

THE MUSES AND THE GRACES

One of the most useful ways of attuning to archetypal forces is through the meditative technique of *personification*—the act of thinking of the archetypal force as embodied by a saint, a goddess, or a mythological persona. By building a strong relationship with the personification, we can intuitively contact and interact with the life, intelligence, and quality of the archetypal force. The potential of working with personifications is so great that we have taken the traditions of the Muses and the Graces from Greek mythology and updated them for modern use as aids to creative inspiration (the Muses) and more gracious and poised living (the Graces).

We first introduced our updated treatment of these ancient traditions in two essays in *The Art of Living* series. The Muses made their debut in "The Act of Human Creation" in volume IV and the Graces followed in "Becoming Graceful" in volume V. Because many of the readers of our original reports on *Forces of the Zodiac* were familiar with these two traditions, we often suggested helpful Muses or Graces to invoke when working with the archetypal forces of a sign. We have gathered these references here and list them on the following two pages. It should be kept in mind, however, that these lists are meant to be suggestions only. Any of the twelve Muses or the nine Graces can be invoked during any of the signs of the zodiac, not just the ones we have listed.

The purpose of working with personifications is *not* just to have a pleasant fantasy. The idea is to build up a strong relationship with the power and essence of an archetypal force. As such, working with the Muses and the Graces can help us appreciate more fully one of the key themes of this book—that the forces of the zodiac are meant to be companions of the soul, as well as our companions in daily living. They are meant to become alive in our own awareness, goodwill, talent, and hard work.

THE MUSES AND THE TWELVE SIGNS

Aries
: **Dominion,** the Muse of leadership. Her symbol is the white marble pillar of strength.

Taurus
: **Vela,** the Muse of discovery. Her symbol is the veil of darkness being lifted at dawn.

Gemini
: **Erato,** the Muse of right human relationships. Her symbol is a magenta rose in full bloom.

Cancer
: **Lyra,** the Muse of music and harmony. Her symbol is the lyre.

Leo
: **Persona,** the Muse of the performing arts and self-expression. Her symbol is the actor's mask.

Virgo
: **Zoe,** the Muse of healing. Her symbol is a mother with a child in her arms.

Libra
: **Juris,** the Muse of justice. Her symbol is blind-folded justice balancing the scale.

Scorpio
: **Lumen,** the Muse of literature and enlighten-ment. Her symbol is the lighted lamp.

Sagittarius
: **Laurel,** the Muse of teaching. Her symbol is the laurel wreath of honor.

Capricorn
: **Fortuna,** the Muse of commerce and business. Her symbol is a fountain that is the source for all the tributaries of the earth.

Aquarius
: **Oracle,** the Muse of intuition. Her symbol is a woman carrying a radiant globe of light.

Pisces
: **Iris,** the Muse of beauty and the fine arts. Her symbol is the rainbow.

447

THE GRACES AND THE TWELVE SIGNS

Aries   **Hero,** the Grace of fortitude and endurance. Her symbol is a winged white horse.

Taurus   **Merry,** the Grace of cheerfulness and joy. Her symbol is a woman setting the centerpiece on a banquet table, preparing for a celebration.

Gemini   **Amie,** the Grace of affection. Her symbol is the embrace of genuine friendship.

Cancer   **Enthea,** the Grace of enthusiasm. Her symbol is a torch that burns through apathy.

Leo   **Charity,** the Grace of helpfulness and goodwill. Her symbol is a woman assisting an ill person.

Virgo   **Dawn,** the Grace of optimism. Her symbol is a woman facing the rising sun, absorbing light.

Libra   **Pacifica,** the Grace of peace. Her symbol is a woman of supreme patience weaving a tapestry.

Scorpio   **Piety,** the Grace of kinship and gratitude. Her symbol is a woman kneeling in prayer.

Sagittarius   **Corona,** the Grace of dignity. Her symbol is a woman with a golden crown and halo.

Capricorn   **Enthea,** the Grace of enthusiasm, who helps us generate our eagerness to act.

Aquarius   **Charity,** the Grace of helpfulness. She helps us understand the true nature of service.

Pisces   **Piety,** the Grace of inspired humility. She helps us learn to love God.

THE PLANETS AND THE TWELVE SIGNS

(Extracted from *Esoteric Astrology* by Alice Bailey)

Aries	Mars, Mercury, and Uranus.
Taurus	Venus and Vulcan (veiling an unnamed planet).
Gemini	Mercury, Venus, and the Earth.
Cancer	The Moon and Neptune.
Leo	The Sun.
Virgo	Mercury, the Moon, and Jupiter.
Libra	Venus, Uranus, and Saturn.
Scorpio	Mars and Mercury.
Sagittarius	Jupiter, the Earth, and Mars.
Capricorn	Saturn and Venus.
Aquarius	Uranus, Jupiter, and the Moon.
Pisces	Jupiter and Pluto.

THE NATURE OF THE SEVEN RAYS

Ray One—will, power, authority, strength, and leadership.

Ray Two—love, wisdom, brotherhood, teaching, and healing.

Ray Three—intelligence, civilization, law, and adaptability.

Ray Four—integration, harmony, creativity, and cooperation.

Ray Five—practical knowledge, science, truth, and discovery.

Ray Six—devotion, idealism, mysticism, faith, and aspiration.

Ray Seven—constructive activity, ritual, order, and prosperity.

449

INDEX

451

Recommended Study

The following are other books and tapes which will enrich the study and use of the forces of the zodiac:

Esoteric Astrology, by Alice A. Bailey

The Labors of Hercules, by Alice A. Bailey

The I Ching Workbook, by R. L. Wing

Active Meditation: The Western Tradition
by Robert R. Leichtman, M.D. & Carl Japikse

The Art of Living, by Leichtman & Japikse
Especially recommended are the essays:
"The Practice of Detachment" in Volume I
"Seeking Intelligent Guidance" in Volume II
"Cooperating with Life" in Volume III
"The Act of Human Creation" in Volume IV (describes the Muses)
"Becoming Graceful" in Volume V (describes the Graces)

The Life of Spirit, by Leichtman & Japikse
Especially recommended are the essays:
"The Spiritual Person" and "The Spiritual Path" in Volume I
"Psychic Dimensions of the Life of Spirit" in Volume II
"Invoking Divine Life" in Volume III

Exploring the Tarot, by Carl Japikse
A set of 16 cassette tapes. Especially recommended are:
"Harnessing the Subconscious"
"The Pressures of Mass Consciousness"
"Working with Archetypal Forces"

ABOUT THE AUTHORS

In the late 1960's, Dr. Robert R. Leichtman's interest in intuition and spiritual growth caused him to close his medical practice and devote his energies to lecturing, teaching, and writing. Out of his experiences and personal insights, he developed the basis of "Active Meditation," a comprehensive course in personal growth and meditative techniques which he has now been teaching for seventeen years. In addition, he has devoted much of his time to refining his intuitive skills. His pioneer work as a psychic consultant to medical doctors, psychiatrists, and psychologists has earned him recognition as one of the premier psychics in America today. Dr. Leichtman currently resides in Baltimore, where part of his time is spent participating in the healing services of the New Life Clinic.

A graduate of Dartmouth College, Carl Japikse began his work career as a newspaper reporter and freelance writer. He has worked for several newspapers, including *The Wall Street Journal*. In the early 1970's, he left the field of journalism to pursue his current interests: teaching "Active Meditation" and other courses in personal growth, writing, lecturing, and consulting psychically with businesses and individuals. It was a series of intuitive observations made during 1977 and 1978 that led Mr. Japikse to develop the idea for *Forces of the Zodiac*. He is also the developer of The Enlightened Management Seminar.

Dr. Leichtman and Mr. Japikse are the authors of *Active Meditation: The Western Tradition, The Art of Living*, and *The Life of Spirit*, all published by Ariel Press. In addition, Dr. Leichtman is the author of *From Heaven to Earth*, a series of 24 interviews with the spirits of famous individuals, and Mr. Japikse is the author of *The Hour Glass: Sixty Fables For This Moment in Time*, a book of esoteric fables and parables.

The illustrations for the twelve signs included in this book are the work of D. Kendrick Johnson of Carmel, California.

THE WORK OF LIGHT

Forces of the Zodiac: Companions of the Soul is issued by Ariel Press, the publishing house of Light, a nonprofit, charitable foundation.

The purpose of Light is to stimulate the growth of the mind and the creativity of people throughout the world. It was founded by Dr. Robert R. Leichtman and Carl Japikse, two authorities on human consciousness, personal growth, and the creative process. The work of Light is to enrich the human capacity to use the mind and spirit wisely and productively.

The activities of Light include the publications of Ariel Press, a series of taped lectures, the development of new classes, the Books of Light book club, and the presentation of lectures and forums.

Contributing members of the work of Light receive a series of lessons in personal growth called *Enlightenment*. Each issue of *Enlightenment* focuses on one specific aspect of the development of the mind, creativity, or the intuition. In addition, members receive a newsletter, "The Work of Light," and automatically become members of Books of Light, thereby entitling them to discounts on a wide range of books.

The cost of a contributing membership is $25 a year for an individual, $40 a year for a family. There are also three other levels of contributing membership: the *fellow*, who contributes $100 a year or more; the *benefactor*, who contributes $250 a year or more; and the *angel*, who contributes $1,000 a year or more. Fellows, benefactors, and angels receive all the benefits of the contributing membership, plus several more. A brochure describing the work of Light will be sent on request.

To become a contributing member of Light, send a check and a letter of application to Light, 3391 Edenbrook Court, Columbus, Ohio 43220. All contributions to the work of Light are fully tax deductible.